Language Pedagogy and Language Use in Africa

By

Lioba Moshi & Akinloyè Òjó
(eds.)

Published by

Adonis & Abbey Publishers Ltd
P.O. Box 43418
London
SE11 4XZ
http://www.adonis-abbey.com
Email: editor@adonis-abbey.com

First Edition, October 2009

Copyright 2009 © Lioba Moshi & Akinloyè Òjó

British Library Cataloguing-in-Publication Data

A catalogue record for this book is available from the British Library

ISBN: 978-1-906704-605 (HB)978-1-906704-612(PB)

The moral right of the author has been asserted

All rights reserved. No part of this book may be reproduced, stored in a retrieval system or transmitted at any time or by any means without the prior permission of the publisher

Layout Artist/Technical Editor: Jan B. Mwesigwa

Language Pedagogy and Language Use in Africa

By

Lioba Moshi & Akinloyè Òjó
(eds.)

To all
Speakers, Teachers and Scholars of African languages in Africa and in the African Diaspora

CONTENTS

Chapter 1
The Pedagogy and Use of Language in Africa: A Foreword
Lioba Moshi and Akinloyè Òjó 1

Chapter 2
The Plight of Indigenous Languages: A Prognosis
Lioba Moshi 11

Chapter 3
National Languages and National Development
Ben Ohi Elugbe 39

Chapter 4
Swahili versus English in Tanzania: The Win-Win Situation
Josephine Dzahene-Quarshie 53

Chapter 5
Confronting the Dialectics of Nigeria's Language Policy Laws: The Constitutional Solution
Olaoba F. Arasanyin 75

Chapter 6
Language-Based Problems and National Development in Nigeria
Akinloyè Òjó 121

Chapter 7
Language Planning: The Bane of Yoruba Language Education in Southwest Nigeria
B. A. Amoloye 147

Chapter 8
Kanga Captions: Social and Political Communication with Application to Kiswahili Language Teaching and Learning
Alwiya S. Omar 161

Chapter 9
Language Contact and Language Use: A Study of Igbo Undergraduates in selected Nigerian Universities
Harrison Adéníyî and Rachael Bello 181

Chapter 10
Language Restriction in Radio Programming as a Source of Indigenous Language Promotion: The Orisun FM as a case study
Adeola Adijat Faleye 193

Chapter 11
The Oriki (Panegyric) Phenomenon as Archival Material for Yoruba History
Oladayo Akanmu 207

Chapter 12
Phonological Deviation in Spoken English among students in Nigerian Tertiary Institutions: Drama and Theatre to the Rescue
Ezekiel Tunde Bolaji and Kehinde Abimbola Adeniyi 219

Chapter 13
Interpreting the Language of the Drums: A Case Study of Yoruba Traditional Bata and Dundun
Jeleel Olasunkanmi Ojuade 235

Chapter 14
African Languages Use and Pedagogy: The Road Ahead
Lioba Moshi and Akinloyè Òjó 245

About the Contributors 261
Index 263

Chapter 1

THE PEDAGOGY AND USE OF LANGUAGE IN AFRICA: A FOREWORD

Lioba Moshi and Akinloyè Òjó

Introduction

The study of African languages in the world was prompted by the interest of missionaries who, as early as the 15th Century, realized that in order to win the souls of their converts, they needed to communicate with them in their indigenous languages. Many of these missionaries engaged in the translation of the bible in the languages of their converts and in the process inspired the early African linguistics scholars who developed an interest in the development of grammars and dictionaries. Many African linguistics scholars of later days were inspired by the works of early scholars like Koelle (1854: Polyglotta Africana); Meinhof (1905-1906) on the phonology of Bantu languages; Migeod (1911) on the languages of West Africa; Doke (1943, 1945) on the grammar of Bantu, phonetics and lexicographical studies; Pike (1948) on tone languages; Bamgbose (1966) and Abraham (1967) on the grammar of languages such as Yoruba and Igbo; Guthrie (1967) who authored two volumes on Comparative Bantu; Greenberg (1955, 1963) on African linguistics classification, and the languages of Africa; Meeussen (1967) on the reconstruction of Bantu grammar; and Welmers (1973) on the structures of African languages, to name only a few. Their work became the foundation of field research on African languages pedagogy and linguistic research. Their works and that of others have been instrumental in interrogating linguistic theories that had for a long time relied only on Indo-European languages.

Emergent scholars in this new tradition used data from African languages to test pre-conceived theories on universal grammar and introduce new questions to the field of linguistics that interrogate theories that are specific to Indo-European languages but are posited as assumptions about all languages of the world. The new data from African languages has forced linguists to abandon analyses that do not do justice to African languages and to devise explanations that make particular sense to specific language or a group of languages. In addition, the social and cultural realities within which these languages exist also became relevant to the study of these languages. These *social and linguistic* efforts have influenced the study of African language pedagogy and use in the Diaspora dating back to the 1960s, the dawn of independence for many African countries. The interest shown in the Diaspora on African languages has also allowed scholars in Africa to maintain their scholarship through research on many of the indigenous languages. However, as some of the contributors in this book contend, the enthusiasm for the use of indigenous languages and scholarship has remained relatively moderate as scholars are conflicted in their loyalty to imperial languages. The lack of enthusiasm seems to be influenced by the attitude towards the use of African languages by African leaders who have hampered scholars' efforts to create and sustain the needed visibility for African languages around the world.

The contributors in this book show by their research and discussions that the study of African languages is not only critical to the study of language theories but also important in changing Africa's overwhelming reliance on European languages to communicate with each other. The reliance has not only affected the politics of the continent but also its economic well being. An analysis of the enormous developmental challenges facing the African continent will reveal that many of the economic, social, political and cultural challenges have major language components.

It can actually be said that the challenges of development in Africa are either outright language challenges or language-based. More significantly, at the social level in many parts of the continent, African languages are now perceived as inadequate means of communication. These aspects are highlighted in the various discussions offered by the authors on language policy in different African countries. The discussions clearly show that the struggle to sustain and raise the visibility profile of African languages in the world is not only important but also necessary due to the contribution of the study of world languages and cultures (see Moshi Chapter 2). It is without doubt that once a language dies the nation also loses the associated culture and a valuable part of the history of its speakers. Examples of nations that lost their language and cultures are ample. Similarly, there are some that have elevated the visibility of their cultures, history and enhanced heir economic wellbeing through the promotion of their indigenous languages. Countries that claim English, French, Portuguese, Japanese, Chinese, and Arabic as indigenous languages have managed to convince its people to revere and promote the languages through education, communication/technology and trade. These three aspects are the bedrock of a nation's economic survival in the 21st Century that has proved globally challenging.

Scholars are aware that there is enough blame to be shared for the demise of Afro-ethnic languages but they single out colonialism and the lack of commitment to these languages by the African elites, leaders, and the speakers at large. Moshi (Chapter 2) notes that it is rather unfortunate that African countries have never been able to do what other colonized nations have done, namely sustaining and maintaining the visibility of their ethnic languages despite the imperial language influences that are associated with colonialism. Countries like Japan, China, and India use ethnic languages in all critical medium of communication while imperial languages are reserved for inter-continental and business communications. She continues by outlining the historical background for the demise of ethnic languages pointing out that there are three main factors that contribute to the growth or demise of ethnic languages, namely historical, emerging national languages, and the African consciousness.

The discussion on national languages and national development by Elugbe (Chapter 3) extends the view point by pointing out the way nations interpret the idea of a national language and how that could influence issues of national development. Elugbe notes that every language which is indigenous to Nigeria, which has a definite location or locations, and is part of an indigenous culture, is a Nigerian language and that English should not be included in the mix even though there have been attempts to claim Nigerian pidgin (English) to have sufficient cultural value that enhances its status as an indigenous language of Nigeria. He points out an interpretation of a national language based on its ability to unite a nation (as is the case of Swahili in Tanzania), and as an instrument that allows for the achievement of independence and nationhood (of Fishman 1968:6, Bamgbose 1983:3). Elugbe also refers the reader to Amayo (1983:11)'s quote from Ikara 1981 that points out that the Obasanjo administration designated Hausa, Igbo, and Yoruba as national languages and inserted them into the 1979 constitution. Elugbe contends that it is going to be exceedingly difficult for political leaders to sell to the nation, at this stage of Nigeria's political development, the idea that English should continue to serve as the only national language because English does not qualify as a national language in Nigeria. It can be considered as one of the Nigeria's Lingua Francas and can continue to assume its role as an official language considering its role as the language of administration, business, communication, technology, and education (secondary, and tertiary). Elugbe also notes that the Nigerian people would be naive to think that English should remain a national language just because it is taught nationally and exploited across the country. As the language of the elites, English serves a very small geographical constituency.

Similar arguments are highlighted by Dzahene-Quarshie (Chapter 4) on her discussion on the status of English and Swahili in Tanzania. As she notes, Tanzania is only one of a very few independent African states that declared an indigenous language, Swahili, both a national and official language in the post-independence era. However, despite the fact that the Swahili language has attained a very reputable status and a strong global presence over several decades; Dzahene-Quarshie pointed out that there are glaring pieces of evidence that indicate that it is facing challenges that may have serious implications for its position in Tanzania in the near and distant future. She points out facts that show the presence of a long standing competition between Swahili and English especially where language policy in Education is concerned. She also notes that Tanzania's early policy of *Ujamaa* and the subsequent retreat from *Ujamaa* as the nation moved towards democracy and liberalization has created an ambiguous status for English and somehow minimized the visibility that Swahili needs in the global market.

Another take on the influences of language policy on indigenous languages is evidenced by Arasanyin (Chapter 5) in his discussion on language policy, the law, and solutions from the Nigerian constitution. Scholars pay attention to language policy in Nigeria because of its unique political experience and economic standing in the continent. Arasanyin notes that Nigeria has been able to survive the struggle for political integration in spite of its tumultuous struggle with political identity and social cohesion because it has adopted a prudent constitutional philosophy that drives its political establishment and management as a *quasi-federalist* state. He points out this philosophy that is constructed on a centralist principle of promoting national loyalty and harmony through a singular law: the federal character statute *(sec. 277 (1)* of the 1979 constitution; and *chapt. II, sec. 15 (3)* of the 1999 constitution)). This law is predicated by three sets of social management laws that provide political context and character to this statue: (i) the social order laws (founded on ideals of freedom, equality and justice: *sec. 17 (1):1979*, and *chapt. II, Sec. 18 (1):1999*); (ii) the educational policy laws (based on the principles of equality of educational opportunity: *sec. 18:1979*, and *chapt. II, sec.*

19(1):1999); and (iii) the economic objective laws (assigned to national wealth distribution: *sec. 16:1979*, and *chapt. II, sec. 17(2):1999*). By understanding the functional paradox that the federal character law supports through its conceptual predication allows scholars like Arasanyin to examine the Nigerian language policies in the context of legal and political imperatives embedded in the supporting laws as they converge mainly to define the nation's federal character principle.

This discussion is furthered by Ojo (Chapter 6) in his discussion on language in education and the ensuing challenges with policy implementation in Nigeria. Ojo contends that despite the fact that it is over a decade since Nigeria attempted to return to participatory democratic rule, a significant number of Nigerians have not taken advantage of it to effectively participate in the national debate due to two enduring challenges: language use and language in education. These two challenges are decidedly linked and have continually contributed to the demise of various development plans and national integration efforts in the country. The majority of Nigerians, due to their low level or lack of education (often translating into identical low level or lack of economic opportunities) have incessantly lacked the means for full participation in the social, economic and political development of the country. This challenge has continually been complicated by the multi-lingual nature of the Nigerian federation, the dominance of the English language (one of the least widely spoken language in the country) in official domains and the ineffective role of the government in implementing the viable language in education policy. Language in education embraces the wider questions of the languages taught and learnt in the educational system, and the languages used for educating at various levels and sectors of a national system (Obanya, 1992). Ojo further discusses language related issues in Nigeria's quest for development and national integration and suggests that the major problem that needs to be fixed is the language policy outlined in the Nigerian National Policy on Education (NPE) and which shows critical flaws in its implementation.

Following from the same trend of thought is Amoloye (Chapter 7) who focuses on language planning in Nigeria with special attention to the Yoruba language as a language of education in the southwest part of Nigeria. His discussion focuses on the nature of Nigeria's dense multilingualism and multi-dialectism. He contends that there is no single language that can be considered predominant in the country. Yoruba serves as dominant languages of the southwestern states of the country (encompassing Lagos, Ogun, Ondo, Ekiti, Oyo, Osun and some parts of

Kwara and Kogi states) where it has maintained a visible status since the introduction of formal western education in Nigeria. Its influence can be seen in the major education policies of Nigeria (Adegbija 2004).

Often times, when language policy and implementation is discussed, scholars make reference to Tanzania's approach to national language policy. This is because Tanzania declared Swahili a national language in the early years of independence and has never stopped advocating for the language as a learning tool and a symbol of national unity. Omar (Chapter 8) shows one of the covert ways Tanzania has been able to mobilize the nation on language policy without alarming the people. Omar shows how Swahili speakers utilize fabrics as a pedagogical tool to spread the language both at home and in the Diaspora. Her discussion focuses on the implications of Kanga captions in social and political communication and the link to the teaching and learning of Swahili. Khanga is a social garment worn in Tanzania, predominantly by women as everyday day attire. However, it has also been utilized as a teaching tool to meet cultural, political, and social functions. Omar provides a brief history of the 'kanga' also known as 'leso'. By using data from previous literature, her own personal kanga collection as well as personal communication, she provides a detailed discussion of socio-cultural and socio-political uses of the 'kanga'. Women, sole users of the 'kanga' in public places, communicate with each other indirectly using 'kanga' captions. They use kanga captions to argue and to provide warning, advice, as well as expressions of love and appreciation. Kanga captions are also used to support different political views and promote governmental as well as non-governmental programs. The kanga, as a cultural product can be used in the teaching of Swahili in the Diaspora to reinforce the 5Cs of the National Foreign Language Standards, namely: (1) Communication: the use of language for communication in "real life" situations; (2) Cultures: experiencing other cultures to develop a better understanding and appreciation of the relationship between languages and other cultures; (3) Connections: to connected with other subject areas; Comparisons: to compare and contrast languages and cultures; (4) Communities: to extend learning experiences from the world language classroom to the home and multilingual and multicultural community in order to emphasizes living in a global society.

Adeniyi and Bello (Chapter 9) discusses language contact and language use with focus on the acquisition of Igbo by undergraduate students in Nigerian Universities. For the most part they discuss the concept of language in contact noting that the concept brings to mind the bidirectional effects the two languages have on each other when they come in contact. Evidence comes from looking at language use by the Nigerian Igbo-English bilingual speakers, (undergraduate students) from selected Southwestern universities in Nigeria. These were mostly minority bilingual speakers in the communities and the investigation involved how they were able to socialize while they retain and/or maintain their indigenous identity. The framework was based on Winford's (2004) in which Winford contended that language contact situations are generally subject to two often conflicting forces which are the need to achieve communicative efficiency adequate for the purpose of interaction and the need to preserve a distinct sense of group identity. This research brings to bear what is needed from the field of African languages to enrich the pedagogy.

Radio programs are important in preserving and promoting indigenous languages both for communication and classroom use. Faleye (Chapter 10) discusses the danger in restricting the use of indigenous languages in radio programming. Radio plays an important role in education when it promotes the use of languages amongst people in a particular society. Programmers and presenters on a radio station can be linked to linguistic field research assistants while they educate the rest of the community. It is, therefore important for radio programs to consider the use of indigenous languages and provide the service to a variety of listeners. Faleye discusses data obtained from *Orísun* FM radio station that promote the sustainability of the Yoruba language to its listeners.

Following this is a discussion by Akanmu (Chapter 11) on the oriki (panegyric) phenomenon as archival material for Yoruba history, a valuable contribution to pedagogical studies. Oriki is one of the most popular Yoruba oral and poetic genres that are often featured in the performance of all Yoruba chanters as they address members of their audience. Oriki is basically panegyric i. e. praise poetry. Although it is very difficult to analyze, oriki exhibit apparent truths reflecting human experiences; represent the philosophy and worldview of a people, and are used in various occasions. Oriki can be used to reveal people's origins, their ancestry, and wealth, nobility, and life accomplishments. The importance of infusing this knowledge in pedagogy comes from the fact that oriki is gradually losing popularity among the Yoruba people due to the effects of globalization. The author hopes that by investigating its history and use, its plight as a useful linguistic genre would prompt additional research and connect it to pedagogy to enrich the Yoruba language and culture studies.

Bolaji and Adeniyi (Chapter 12) focuses on the expectations from learners of a second language in Nigeria in light of the fact that English which is often considered a second language by many Nigerians is also the government's official language. It is thereof not only required but also a necessary tool for advancement which makes the learning critical to many Nigerians. The authors look at these goals in light of the errors that are made by learners as they strive for near native proficiency and how their first languages affect these efforts. They also recommend strategic measures to overcome the errors while they suggest theatre and drama which emphasize action, vision and imitation as valuable strategies for teaching language and improving spoken language.

Finally, another concise discussion that contributes correspondingly on the assorted uses of language in Africa is presented by Ojuade (Chapter 13) on interpreting the language of the drums: a case study of Nigerian Yoruba traditional bata and dundun dancers. The discussion concerns specific traditions of the Yorubas of the Southern part of Nigeria and their interpretations through dance movement in Nigeria. It examines the interplay of the ensuing communication and variations that occur occasionally between the drummers and dancers in performance(s). This discussion raises questions about the dancers' ability to easily decode the assumed knotty, difficult, and complex language of the drums using his or her body. It equally compares the Bata and Dundun drum patterns in word formations/interpretations while making a comprehensive recommendation for the further inclusion of the drums (usage and application) in day-to-day activities.

The papers collected here focus on the diverse uses of language, especially the indigenous African languages and English, on the African continent. In addition, they share concern about the less often discussed language related issues in education, communication, history and development in Africa. From the prognosis provided on the plight of indigenous languages on the African continent (Moshi: Chapter 2) to the explication of national language policies and their impacts on development in different African countries (Elugbe: Chapter 2; Kyei-Mensah: Chapter 4; Arasanyin: Chapter 5; and Ojo: Chapter 6) as well as the pronunciation challenges facing African speakers of European languages (Bolaji and Idowu: Chapter 12), the collection lays out helpful arguments for the increased teaching and use of indigenous African languages on the continent. Additionally, the collection further provides illustration of the importance and valuable roles of indigenous African languages in areas such as indigenous language education (Amoloye: Chapter 7; and

Omar: Chapter 8), higher education (Adeniyi and Bello: Chapter 9), mass media, particularly community based radio programming (Faleye: Chapter 10), historical records and cultural archiving (Akanmu: Chapter 11) and performance (Ojuade: Chapter 13).

In all, *Language Pedagogy and Language Use in Africa* highlights some of the vital and highly applicable uses of indigenous African languages for development. The illustrations provided of both direct and indirect use of African languages on the continent and beyond as a result of both historical and contemporary contacts, language planning policies and pedagogical concerns would be of interest to all scholars and practitioners interested in the teaching, development and utilization of African languages both in Africa and elsewhere.

References

Abraham, R. 1967. The Principle of Ibo. Ibadan, Nigeria: University of Ibadan Press.

Bamgbose, Ayo. 1966. A Grammar of Yoruba. Cambridge: Cambridge University Press.

Bendor, John. 1989. The Niger Congo Languages. Lanham, NY: University Press of America.

Doke, C. M. 1943. Outline grammar of Bantu. Johannesburg, South Africa.

_____1945. Bantu-Modern grammatical, phonetic, and lexicographical Studies Series 1860. London Percy Lund.

Greenberg, Joseph H. 1948. The Tonal System of Proto Bantu Word: 4-176-208.

_____1955. Studies in African Linguistic Classification. New Haven, CT: Compass Publishing Company.

_____1963. The Languages of Africa. The Hague: Mouton; JAL 29. 1 Publication 25 of the Indiana University research Center in Anthropology, Folklore and Linguistics. Bloomington, Indiana University Press.

Guthrie, Malcomn. 1967. Comparative Bantu, Volume 1. Gregg Press LTD.

_____1971. Comparative Bantu, Volume 2. Gregg International Publication LTD.

Koelle, S. W. 1854. Polyglotta Africana. (Republished in 1963). London: Gregg International.

Meinhof, C. 1904- 1906. Linguistischen Studien in Ostafrika. Mitteilungen Des Seminars Fur Orientalischen Sprachen Zu Berlin Vol. VII – IX.

Meeussen, A. E. 1967. Bantu Grammar reconstruction. Africana Linguistica, 3. Annasen van het Koninklijk Museum voo Midden-Africa 61:79-121. Tervuren.

Migeod, F. W. H. 1911. Languages of West Africa. London: Kegan Paul, Trench, Trubner & Co.

Pike, K. L. 1948. Tone Languages. Ann Arbor: University of Michigan Press.

Welmers, W. E. 1973. African Language Structures. Berkeley: University of California Press.

Winford, D. 2003. An introduction to Contact Linguistics. Malden. M. A. Blackwell Publishers.

Chapter 2

THE PLIGHT OF INDIGENOUS LANGUAGES: A PROGNOSIS

Lioba Moshi

Introduction

The struggle to sustain and raise the visibility profile of African languages in the world is not only important but also necessary due to the contribution study of world languages and cultures. Once a language dies, so does its culture and history of its speakers. There is shared blame for the demise of Afro-ethnic languages, on colonialism and the lack of commitment to these languages by the African élites, leaders, and the speakers at large. It is disconcerting that African countries have never been able to do what other colonized nations have done, namely sustaining and maintaining the visibility of their ethnic languages despite the imperial language influences that are associated with colonialism. Countries like Japan, China, and India use ethnic languages in all critical medium of communication while imperial languages are reserved for inter-continental and business communications. In this paper, I will explore some of the aspects that seem to create such discrepancies with specific examples from East Africa and more so from Tanzania.

Influences on the Status of Ethnic Languages

There are three factors that contribute to the growth or demise of ethnic languages, namely historical, emerging national languages, and the African consciousness.

Historical factors

Many African languages do not have a documented history other than passing references when discussing other world languages particularly the introduction of imperial languages and their connection to religion, education, and governance in different regions of African. A few, like Kiswahili have a substantial history documented because of the role the language played in either counteracting colonialism or enhancing colonialism. For example, scholars have for a long time debated the origins of Kiswahili, taking a stand in defense of the central role of Arabic in Kiswahili language and civilization (e. g. Stigan 1913, Kirkman 1964 and others). Marzui, Mazrui, and Sharif (1994) had also posited a hypothesis that favored the role of Arabic in the formation of Kiswahili by positing that the roots of Kiswahili were in pidgin Arabic that developed as a result of contact between the native coastal people and Arab traders. This hypothesis was critiqued by Nurse and Hinnebusch (1996) with a claim that favors an exclusive Bantu origin for Kiswahili. Opposition to the exclusive role of Arabic in the formation of Kiswahili language and civilization as espoused by the *'external origin theory'* include: Fitzgerald (1898), Hinnebusch 1976), Nurse 1983, Nurse and Spear 1985, Mutoro 1987, Wilding 1989, Middleton 1992, Horton 1996, and Kusimba (1999). Essentially, the *'external origin theory'*, stated that the Coastal people of Eastern Africa did not exist prior to the arrival of outsiders, bringing with them the culture, civilization, and language. There was a tendency to believe that African cities were built by foreigners, and that the civilization which developed on the Swahili Coast was a by-product of the migration of people and ideas from the Near East. Furthermore, the role of indigenous people in understanding the origins of social complexities was not considered important or relevant. (Kirkman1964:22). Unfortunately the debate caused more harm than good. It impacted and continues to impact the role of Kiswahili in East Africa and globally and it extenuates the demise of other ethnic languages by emphasizing the importance of imported languages to the development and wellbeing of a people.

The demise of ethnic languages started with the introduction of foreign religions in African communities. Both Islam and Christianity imposed foreign language usage on the people. Islam is responsible for the extensive use of Arabic while Christianity introduced the major European languages on the continent: English, Portuguese, German, and Italian (and Latin for religious services in the Catholic Church). Arabic and Islam predated the European languages and it was widely accepted by the start of Christianity and colonialism. The need to introduce colonial languages was largely influenced by a perceived threat to those who wanted to establish colonies. Mazrui and Mazrui (1998) reveal some of the conflicts that ensued, for example, as different colonial powers sought to control the Swahili States that were already under the influence of Arabic and Islam. Mazrui and Mazrui note that the African colonial experience showed a close link between colonialism and religious establishments. Christian missionaries were logical foundations for the establishment of colonies and their ventures preceded colonial military invasions and rule. However, to expedite the control and to ensure a captive audience to the Christian establishment, missionaries downplayed the emphasis on western languages. They saw a need to learn the local languages as they quickly realized that the best way to win the African soul and mind to ensure a deeper interaction with the native people they too had to learn the languages of their converts. Resulting from this venture are the numerous early grammars and bibles written in the local languages. They saw a need to develop an understanding of the culture of their converts in order to communicate effectively to them the "Word of God. " In order for them to explain why they should abandon their own religious beliefs in favor of the new (foreign) religious belief they need to create an atmosphere that is closer to the convert's cultural roots.

The language choice for the spread on Christianity in East Africa was largely influenced by the 'external origin theory' that sought to drive a wedge between the Swahili and non-Swahili speakers as well as the prevailing competition on winning converts. While the Protestants (mostly Germans) utilized the 'external origin theory' the Catholics (mixed sources) overlooked this aspect. Thus many of the hymnals, bibles, and some grammars translated into local languages were done by missionaries who were competing for Protestants converts. Catholics used Latin (traditional service) and Kiswahili (sermons/other teachings). This division provides for the argument on the one hand, that could support the 'eternal origin theory' whose intention was to show non-Kiswahili speakers that Kiswahili was just as foreign as any of the other foreign languages. Such an argument would also strengthen the belief that the Western forces were looking out for the natives by encouraging the development of their own languages to counter the Islamic-based Kiswahili language. Present day scholars could argue that if the controversy had been allowed to grow roots, the role of indigenous languages in East Africa would have developed to match that of present day Kiswahili. However, when we look at competition between Kiswahili and English in the region, it is clear that there are no guarantees that any of the favored indigenous languages during the establishment of Christianity would have withstood the strong winds of the imperial English language or whether a linguistic scramble for Africa would have ensured in the process of competing for converts for the different religions. English has attained a priority status in all aspects of communication in East Africa and has become a preferred language of communication by the academic élites and political leaders. In Tanzania the competition is exemplified by the mushrooming of English-based private elementary schools which feed into English-only secondary schools.

With respect to colonial languages in Eastern Africa, one aspect of interest is the competition encountered between Islam and Christianity. Islam was considered a great influence on Kiswahili causing suspicion among advocates of Christianity especially westerners who did not trust the growing relationship between the language and Islam. The deep fear of the spread of Islam across the continent of Africa by westerners influenced their concern on its link to the language of the Coastal states that had the potential of influencing the hinterland through trade and other social and cultural interactions. The 1905 attempt by Germany to obstruct the penetration of Islam into different territories in Africa especially emerging ones like the Coastal States that spoke Kiswahili resulted from the antagonism between Islam and Christianity. Julius Richter, a member of the Berlin Committee on the expansion of Islam, adopted and expanded the opposition to the influence of Islam everywhere in Africa. East Africa was seen as a new area of interest and was designated the scene of the most danger due to the association of Kiswahili with Islamic culture. To limit the spread of Kiswahili from the Coastal States to the hinterland, a claim was made that Kiswahili was not indigenous to the coastal people but rather imported and had its origins in Arabic. The claim was supported by the Arabic elements in the language that largely resulted from Kiswahili's heavy lexical borrowings from Arabic. By making such a claim, the destructors were able to discredit Kiswahili making it impossible for polities to advocate it as a lingua franca for the hinterland. It was also discredited as a possible language of the gospel that was used to spread Christianity. Because the missionaries were suspicious of Kiswahili they embarked on learning the local languages, translated the gospel and hymnals in local languages to counter the use of Kiswahili and its Islamic influences.

The distrust of Kiswahili and the subsequent campaign to dissociate it with Islam damaged the status of Kiswahili as a revered ethnic language. It also paved the way for the disregard for other ethnic languages in favor of imperial languages that were seen as an alternative to a single unifying continental language. It is without doubt that Kiswahili could have grown to a stronger regional language considering its historical importance to the East African Coastal States. The earliest known documentation that establishes Kiswahili as an indigenous language in the Coastal States dates back to the 2nd century AD. Kusimba (1999) notes that merchants visiting the East African coast at that time from Southern Arabia, found natives speaking the language, spreading from southwards of Somalia and Kenya all the way to Zanzibar and Kilwa. It is also believed that the Kiswahili civilization carved out a small territory even further south around Sofala in Zimbabwe.

External trade and social interactions are essential elements in civilizations. There is no doubt that visitors to the Swahili coastal states namely the Arabs, Persians, and the Portuguese, played a significant role in the growth of Kiswahili civilization. They played a prominent role in the triangular mercantile trade, establishing cultural and commercial relations with the East African interior, the Persian and Arabian Gulf, the Indian subcontinent, and Indonesia. As such, they were very important in the world trade as early as 1 B. C. At the same time, they destroyed successful polities that were highly respected by the people and nobilities that were African in origin and enslaved the indigenous people. They also disrupted a vibrant trade that had established them as sophisticated merchants who traded with other coastal people and those who lived near and far. Before it was infiltrated, the Kiswahili language and culture of the Coastal people was vibrant and later became multi-textured because of a number of factors including an extensive and dynamic interaction between the indigenous people of the Coastal States and towns with the majority culture, the cultures of the rural people who traded and interacted with them, and non-Africans who ventured into the Coastal States from across the oceans.

The question is: What would have happened if the Swahili Coastal States were never infiltrated and subjected to the negative forces? Proponents of Kiswahili's ethnic origins would contend that if infiltration by outsiders had not happened, the people would have emerged differently due to their savvy trading skills of the time. Such savvy skills would have influenced a unique type of civilization that had already started to show in the southern coastal city of Kilwa. This Tanzanian city was described by Ibn Battuta[1], in his 1332 visit, as one of the most beautiful and best-constructed towns he had visited. The city also endowed with tremendous wealth as a result of its trade with merchants from the near and far east. However, the arrival of the Portuguese at the beginning of the sixteenth century brought an abrupt end to the civilization and prosperity of the city. It is without doubt that if the destruction had not occurred, the indigenous Coastal States could have contributed to world civilizations in a more significant way while developing global visibility that matches that of the Asian countries of today.

The *'external origin theory'* that excluded Kiswahili from the list of ethnic languages of East Africa affected the way the Swahili Coastal States were perceived and continue to been viewed in history. It allowed the distinctive cultural and ethnic character of the Swahili people who are urban, literate, and Islamic, and seemingly unlike the others who are rural, farmers, non-literate, and traditionally African, in their beliefs, to be used as evidence of their separate identities and cultural origins, reinforcing the theory and the class system that we will discuss shortly. By not according the origins of Kiswahili and the civilization of the Coastal States to the indigenous people, the debate generated negative views that, undoubtedly, contributed to the view that placed Kiswahili and many other ethnic languages on the margins of world history and interests of western science. Kiswahili was not given the chance to develop similarly to languages in other formerly colonized nations such as in Asia. Asian countries that were colonized by the English (such as China, India, Malaysia) or the French (Vietnam, Cambodia Laos) have never been identified as Anglophone or Francophone or referred to by the imperial language. Without doubt, the external origin theory of Kiswahili made it easier for foreign languages and language policies to be imposed on the people, minimizing its importance and creating its lasting demise globally and in general the demise of all other ethnic languages of the region.

The decline of the Coastal city-states, their languages and cultures began in the 16th century; the advent of the arrival of the Portuguese who caused the most disruption of the old trade routes making the Swahili commercial centers obsolete. The Portuguese were not interested in including native Africans in what we could term *'early free trade practices'*. Because the Arabs had enslaved and converted the locals into Islam, the Portuguese set out with a mission to conquering the Islamic city-states along the eastern coast. Although the Omans (from south of Arabia) returned in the 17th Century and conquered the Portuguese cities along the coast, the natives did not sigh with relief because slavery and subjugation continued and the new controlling power played as much of a major role in the destruction of individual and collective creativity that had existed prior to their arrival. Destroyed in the process also was the people's linguistic and cultural confidence and diversity. Trade, friendship, and alliances between many different communities that led to the exchange of ideas, information, and genes through shared language and cultural beliefs were also destroyed.

To be fair, I must point out that there were some desired gains. Many of the ethnic languages benefited from the language of the rulers through lexical borrowing. This was necessary because it enhanced trading activities. For example, Kiswahili demonstrates a lexicon that has been enriched by the various encounters with the outside world. Such influences include number terms like: sita 'six' saba 'seven' and tisa 'nine' that are considered borrowed words from Arabic to add to the Bantu numbers: moja 'one', mbili 'two', tatu 'three', nne 'four', tano 'five', nane 'eight', kumi 'ten. Needelss to say tisa replaced the Bantu word kenda which is still used to mean 'nine'. Furthermore, the Kiswahili words: serikali 'government', diwani 'councilor', and chai 'tea', are among some of the words considered borrowed from Persian. Borrowings from Portuguese include meza 'table' gereza 'prison', and pesa ('peso'), 'money'. The German rule introduced into the language words like shule 'school' and 'hela' a German coin rupee. Likewise, English (British) introduced words like baiskeli 'bicycle', basi 'bus', penseli 'pencil', mashine 'machine', and koti 'coat', and continues to influence the language to date. However, this is not to say that this rich resource would not have developed through other means considering the pre-existing trade relations that involved different polities, both near and far. Another influencing factor is the interpretation of cultural behavior, cultural values, cultural attitudes, and perspectives that were introduced to the indigenous people. The Arab control brought Islam and its culture that emphasized the Koran and the strict observances of the Islamic culture. It also instituted a social class system that valued those who were direct descendants of the rulers and demeaned those who were not. There were four main social classes (Kusimba 1999: 140-141):

1. *waungwana* 'élite' (the ethic of possessing high culture) which included the free, or nobly born--- descendants of the Sultan (Arab ruler)

2. *wazaliwa* 'free-born'/descendants of freed slaves or at least one of their parents (often the mother);

3. *watumwa* 'slaves' those who were enslaved;

4. *wageni* 'visitors' - included recent immigrants and other inhabitants from the non-Coastal States.

These terms made reference to the rights and privileges that depended on one's social status. The *waungwana* were predominantly in the urban areas and led an urban life. They also controlled the socio-political and economic structures of the community. Because they were considered to posses the high culture, intellectual, and artistic sensitivity, they also acquired the ideological support to their control of wealth-creating activities, including land and labor; had exclusive ownership of the fertile land, stretches of beach, and mangrove swamps. They had a right to slaves who worked these lands and had a right to make policy decisions in the affairs of the town. Not everyone could claim membership to the *uungwana* social group, only those who were able to demonstrate blood ties to a well-respected ancestor, who could supplement their kin-based claims to status with wealth. Ownership of a stone house in an élite section of the town enhanced that affiliation and stamp of approval. This social status were translated to other languages and are responsible for the changes in the rural chiefdoms where the chief and his immediate acquaintances assumed a privileged status that was emerging in the areas most affected by the foreign influences. The chiefdoms included separate categories: (1) immediate members of the chief and the chief bearers, (2) adopted members by the chiefdoms to attend group 1, and (3) laborers (those who worked on the chief's farms and property).

Kusimba (1999) notes that *ungwana* privileges included the right: to religious scholarship, to own property such as fertile farmland, stretches of beach land, mangrove forests, and fishing areas, to own cattle, to build and live in stone houses in one's own neighborhood, to receive, entertain, and trade with foreign merchants, to elect town, and mosque officials, and to hold hereditary offices such as a prison warden or the town treasurer. Even the sea was owned by the *waungwana* and was designated a hereditary office with a warden. A stricter consideration for the inclusion of members outside groups 1&2 was influenced by the change of property ownership. The subjugation of the chiefs by the colonial powers resulted in the community losing much of their property, especially farmland, if they did not belong to groups 1&2. Likewise, left with limited land to distribute to the people, the chiefs had to focus on class and status when distributing land to the community. By doing so, the community's cultural and social fabric fractured and promoted individualism rather than encouraging collectivity.

In East Africa, particularly Tanzania, the British colonial era introduced the English language as part the governing system, educational system, and the English cultural values. English was given a priority, in the urban cities and schools and later infiltrated the rural areas through the school system. One could start learning English from the third grade and schools offered at least three hours of English classes a day with only one hour for Kiswahili. The medium of instruction for other classes was Kiswahili in primary school while English took over Middle School, High School, and College. Emphasis was placed on excelling in English as a prerequisite to excelling in other subjects and advancement into the élite group of the society. This affected the language attitudes of the people, something that has persisted to date. The importance of local languages in shaping the cultural and social attitudes of the community was lost in this case and to some extent also the attitude toward Kiswahili as a local language with a lingua franca status. Thus the emphasis of English contributed to the demise of not only the ethnic languages that were already being used in the house of worship but also Kiswahili that was trying to grow its viability as a national language. Culturally, the English language created a social class system, with subtle rights and privileges. As it will be shown later this attitude and the creation of an inferior mind set has proved to be a major challenge, even in a country like Tanzania where tremendous effort has been undertaken since independence to eliminate the inferior/superior perception and status espoused by fluency in an imperial language.

The rise of a unifying language

As noted earlier, colonialism had major effects on both ethnic and emerging national languages. On the one hand colonialism encouraged the development of ethnic languages by giving its speakers more autonomy during the colonial period. This changed after independence. In Kenya, for example, the British encouraged the natives to speak their own language and promoted Kiswahili (Kiunguja) as a medium of communication. There are those who evaluated this gesture not as an encouragement for the preservation of ethnic languages and cultures but rather a subtle element of racism. This thinking is derived from the belief by the colonial masters that the Africans were not good enough to speak the imperial language and therefore did not want their subjects who worked for them as house servants or farm laborers to use their English instead of their own ethnic languages. To bridge the linguistic gap, the English attempted to learn the local languages, especially Kiswahili to enforce the rule that limited the locals' need to use English when communicating with their masters. Lord Lugard's[2] a British bureaucrat asserted that the native Kenya's were not good enough to speak English.

Incidentally this is very similar to an earlier stance by the Germans during their colonial rule because they did not want the natives to learn and speak German because that would have made them equals. By contrast the French emphasized the importance of its subjects learning French but motivated differently. The reason, which could be construed just as much a sense of indifference as the case of the Germans and British in Kenya, was that they did not believe that a native was good enough until he/she spoke French fluently (Mazrui & Mazrui 1998, 1999).

With Kiswahili well utilized during and before independence in Tanzania, it was enhanced and thus independence fostered the emergence of Kiswahili as a lingua Franca. With the role of a lingua Franca, Kiswahili rapidly spread from the Coastal States to the hinterland crossing borders to other parts of sub-Sahara Africa. The rapid nature of its spread and the ease at which it was accepted by other communities stems from its adopted role in the early 50s when it assumed a political function of fostering nationalism. It was used to advocate for African nationalism, the right to self-determination, and independence by the African political leaders who assumed leaderships of their countries both in pre and post independence from colonial rule.

The Uganda experience is interesting because of the relationship between who ruled the country and who dominated the armed force. At the onset of colonialism, English was adopted by the Royale Family that sought to make its off-springs the élites of the kingdoms. Consequently, the ethnic languages grew as a medium of communication and services among the citizenry while English became the language of the Royal family and the élites after it was embraced in education to benefit the nation. Nevertheless, ethnic languages remained a symbol of cultural pride. Kiswahili entered Uganda through the military. Both Milton Obote and Idi Amin who ruled Uganda at different times, come from the northern part of Uganda and were linked to the Nilotes. Consequently, the armed forces looked to the north for recruitments making the Nilotes the largest in numbers in the army. The Nilotes were very conscious of their separateness from the Bantu groups that were predominantly settled in the southern parts of Uganda and were especially alienated from the Baganda (Mazrui & Mazrui 1999). This relationship created ethnic rivalry among the groups (Acholi, Langi, Kakwa, Lugbara, Baganda, and Nilotes). It is also interesting to note that the rivalry necessitated the use of a common language for communication within the army. To build and sustain camaraderie, Kiswahili became the language of choice across ethnic boundaries and even when Idi Amin came to power and eliminated many of the Acholi and Langi members of the armed force, Kiswahili remained the language of choice in the army. Outside the army, Kiswahili gained political importance during Idi Amin's reign despite the hostility and political decline associated with his brutal regime. This is because the Baganda saw wisdom in changing their resistance to Kiswahili and became the propagators of Kiswahili and its integrative functions in the army. Needless to say, that move did not affect the sustainability of their ethnic languages.

The role of ethnic languages in Kenya and Uganda is demonstrated by their *right to language* mandate. This is an allowance for individuals to determine the language for effective communication. This right explains the mode of operation in the Kenya parliament. While the constitution in Kenya is written in English it can be discussed in English or Swahili in parliament. Furthermore, a President in Kenya has to be trilingual: competent in the imperial language (English), the preponderant language (Kiswahili), and the language of the major ethnic constituency (Kikuyu, Kalenjin, Luo, or other). A trilingual President in Kenya is a *de facto* requirement. In Uganda, English is very visible and it is considered a qualification for the presidency because any Afro-ethnic language is seen as a political risk in the deeply divided society. Kiswahili is still more popularly accepted among the northerners and the military than among the more numerous Bantu. However, while a Ugandan president could be unilingual -- simply competent or at best brilliant in the English language – Ugandans, unlike their counterparts the Kenyans and Tanzanians, revere ethnic languages and for that matter learn and speak each other's Afro-ethnic languages more readily.

Interestingly, both Kenya and Uganda look at Tanzania with envy due to the success Tanzania has attained in uniting its citizen both linguistically and culturally through the use of Kiswahili. However, while ethnic languages in Kenya take a second place to English, Tanzania's ethnic languages take a third place. Kiswahili takes a second place a strong competitor to English in urban areas but remains very strong in rural areas. IN other words, English has taken over Kiswahili in urban areas while Kiswahili has taken over ethnic languages in rural areas. It is possible to find rural communities where children are expected to grow up bilingual (Kiswahili and an ethnic language) but are now growing up as monolingual (Kiswahili only) speakers, a phenomenon that was considered more common in children born of parents who moved to the city cities during colonial and early post independence eras.

It is interesting to also note that colonialism allowed Kiswahili to penetrate and influence areas beyond the rural boundaries of the hinterland from the original coastal states to neighbor countries, namely the Francophone countries of the Democratic Republic of the Congo (DRC), Rwanda, and Burundi, where French was introduced through the Belgians. The penetration was influenced by trade and later by other linguistic implications of the Belgians and the French with respect to the introduction of the French language to the people of these countries.

Because of the Belgian's linguistic composition (had two languages at their disposal: French and Flemish) there was a period when it was not clear, in Belgian Congo, whether French or Flemish would be the language to be adopted. The perception and association of the French language made the Belgians both fear and revere the French. However, they used their Flemish cultural affiliations with German to create a linguistic distance from the French. Interestingly, in the African context, the French language thrived even though it was sandwiched, in some parts, between indigenous African languages and Flemish. Nevertheless, the ambiguity gave Kiswahili an opportunity to fill the void by penetrating the Eastern and Southern parts of the Congo. Kiswahili became the unifying element between the people, a much needed cultural bond. When the DRC achieved its independence a substantial number of Congolese had acquired a high proficiency in Kiswahili even though it never attained an influential status. It was, nevertheless Kiswahili was adopted by a majority of Congolese but it did it was not powerful enough (as it was the case in Tanzania) to threatened indigenous languages of the area. While Lingala and Kikongo are primary languages in the DRC, Kiswahili has remained one of the important languages for the people who adopted it during the colonial period. The expansion and the bond that Kiswahili has been able to cultivate among different speakers support my earlier comment that if relationship between Kiswahili and Islam had not been used as a wage issue by the imperial powers, its influence was powerful enough to create a large impact anywhere in Africa, let alone east Africa.

National Consciousness

Linguistically, Africa is divided into: Anglophone (English affiliate), Francophone (French/Belgian Affiliate), Lusophone (Portuguese affiliate). Many of the countries in these categories are geographically referred to as such. No other colonized nation ever received this kind of geographical categorization or is still referred to by the imperial language. Mazrui and

Mazrui (1998) explain this anomaly as inevitable consequently to Africa's political dependence on the imperial languages. They also link the anomaly to the power of the colonial masters, and their relationship with those they ruled. This relationship created a type of nationalism that did not lead to the demand of less English but rather more especially in Kenya and Uganda. This demand for more rather than less English for the middle class was (and to some extent presently too) interpreted as a struggle for equal opportunity for 'good' education. Mazrui and Mazrui point out, for example, there is evidence for a stronger ethno-linguistic nationalism among the Baganda due to their support of Luganda, one of the major languages in Uganda than can be claimed by speakers of Gikuyu in Kenya. To some extent this can be explained by the fact that the Baganda succeeded in their opposition to the promotion of Kiswahili in Uganda while the Gikuyu speakers have done the opposite. Needless to say, the campaign against Kiswahili enhanced the promotion of English in Uganda while the acceptance Kiswahili for national purposes by the Gikuyu speakers somehow affected quest for the English language in Kenya. The opposition resulted from the Baganda's (mainly the royals) regarded of Kiswahili as the language of 'the lower classes' or the 'lesser breeds' with its use at the workplace, the market, and by soldiers from the barracks (mostly composed of men from the northern part of the country). As such, English was promoted for 'class' distinctions.

In Kenya, the image of Kiswahili was and continues to reflect a more class-neutral status. It was once the language of 'sultans' at the coast. It later became the preferred political language of independent Kenya (as promoted by the first President, Jomo Kenyata). Along the coast, it was preserved by poets and creative writers, an aspect that served to affirm the dignity of Kiswahili as an indigenous language of the coastal states and to counteract the pervasiveness of English with local languages. It is factors like these that have enhance the national consciousness of the need for a national language with Kiswahili catching up in the politics of class consciousness in both Uganda and Kenya. However, there are still signs of the effects of the power of colonialism on the colonized. The environment created continues to sustain, on the continent, a heavy reliance on foreign languages. In most of the sub-Saharan African countries governments conduct their business, legislate, and conduct judiciary processes primarily in European languages. Even Tanzania that had made strides in changing this trend, are slipping back to over reliance on English. Mazrui and Mazrui explain such trends as a consequence of an absence of linguistic loyalty by a people to indigenous/national languages. They note that over relying on imported imperial languages robe Africans the legitimacy of questioning the inappropriate use of the terms 'Anglophone', 'francophone', and 'Lusophone' to describe different regions of the continent.

In Tanzania, Swahili gained prominence in the 60s, shortly after its independence from the British. It was the language of politics and governance. In 1967, it was declared the language of instruction at elementary and middle school levels. Julius Nyerere, the first President of Tanzania championed the change and in identifying an indigenous language as the national language. His efforts were supported by those of the other leaders in East Africa in developing Kiswahili. Their enthusiasm stemmed from a national patriotic understanding and belief in specific ideals. In Tanzania, for example, the citizenry believe that *nationalism* and *cultural revolution* relies heavily in the development of Kiswahili, the single unifying language. In this respect, we can claim that Tanzania made a conscious decision to overlook the cultural importance of their various ethnic languages in order to develop a nation consciousness that unites the country for a common good. It is important, however to understand that there was no institutional moratorium on the ethnic languages in order to promote Kiswahili. However, the collective need for a national language gradually affected the status of ethnic languages by reducing their visibility both locally and nationally. Gone with the linguistic visibility are also the cultures that contributed greatly to the social values espoused by different communities. Today, both in rural and urban communities show traces of cultural adaptations that have prompted the nation to accept and emphasize a Tanzanian culture rather than a Sukuma, Chaga, Nyakyusa, or Gogo to name only a few. As noted earlier, rural communities that used to be bilingual are more and more becoming monolingual. It is no secret that Kiswahili is the preferred language of the home, especially among the younger generation despite heavy competition from local and other indigenous languages.

Credit to the *national consciousness* development goes to President Julius Kambarage Nyerere, the late and first President of Tanzania. It was during the early years of his governance that Kiswahili gained popularity at home, regionally, and in the Diaspora. He was seen as a revolutionary leader who wanted to rid his country of dependency and colonial mentality. He joined forces with Kwame Nkrumah, President of Ghana, to champion Pan Africanism which appealed to a lot of Africans in the Diaspora. With his writing on Freedom, Unity, and Familyhood and his efforts to translate major writings by Shakespeare[3] into Kiswahili won him respect in the Diaspora and generated an enthusiasm to learn Kiswahili. It was during this era that Kiswahili was institutionalized in many institutions abroad. It is without doubt that he will be remembered for his advocacy of *National Consciousness* to his people and the world. The popularity of his ideas won him much respect from his people a valuable asset in the later years of his reign factor that kept Tanzania free of ethnic strife over the promotion of Kiswahili at the expense of ethnic languages.

It can be argued that Nyerere's success in instilling a *national consciousness philosophy* to his people a national *cultural consciousness* was inevitable. Such a consciousness would have to borrow from different ethnic backgrounds and each group has to compromise in order to make it work. Indeed, Tanzania's *national consciousness philosophy* promoted Kiswahili at home and beyond. Because ethnicity was suppressed in order to promote a national unity, the love and pride of ethnic languages were lost in the process. Ethnic cultures were not completely lost but the power associated with a strong sense of ethnicity was minimized, a factor also that can be used to explain the fact that Tanzania, unlike its neighbors, has never been engaged in ethnic rivalry. It is, therefore, an understatement to assert that advocating for ethnic languages in Tanzania would be a daunting task compared to her neighbors. As national language, advocating for a national consciousness and promoting a national cultural consciousness, Kiswahili has gain unbeatable power. It has benefited greatly, both linguistically and culturally, by borrowing from different sources both locally and from other Bantu languages within the region (East Africa) in addition to foreign languages. As such, Kiswahili has been able to show linguistic inclusiveness that other global languages have failed to do. Thus its popularity is here to stay and no amount of advocacy for ethnic languages in Tanzania can diminish the ability for Kiswahili to continue to grow. The popularity of Kiswahili in Tanzania has a profound influence on the neighboring countries, a language of choice in many homes of mixed ethnicity, refugee campus and now expanding to western nations where the refugees from Somalia, Rwanda, Burundi, and the democratic republic of the Congo are being settled (mostly the US and Europe).

The debate that would ensure in the near future is whether Kiswahili is sustainable as an indigenous language in the absence of the other indigenous languages that contributed to its lexical growth. It is important that as we continue to develop Kiswahili to a global status that it continues to borrow from like Bantu languages and cultures that are within the confines of its regional distribution. The inability to borrow from other regional Bantu languages would force Kiswahili to borrow more heavily from foreign languages and thus increase the potential to succumb to losing its status to its competitor, the English language. There is also a need for the nation to advocate for the retention of ethnic cultural consciousness through indigenous languages. Such retention would enhance the national cultural consciousness. The task of developing, promoting and sustaining ethnic cultural consciousness through indigenous languages cannot be assumed by any one person. It has to be a partnership between the government, scholars, and speakers of those languages. Just as Nyerere was able to promote a *national consciousness philosophy* without antagonizing the nation, the post-Nyerere generation of leaders should find a way to re-define the *cultural consciousness philosophy* of the nation that does not seek to pity one ethnic group against another, define or establish one culture as superior or better than another and yet allow each culture to promote and advocate for its ethnic language that informs the ethnic cultural fabric of the society. The expected outcome should be the ability to instill pride in a people and to show the importance of indigenous languages in framing the national culture. Culture should be describe in light of a society at a particular time and place; "a way of life mannerisms that are favored by a social group, and the knowledge and values that a society share. Culture should be defined as a 'total sum of different ways of doing' rather than a manifestation of a 'singularly way of doing'. In other words, culture should be defined as the cumulative deposit of experience, attitudes, beliefs, meanings, all kinds of values, hierarchies, religion, notions of time, roles, spatial relations, knowledge, concepts of the universe, and material objects and possessions acquired by a group of people in the course of generations through individual and group striving.

Implications for Africans and Africanists

There is a tendency for scholars to look outward rather than inward when discussing the demise of African languages and cultures. It is not true that what has happened to African languages was solely influenced by forces external to the continent. As noted by Mazrui and Mazrui (1998), speakers' lack of linguistic nationalism that grew roots during colonialism and continues to be sustained by African élites has contributed to the demise of indigenous languages. Those who might want to claim that the demise of African languages in Tanzania is a consequence of the drive to spread Kiswahili as a lingua franca, I would remind them that Kiswahili is in competition with English forty seven years after independence and the intensity is almost equal to that shown before independence. This is only possible despite the efforts made by the government to inculcate a national linguistic pride using Kiswahili. There is a segment in the society that still thinks that Kiswahili is ill equipped to deal with complicated philosophical and scientific issues. As such, one is considered not well educated unless they have a good command of the English language. Such a pressure forces parents and guardians to seek out English medium schools and are willing to pay top dollar to send their kids to English medium schools, sometimes outside the country and as early as age five. With that kind of pressure, the place of ethnic languages has been pushed further and further with limited chance of survival. The author will contend that it would be refreshing if at least Kiswahili sustains the momentum it had a couple of decades ago and remains the national unity symbol that it was immediately after independence. This can only be done if scholars and speakers advocate for the importance of a linguistic nationalism.

It is without doubt that regionally (i. e. East Africa), Kiswahili still commands a good linguistic lead among indigenous languages and it is fairly secure as a national language for Tanzania with a possible chance of attaining a global status. It has gained ground as a language of choice by millions of people in East Africa and its neighbors. It has also been transported to different parts of Africa and the West due to migration, both voluntary and as a consequence of ethnic wars, including the fight against colonialism and apartheid. Refugees from neighboring countries learn Kiswahili during their short stay in Kenya or Tanzania and keep the language when they finally immigrate to England, the United States, or other western countries. This is evident in the increase in demand for Kiswahili translators for agencies like the American based Language Line Inc., and Pacific Interpreters Inc., that offer services to law enforcement, hospitals, legal services, social services, immigration services, airline companies, and schools. Furthermore, the number of people learning Kiswahili at institutions of higher education in the United States has also attained impressive numbers but the enrolments are only high at the elementary and in special cases intermediate levels. Scholars in a position to advocate for serious language learning, in the likes of the commonly taught languages, should seize that opportunity.

It is also encouraging when we look at Europe and Asia where the enthusiasm in teaching and researching on African languages is strong with well defined objectives. For example, many European institutions of higher education, including private organizations, teach Kiswahili more intensely and purposefully. Their programs are usually tied to development projects that are sponsored by the European Economic market, and specific agencies such as DANIDA and NORAD, to name only a few. The United States institutions could exploit this opportunity for programs such as Peace Corps, UNCEF, UNESCO, various NGOs associated with projects on global health, the World Bank, USAID, other independent agencies and missionary organizations. Currently, most institutions focus on academic related programs for the purposes of research projects that relate to the publication of books and graduate theses. This is a very narrowly defined market for the purposes of advocating for African languages especially the popular ones like Kiswahili.

Available examples that demonstrate that Kiswahili is attaining prominence are ample as we experience the growing use of Kiswahili in world media such as the *Voice of America,* and *Radio Deutsche Welle, BBC radio and Television,* and *Asia radio and TV* programs that come to many homes in East Africa. Some of these programs are broadcasted to East Africa (especially Kenya, and Tanzania) on a regular basis (in some cases twice a day). In addition, Kiswahili has been identified by Microsoft for the development of scanner OCR that would identify Kiswahili text. The Nairobi Microsoft office (cf. Majira Newspaper, June 2004:2) noted that Kiswahili was selected because of its status, a strong African language that can stand a global test as a language of business and communication in East Africa. Other African languages that are being targeted include: Yoruba, Hausa, Somali, and Amharic. The growing interest to expose Kiswahili to technology is also demonstrated in the move by Vodacom and Celtel phone companies to regularly place advertisements in newspapers in both English and Kiswahili to advertise their services. Both companies have seen the wisdom of reaching all sectors of the public since the buying power or usage does not reside in the affluent only[4]. The challenge is to prevent these signs from remaining as signs and symbols that make us feel good for the moment. Establishing a sustainable global need and importance among other global languages is what Kiswahili needs (also other African languages). This can only be done by scholars and speakers. They should be the champions of establishing the need rather than discouraging it by inadvertently demonstrating that fluency in Kiswahili (or other key African languages) is unnecessary and therefore a low priority. Thus, as an Afro-ethnic language, Kiswahili has done very well and leaders like the late President Julius Nyerere are to be commended for their efforts to promote and advocate for the language.

What has not done so well are the millions of ethnic languages in Africa and those that Kiswahili has semi-replaced in the Coastal States of east Africa and more so mainland Tanzania.

The burden of promoting and sustaining ethnic languages should follow examples from Kiswahili. The responsibility lies with speakers, scholars, as well as the community and political leaders. The demise of ethnic languages is a consequence of speakers of African languages tendency to seek the prestige of speaking imperial languages as a way to show that they are educated. Speaking English, French, or Portuguese on the continent of Africa gives one an élite status, even in places like Kenya and Tanzania where Kiswahili has gain grounds and needs to be promoted to a global status. Only a handful of scholars write in their own languages (e. g. Ngungi wa Thiongo, Ruhumbika, Kezilahabi, etc…). The majority of scholars publish their researches exclusively in imperial languages. The only leaders, who give their speeches abroad in languages other than their own ethnic languages, even where they run a risk of embarrassing themselves because of limited fluency, are Africans. Other leaders take pride in their languages and cultures and are generally provided with translators when they need them. If African leaders can be provided with translators when speaking in a foreign environment with non-English, or to an English speaking audience when their repertoire is French or Portuguese, why don't they use their own languages instead of English, French, or Portuguese? The answer could be attributed to Mazrui and Mazrui's (1998) observations that the African leadership and the élites lack linguistic loyalty to their indigenous languages and cultures. Many of these leaders were trained exclusively in a foreign language and feel more confident in expressing their ideas in that foreign language than in their own ethnic languages. Leaders and scholars are expected to lead the way in rectifying the neglect that their ethnic African languages suffered during the colonial period and subsequently after independence. However, the lack confidence and cultural pride in their own ethnic languages continues to influence the trends among the younger generation to distance themselves from ethnic languages and to align themselves more and more with foreign languages in their daily repertoires.

With respect to maintaining the advances that Kiswahili has made, speakers have to consider its expansive development and world status as a motivation to advocate for it to be considered an emerging global language. There is no excuse for example for Tanzanians and Kenyans not to promote the use Kiswahili when it is the language of official business and in the case of Tanzania, their national language. There are examples of African leaders who have defied the norm by flaunting their African cultural pride. For example, President Joachim Chisano of Mozambique is not a native speaker of Kiswahili but chose to use it at the African Union (AU) Assembly in Addis Ababa in 2005 when addressing the AU Assembly. Mozambique borders Tanzania and based on the archeological studies of the Coastal States, it was once considered a part of the Coastal States (Kusimba 1999, Mazrui & Mazrui 1998, Mirza & Strobel 1989). Many of the coastal cities have communities whose ancestral land is Mozambique but ended in Zanzibar, Mombasa, Malindi, or Lamu through normal immigration process, slavery, or inter-ethnic marriages. President Chisano's decision to address the Assembly in Kiswahili was intended to demonstrate to the Assembly that they should not be addressing each other in imperial/colonial languages. The Assembly was not prepared for this bold move and there was a brief moment of panic as the delegates scrambled to get translators to provide simultaneous translation. Needless to say, President Chisano was not swayed and continued with his remarks without worrying about the inability of the delegates to comprehend what he was saying. President Chisano's bold move, prompted President Obasanjo of Nigeria to follow suit by greeting the delegates in Kiswahili and thanking President Chisano for his bold move. Though symbolic, gesture was also a demonstration of cultural pride. What was not impressive though was that President Obasanjo did not give his address in a Nigerian ethnic language, but rather in English. All other Presidents who spoke after him, followed in the same fashion, even those presidents from the Kiswahili speaking states. President Chisano demonstrated the uniqueness of Kiswahili, both as an ethnic African language and as a regional language. He wanted to remind the delegates that they have been debating on the use of African languages at the assembly for over a decade and yet they had not moved to implement it. He also wanted to show that this was the time to implement the resolution to use African languages at the Assembly, at the birth of a new organization, the African Union (that replaced the Organization of African Unity – OAU). Needless to say, President Chisano wanted to emphasize that the organization has reached a point where they cannot continue to do business as usual and that they should lead by example, beginning with a demonstration of their linguistic nationalism.

In essence, President Chisano was following the footsteps of Ngugi wa Thiongo and many others who have followed him in affirming the dignity of African languages. Ngugi asks a question that all African leaders as well as scholars need to ask themselves, whether the foreign (European) cultural that is manifested in those Africans who have acquired European languages is merely superfluous or there are deeper cognitive controls that the languages impose on their minds. Fanon (1967) explains this as a case of intellectuals are alienated in their social categories and are also detached from their own thought to the extent their consciousness is trapped in foundations that mainly foreign.

Conclusions

Langer (1953, 1979) notes that language transforms speakers from biological creatures, who respond to the concrete world as it exists, into thinking beings that interpret, interact with, and remake the world through symbols. The symbols used shape our understanding of the world and our own places within it. The power of symbols lies in the kind of thought and action they enable. Symbols allow us to define, organize, and evaluate experiences and people. At the same time, they enable us to think hypothetically and to reflect on ourselves. Thus, the language that we use, selectively, shapes our perceptions and the names we apply emphasize particular aspects of reality and neglect others. Language names what exists and those with power name and define the world in their own terms. Furthermore, those with power to name the world use names and words rooted in their language to acknowledge what affects them. Therefore, when we talk about "the power of a language" we are talking about how it reflects its speakers and how the speakers exploit that power. It is also important to note that language conventions and acceptance replicate and validate the existing power structures. It is without doubt that African leaders and speakers of the various languages have misinterpreted linguistic determinism for the continent by not focusing on the power of indigenous languages and by extending determinism situations in which European languages inherited from the colonial tradition classroom situations have and continue to exercise great control on African thinking and perceptions.

Ngungi wa Thiongo (1986) sums up the effects of this extensions. He notes that the language that an African child's acquires for his/her formal education and the books he/reads read are not only written in a foreign language but the concepts learned are devoid of local conditions and emphasize the foreign ones. From the onset, thought in him/her takes a visible form of foreign language influenced by the foreign culture. Inevitably this dominates the mental universe of the (colonized) learner.

Ngugi's evaluation of the situation is substantiated by his observation that the African élite whose elitism is measured by their proficiency in a foreign language are also culturally very westernized. Trying to disassociate himself from this group and in his quest to lead by example, Ngugi's has write in his own native language of Gikuyu. His actions are motivated by his want to affirm the dignity of African languages and most of all, even though in a very small way, counteract the influences of European languages on the mind of the African. Ngugi realizes the power of influence leaders and élites have on the general masses. Generally, the powerful can control and constrain the effectiveness of language as used by the non-powerful by constraining the contents of usage as well as the relations entered into through the use of language. Consequently, what becomes of a language depends largely on its users and the way it is advocated. That is why the role of leaders and élites is critical in the preservation and sustainability of indigenous languages. It is incumbent upon, first and foremost, speakers and then scholars to look for ways to grow the languages that are the root of the African symbolic place in the world. Part of the goal of making a language visible should be to expose its existing powerful achievements as well as its global role even if limited. Kiswahili was not known before traders ventured to the east coast of Africa. It played an important role in trade (global use within its locale) and it grew because of the need to extend the trading routes to the hinterland.

There is need for Africans to reduce dependence on western language and develop the mindset that respect and the power of negotiation is enriched by observing the cultural understanding of the process. The dependency legacy that the continent inherited from colonialism is the sole factor behind its economic misfortunes, its inability to create sustainable development and most of all attaining the respect owed at the table of global understanding. The heavy reliance on European languages for technological advancement and modernization negates the fact that Africans practiced some form of indigenous technology that served the continent for many years before it was discouraged by colonial powers. Some communities have resorted to those indigenous technologies, especially where modern technology has not been extended. These communities use indigenous technologies to solve everyday problems that result from specific local conditions. Marzui and Mazrui note that the over reliance on foreign languages by African leaders and the élites is a result of the fear that if they transform their communication strategies from the use of foreign languages to African languages they would diminish their standing in the world of foreign expertise which would also make it more difficult to seek support in financial aid at various levels (research, development, and even governance). Mazrui & Mazrui notes that catering for such a fear disables more than enables the individual and it reduce the ability to develop critical aspect of the continent's economic vitality.

David Latin (1977) provides the examples of Asian countries such as Japan and India where 'technical' and 'western' have been separated to allow the development of non-western market strategies in order to eliminate the domination of the hegemony of the economic order by the western countries. He notes that this was achieved through Linguistic dislocation. The Asians were able to put in place policies that favored the use of indigenous languages. African countries should be encouraged by such examples. The use of ethnic languages as symbols of solidarity and support of cultivating a patron-client relationship reside in national (political) and community (social) settings. The only danger that has to be avoided is in the use of ethnic languages for the purposes of inciting violence and descent. Examples can be drawn from the Rwanda genocides, and the recent political strife in Kenya. To eliminate the use of ethnic languages for the purposes of dividing rather than uniting a people national leaders have declare a national language in the likes of Kiswahili, or a selection of a representative sample of languages that could be used as national languages that units the people as a nation. Following from the examples set by Kiswahili, such a language(s) would be entered into the national language policy requiring all citizens to learn the language(s). The language(s) would also be required in the educational curriculum of the nation.

The pertinent question is the one associated with what Mazrui and Mazrui observed with respect to the attitude leaders and scholars have towards the need for foreign language dependency. They contended that leaders and élites are afraid of transforming their communication strategies that heavily rely on the use of foreign languages because it would diminish their standing in the world of foreign expertise. By extension, they fear losing vital links to the outside world. The question to ask is: How does Japan, India, China, relate or access the rest of the world? There is a lot to be gained by African countries if they could learn from the examples set by these Asian countries. In actual fact, Africa is a mile ahead of Asia and many other nations of the world. Not only do Africans speak multiple languages on the continent but also a number of foreign languages. A good example is the Democratic Republic of the

Congo. Many political leaders and élites as well as ordinary can speak at least four languages: an indigenous language (e. g. Lingala, Kikongo, Kituba-Kikongo), Kiswahili, English, French. Thus multi-lingual ability is a common phenomenon in Africa. Another good example is South Africa which has about twelve ethnic languages that are national languages because the majority of South Africans speak or understand a variety of these national languages in addition to English.

The Asian countries like Japan and India have been successful because of their affinity for their ethnic languages and because the political and scholar leadership have encouraged the speakers to create and maintain effective communication in both their indigenous and foreign languages. African languages that facilitate the process of developing effective communication at a national level and which allows the élite and the masses to penetrate each other's spheres adequately provides a definite advantage in vertical integration[5]. A society that is able to foster a linguistic medium that allows interaction across ethnic lines (horizontal) and across class lines (vertical) would produce a more integrated society, a democratic society. The Continent of Africa can learn from both China and Japan where they have been successful in undergoing and ideological conversion without the mediation of mediation of a foreign language. Their efforts go beyond the creation of critical ideological and political literature. With the exception of Arabic speaking African countries only Tanzania can claim to have devoted substantial capital in the development of an ideological conversion without the mediation of a foreign language. It is not easy to find across Africa, scholars who are able to discuss their disciplines in their native language.

To conclude, Africa cannot claim intellectual independence without disclaiming linguistic dependency. Thus, in order for the continent to achieve linguistic liberation it must not focus on the need to free itself fem the use of European languages but must seek to ways to promote African languages, especially in academia. The aim should therefore be the development of strategies for promoting greater intellectual and scientific independence from the West. Linguistic nationalism is a way in which speakers affirm their language(s), strive to protect and sustain, and promote its use and growth. Africa is known for its nationalistic tendencies towards race, land, and ethnic background. The same affinity should be placed on language. It is an in-disputed fact that the artificial boundaries created by colonial powers left behind multilingual communities within boundaries. Leaders on the continent have to tread cautiously as they seek indigenous language to promote as the national language within those boundaries because such moves carry the danger of internal ethnic rivalry (e. g. Nigeria, Kenya, and South Africa). Those countries need to learn from India's experience in their attempt to make Hindi (northern language) the national language. The outcome was undesired riots.

Notes

[1] Ibn Battutah is best known as a traveler and explorer, whose account documents his travels and excursions over a period of almost thirty years, covering some 73,000 miles (117,000 km). These journeys covered almost the entirety of the known Islamic world and beyond, extending from North Africa, West Africa, Southern Europe and Eastern Europe in the West, to the Middle East, Indian subcontinent, Central Asia, Southeast Asia and China in the East, a distance readily surpassing that of his predecessors and his near-contemporary Marco Polo. Cf also Ibn Buttuta, Travels in Asia and Africa 1325-1345, Published by Routledge and Kegan Paul, The Introduction to the "Voyages of Ibn Battutah" by Vincent Monteil in The Islamic Review and Arab Affairs. March 1970: 30-37.

[2] Frederick John Dealtry Lugard, 1st Baron Lugard was a British soldier who explored Africa extensively and was a part of the colonial administration, governor of Hong Kong (1907-1912) and Governor-General of Nigeria (1914-1919). He is known for pushing for native rule in African colonies. He reasoned that black Africans were very different from white Europeans and should be expected to take second place (middle management) in colonial governance. He also believed that the people of Africa are inclined to look up to someone who looked more like them, spoke their languages, and shared their customs. Lugard was successful in selling this point of view to European colonial leaders. Cf. Middleton, Dorothy (1959).

[3] The merchants of Venice and Julius Caesar.

[4] Interestingly, these and other companies are beginning to feel the pressure to provide service information in different languages. Thus in Namibia, where English is the official language, MTC telephone company decided to advertise in other local languages spoken by Namibians.

⁵ Mazrui and Mazrui (1999) note that African lingua franças s like Hausa in West Africa, Kiswahili in East Africa, and Lingala in Central Africa allows a reasonable degree of contact between the populace and enables them to establish a linguistic basis for interaction that is sustainable across the board. They consider this as an example of lower horizontal integration.

References

Crystal, David. 2005. Globalizing English. In Keith Walters and Michal Brody (Eds.). *What's Language Got to Do With It?* (pp. 504-514). New York: W. W. Norton and Co.

Fanon, Frantz. 1967. Black Skin White Masks. New York: Grove Press.

Hinnebusch, T. 1976. Swahili: Genetic Affiliations and Evidence. Studies in African Linguistics supp. 6:95-108.

Kusimba M. Kusimba. 1999. The Rise and Fall of Swahili States. California: AltaMira Press.

Langer, S. K. 1953. Feeling and Form, a theory of Art. New York: Scriber's.

_____1979. Philosophy in a New Key: A Study in the Symbolism of Reason, Rite and Art. Cambridge, MA: Harvard University.

Latin, David D. 1977. Politics, Language and Thought: The Somali Experience. Chicago: University of Chicago press.

Mazrui, Ali A., Alamin M. Mazrui, & Ibrahim Sharif. 1994. The Swahili: Idiom and identity of an African people. Trenton, NJ: Africa World Press.

Mazrui, Ali A. & Alamin M. Mazrui. 1998. The Power of Babel: Language & Governance in the African Experience. Binghamton, NY: IGCS Publications, Binghamton University.

_____1999. Political Culture of Language. Swahili, Society, and State. Binghamton, NY: IGCS Publications, Binghamton University.

Mirza and Strodle. 1989. Three Swahili Women, Life Histories from Mombasa Kenya. Bloomington: Indiana University Press

Middleton, Dorothy. 1959. Lugard in Africa. London: Robert Hale, Ltd.

Middleton J. 1992. The World of the Swahili: an African Mercantile Civilization. New Haven: Yale University Press.

Moshi, Lioba. 1988. Tuimarishe Kiswahili Chetu (Building Proficiency in Kiswahili) A textbook for 2nd and 3rd Year Students. Lanham, MD: University Press of America.

____1994. The Teaching of African Languages. Penn Language News, Spring Issue.

____1996. KiSwahili Lugha na Utamaduni (A 23 Lesson Video Series for the Teaching KiSwahili Language and Culture). Athens, GA: OISD, University of Georgia.

____1998. KiSwahili, Lugha na Utamaduni (Swahili, Language and Culture). Hyattsville MD: Dunwoody Press, 1998.

Moshi, Lioba & Alwiya Omar. 2003. Kiswahili kwa Kompyuta (KIKO): A series of computer assisted lessons for Kiswahili learners at the elementary, intermediate, and advanced levels. http://www.africa.uga.edu/Kiswahili/doe/

Mwita, A. M. A & D. N. Mwansoko. 1998. Kamusi ya Tiba. Dar Es Salaam, GTZ.

Ngugi wa Tiongo (1986). Decolonizing the Mind: the Politics of Language in African Literature. London: James Currey.

Ohly, Rajmund. 1987. A Primary Technical Dictionary English-Swahili. Dar Es Salaam, Tanzania.

Schleicher, Antonia & Lioba Moshi. 2000. The Pedagogy of African Languages: An Emerging Field. Ohio: Pathways Series. Ohio State University.

Schmied, Josef. 1991. English in Africa: An Introduction. New York: Longman

Tajfel, Henri. 1974. "Social Identity and Intergroup Behavior", Social science Information 13 (2): 65-93.

____1978. Differentiation between Social Groups: Studies in the Social Psychology of Intergroup Relations. London: Academic Press.

____1981. Human Groups and Social Categories. Massachusetts: Cambridge University Press.

Walters, Keith & Michal Brody. 2005. What's Language Got to Do With It? New York: Norton and Company.

Chapter 3

NATIONAL LANGUAGES AND NATIONAL DEVELOPMENT

Ben Ohi Elugbe

National Languages

The title of our topic contains a certain ambiguity which must be straightened out before we can properly discuss the issue involved. There are three possible interpretations of "national" in this context. Firstly, "national may be interpreted to mean Nigeria so that we are here discussing indigenous Nigeria languages and national development. Secondly, we could be discussing national languages in the same sense as of 1979 and 1989 constitutions of Nigeria. Federal Government's Views and Comments on the Political Bureau (1987:62-3) grant the status of "national languages" to Hausa, Igbo, and Yoruba but not to English. Thirdly, national languages may be languages which are national in terms of their geographical spread: their location is nationwide.

In our first interpretation, every language which is indigenous to Nigeria, which has a definite location or locations, and is part of an indigenous culture, is a Nigerian language. The English language does not qualify as an indigenous Nigerian language but Nigerian pidgin (English) does, even though its cultural characteristics maybe difficult to pin down. In our second interpretation, a national language is a symbol of national oneness, of the achievement of independence and nationhood (of Fishman 1968:6, Bamgbose 1983:3). Amayo (1983:11) quotes Ikara 1981 as pointing out that the Obasanjo administration's reason for inserting Hausa, Igbo, and Yoruba into the 1979 constitution as national languages was that it will be embarrassing at this stage of our political development to continue to use English alone' (See also Sections 51 and 91 of the said Constitution). As already mentioned above, English is not a national language in Nigeria. It is one of the Nigeria's Lingua Franca and it is the official language, being the language of administration, business, secondary, and tertiary education etc. While Hausa, Igbo, and Yoruba can be national in so far as they have large constituency in Nigeria, English lacks any such constituency and it is clearly not a rallying point for even a meaningful minority. On the other hand, none of the three major Nigerian languages has official status at the federal level.

It is this third sense that people are been misled into thinking that English is our national language. It is being taught nationwide and so has the whole country as its geographical constituency. However, its ethnic constituency is small – exceedingly small, in fact – and amorphous. Although estimates of the percentage of Nigerians able to speak English are usually of the 30 percent mark, BAmgbose (1983: 5) cut the figure to as low as10. According to him, "perhaps......90 per cent of our people in both the urban and the rural area are the untouched by [the] alleged communicative role [of English]. " In this third sense, then, there is, today, probably no Nigeria qualifies for the title "national" – not even the much-vaunted Nigeria pidgin. Since the issue has twice already been drawn to the attention of Nigerians, I should also point out no artificially develop language can, will, or does, qualify as a national language in Nigeria. During the military era before second Republic, "Wazobia", formed from wa, *zo*, and *bia* for "come" in Yoruba, Hausa, and Igbo respectively, represented the possibility of evolving a national language that would be made up of element of different Nigerian languages. Bamgbose (1983:12) point out that the attempt was "short lived for lack of favorable reaction from language experts".

More recently, a certain Mr. Alex Igbineweka of Nigerian Television Authority, Lagos has been proposing Guosa as an artificial national language. He has received publicity from both the print and the electronic media. Nobody who knows what language is can possibly accept that the combination of *nagode*, 'thank you' in Hausa and *pupo*, 'very much' in Yoruba, can give an artificial 'thank you very much'; or that *na mi hutu uki meta* from Efik, Hausa, Edo, and Yoruba gives a properly national and natural and new form of 'give me three month's leave/holiday. ' In a natural language, infinity of sentences is possible. In the case of Guosa, not even Mr. Igbineweka himself is complete dictionary of the language since he constantly has to toil away at expressing a new idea in Guosa. As Bamgbose has pointed out (1983-13). ' .... we will have to look for Mr. Igbineweka each time we need to form a new sentence [in Guosa]'. In addition, as I pointed out to him once, the loss of the one of the speakers of a language does not mean the end of that language. In the case of Guosa, though, the establishment of Guosa and its possible growth depend on Mr. Igbneweka continued good health. The serious business of national languages and national development must not be stalled by such unproductive proposals as Wazobia and Guosa. In the main, our discussion will focus on the role of indigenous Nigerian languages and the concept of a national language in national development.

A Linguistic Map of Nigeria

Nigeria is a thoroughly multilingual country. Hansford et al. (1976), which represent the best, most documentary compilation of a list of Nigerian languages now contains 394 entries approximate 400. I do know however from my personal contribution to the work that is based on a very elastic use of the term 'language'. So indeed, the actual figure using intelligibility and other practical indices for delimiting language boundaries is definitely going to be higher. Linguistic diversity is one of the better-known attributes of Nigeria, a fact recognized by the original composer of our national anthem who agreed that 'tribe and tongue' differences exist in Nigeria. Since ethnic divisions are often along linguistic lines, it is assumed, that the existence of many languages means the existence of many basically antagonistic ethnic nationalities trying to form a nation. This view of the language problem of newly independent, multilingual, developing nations is recognized and tackled in Fishman et al. (1968).

I do not personally blame language for disunity in Nigeria. Perhaps as a result of my training in comparative historical linguistics, I tend to see fewer languages and ethnic groups in Nigeria than others do. Let me explain why. Greenberg (1963) classifies the languages of Africa into four major phyla; Afro-Asiatic, Khosian, Niger-Kordofanian and Nilo-Saharan. Three of these phyla (excluding Khosian) are represented in Nigeria. Hansford et al. (1976:16) provides a succinct summary of the situation. Within Nigeria, the majority of the languages belong to the Niger-Kordofanian phylum, though there are a substantial number of languages belonging to Afro-Asiatic phylum and three languages belonging to Nilo-Saharan (Kanuri, Dendi, and Zarma). Niger-Kordofanian is divided into Niger-Congo and Kordofanian. There are those who feel that the Niger-Congo languages (covering West, Central, East, and Southern Africa) should be considered separate phylum from Kordofanian (covering only part of Kordofan).

Language is one of the, if not the, most enduring artifacts of culture. Unless forced by conquest or by superior number, or by social, economic, and political domination to give up their language, a people can always have their history traced through their language. This is possible because language changes in a patterned way over times and space. One language beget dialect in space, and then time makes them so divergent that they become separate languages. In this way, one original language can become hundreds. The fact that language changes in systematic manner means that, given a number of related languages, their ancestor form can be reconstructed with varying degrees of accuracy, depending on the availability of indepth synchronic studies on modern descendants (daughter-languages) of that ancestor. It is thus left to Nigerians to see only a few groups or hundreds thereof in Nigeria. It is my belief that the ancestral ties between scores (even hundreds) of these indigenous languages can be exploited to show Nigerians that they have a common history in fact.

Linguists are also very aware of many examples where people who speak different (perhaps unrelated) languages can be united through common and non common linguistic aspect of culture such as religion, trade, agriculture, etc. In Nigeria, an example, per excellence, is that of the much publicized Hausa-Fulani unity. First of all, the Fulani speak a language of the Niger-Congo family more related to Wolof and Serer in Senegal than to any of the Nigerian language. Secondly, within Nigeria, it is, by virtue of its membership of Niger-Congo family, more related to such languages as Yoruba, Igbo, Efik, Edo, Kambari, and Tiv than to Hausa. In fact, as history has it, Hausa were conquered by Fulani warriors of the Jihad and, till today, the ruling house of Emirates in Hausaland (down to Ilorin in the Yoruba enclave) are of Fulani extraction. However, since the Fulani lacked neither the numbers nor the inclination to settlement required to assimilate the Hausa completely, they saw no need and, in fact, lack the means to enforce their rather complex language. So, today in Nigeria, the Hausa and the Fulani are even without any known linguistic ties, seen as a model of unity, oneness, and solidarity.

By contrast, compare the Yoruba and the Igbo. There is no doubt whatsoever that the Yoruba are linguistically related to the Igbo. In fact, members of the two ethnic groups frequently see or notice linguistic similarities. Armstrong (1964) has made the point very clearly and even suggested that the time differences between the two groups is something in the neighborhood of 4-6000 years. Yet I know (thanks partly to my origin in a minority group) that the two most antagonistic groups in Nigeria are the Yoruba and Igbo. I suggest that antagonism which has its root not in linguistic diversity but in more modern political and economic rivalry.

To round off this aspect of our discussion, let me cite a personal experience which showed me that some of our leaders could, if they are willing, emphasize the historical side of linguistic complexity. In 1980, during the launching of Linguistic Association of Nigeria (LAN) at

Ibadan University, a prominent politician who also held a high position in the University Council asked privately if there is any linguistic evidence for linking Kanuri with the Yoruba. He pointed it out to me that facial marks were already been used as cultural evidence of historical connections between the two groups. I told him that there was indeed some possibility of a linguistic connection. However, that connection lays in the thesis that Nilo-Saharan and Niger-Congo may be sufficiently related as to form a Kongo-Saharan super-phylum as Gregersen (1970) has proposed. The time-depth in such a postulated relationship may be no less than 10, 000 years as Welmers (1973) has worked it out. It out that the politician, who was of the National Party of Nigeria (N. P. N), was at the time, worried about the flirtation between Alhaji Waziri's Great Nigeria People's Party (G. N. P. P) and Chief Awolowo's Unity Party of Nigeria (U. P. N).

Multilingualism and National Development

Most Nigerians view Nigeria's linguistic map with make language a ready scapegoat for Nigeria's lack of internal unity and cohesion. But the truth is that linguistic diversity need not always be a serious disadvantage as Das Gupta (1968:19) has argued. In fact, as he pointed out, Nigeria's case is not unique: Most new nations are based on plurality of segmental groups. The natural tie of the people to their segmental group is often valued more highly than their civil ties with the nation (emphasis mine) As he further points out, it is not how cleavage or divisiveness came to occur in society, or the fact that it occurs at all. What is important is what happens this cleavage in the process of National development. On account of the fact that most new or third world countries are faced with linguistic and other diversities, the successful new nation will be that whose leaders acquire 'the political art of holding diverse units together in a national community' Das Gupta (1968:18-19).

Fishman (1968) examines some reports on contrast between linguistically homogenous and linguistically heterogeneous states. The reports consistently associated the good characteristics with homogeneous polities and bad or undesirable characteristics with the heterogeneous. Bamgbose (1982) has pointed out that there is no reason to require the planning of language for national development to be based on the requirement of a western style of parliamentary democracy. In fact, some of the successful decisions in the involvement of African Languages in national development such as Somalia and Tanzania have been taken under peculiar and not definetly western style of governments.

The two points we have been making so far in this section are, to recapitulate, that: linguistic diversity should not scare us; it does not automatically spell doom; and the kind of political system in operation in a country will determine the successful (or other) involvement of national languages in national development.

The Case for National Languages in National Development

National development refers to the growth of the nation in terms of unity, education, economic well being, mass participation in government and so on. The National Policy on Education promulgated by the Federal Government of Nigeria in 1977 and revised in 1981 contains a definite statement on the role of language in education. Government then stated (section 3:15(4) that the language of instruction in the primary school should be initially the child's mother-tongue or the language of the immediate community. Government then pledged itself to ensure that this goal is achieved. Once we accept that education is part, if not the corner-stone, of national development, it will become obvious that Nigerian languages have to be developed so that education may be on a surer footing. Unless we can make it possible for our children to learn the basics of modern technology, science and mathematics, for example in their mother-tongue – i. e. a language they fully understand- then, as Bamgbose (1983:18) has aptly put it 'the seed of transferred technology will fall on barren ground and fail to germinate. ' A mass literacy campaign is on in Nigeria – at least on paper. The quickest way to make majority of Nigerians literate is in their own languages. One of the advantages of mass literacy is that government will reach the people more effectively. For example, a campaign on new farming method should include educating the farmers in their own languages.

In terms of mass participation in government, there is a good case for developing our national languages. Democracy, which is our goal, cannot truly exist where only an elitist few (in this case the speaker of English) can participate. As a matter of fact, trying to make the masses see the issues in election is meaningless where the people can not be reached. Amayo (1983) and Bamgbose (1983) have both made this point in the strongest of terms. One of the advantages of developing the vast majority of our languages is that nobody will be left out of the development process. More importantly, nobody will think or feel that he is being left out (see kelman 1971). This argument indirectly suggests that a feeling of belonging is cultivated in those who feel that they are not left out of the scheme of things. National integration is thus promoted.

Unfortunately as Williamson (1977) has pointed out, some people are often moved by ideological and practical consideration to oppose the development of national languages, 'the ideological argument is that to encourage the reading and writing of a multiplicity of small languages, will seriously hinder the development of the feeling of national unity. On the other hand, as Williamson(1977:81) noted, 'the practical argument is that it will be prohibitively costly, in terms of time [and] expense, to develop written materials and train teachers in a large number of small languages. ' This position leads us to the question of national languages. The assumption is, as already mentioned; that a common indigenous language will foster unity, engender a feeling of oneness, a represent a symbol of unity, a rallying point. It must be stated that neither the lack nor the choice of a national language is guaranteed to cause a national disunity. The point is that the use of national language should not be confused with the need for small languages and their speaker to have a participatory role in the national development. Enemies of small languages look at development only from one rung of the national ladder – the topmost. However, in Federal set-up, State Government have jurisdiction over language matters in the State. So also can the local government initiate and/or execute language policies in its own area of jurisdiction.

The case for Nigerian languages in the development process has been very well stated and so requires no further flogging here (Amayo 1983; Bamgbose 1977, 1983). The point must also be made that developing our indigenous languages does not mean abandoning English. There is, for the foreseeable future, no alternative to the concurrent investment in English.

Challenges and Problems

Languages experts have agreed that the government of Nigeria is not doing enough for Nigerian languages. There are two clear reasons for this. First of all, the role of language in national development can be seen in much the same light as the seed which a farmer puts into the ground in the planting season. The more he put into the ground, the more he can expect. Similarly, the contribution of our national languages to the national development will depend on how much our government put into the development of Nigerian languages. We need to reduce scores and scores of languages to writing and develop materials in them. We also need to train teachers. It is thus true that Nigerian languages can only be developed at great cost. The reward will also be great. This fact is clearly ill digested by our governments. There is another reason why Nigerian government has so far failed to make Nigerian languages serve the rightful role in national development: most government look for quick returns and clearly demonstrable evidence of profit for given programs.

By contrast, investments in language do not yield immediate results. And even when the results come, they are not quantifiable in terms of hard statistics. Yet, wise governments worldwide have invested in language not only because of the benefit of its proper planning and use can bring but also because of the social language in Nigeria; at best, they have paid lip service to it. That will not do; we have to invest massively in language. The option of doing nothing and hoping that the language problem away is not open to Nigeria; it will not go away. Therefore, it should be tackled head-on. In tackling it we should be in no doubt about the slowness of the language investments in yielding fruits. But, as noted by Amayo (1983), the lifespan of a nation is supposed to be eternity. The search for political future lies in a proper examination of our past. And such an examination reveals that our handling of the language problem has been grossly incompetent. If our economy has been handled in the same way, there is no wonder then that the economy is, today in shambles.

It should useful to cite one or two examples of our handling of the language problem over the years as a means of showing the weakness of the managers of our affairs. For some time there was attached to the Educational Services Unit of the Federal Ministry of Education, a National Language Center. Physically, it was located at 6 Obanta Street, Apapa, Lagos. This so-called National Language Centre was ostensibly charged with initiating and coordinating activities relating to language (planning and?) development in Nigeria. It was run by a quasi-executive Secretary and an Advisory Council. The first secretary was a non indigenous Nigerian. It is only in Nigeria, in this whole world, that a multilingual state with acute language problems ignored all her children who are language experts and put the running of her National Language Centre in the hand of someone who is not an expert and has no knowledge of what it means to own a non-European language, be part of its culture and has intense feelings about it.

Over the years, proposals were made to convert the centre into a bigger better organized place, run by an expert Director with proven ability in initiating and coordinating research. None of this proposal has been seen in the light of the day. Some academics refused to serve any further on the Council of the Centre out of sheer exasperation. Such academics span different ethnic and geographic regions of Nigeria. Between the Advisory Council and the authorities what exactly happened to the reports? We do hope that with the re-christening of the centre as the Language Development Centre and its incorporation in the Nigerian Educational Research and Development Council, something serious will now happen in the area of Nigerian languages.

Much is made of the transfer of technology and the problems it involves. In this case, the technology of language planning and development is available here in Nigeria. We have simply refused to use it. Countries with less acute language problems than ours have invested in language in terms of human and material resources. Canada, Somalia and Tanzania are examples. In the early stages of development of Somalia, the government closed all institution of higher learning, including universities for over a year!

My second example is our handling of the national language issue. The Federal Government, in 1979 wisely proposes three languages, rather than one as our national languages. Before then, as far back as 1961, during the first republic, a member of the parliament had moved a motion on the floor of the Parliament urging Government, as reported in Amayo (1983:7):

> 'To introduce the teaching of Hausa, Yoruba, Ibo and other languages into institutions of learning throughout the country with a view to adopting one of them as our official language in the near future.'

In other words this idea is at least a quarter of century old. Yet the Federal Government which has enshrined the idea in a federal Constitution has done nothing to bring it to be. In order to make a Nigeria Language national in practice, we need to develop such a language to enable it cope with the demand of the modern world. We must train teachers who will teach it in the schools from the primary to the tertiary levels. It may be necessary to standardize the language so that a particular dialect is the national one. Considering that the three major Nigerian languages are already very widely spoken in different parts of the country, it is a shame that government has not put in an extra effort required to make them grow more and become truly national. I believe, in fact, that such an effort would lead to the emergence of one of them as the national language in future.

Once more, let me repeat that the time schedule for bringing one of the three national languages to emerge as the national language must not be seen in terms of decades but of centuries. The government which has the foresight to take the necessary steps that lead to this desirable goal in the end will not be around to receive the credit for it. But posterity would nonetheless be grateful for it. Better than that posterity should lament our lack of foresight. Individual Nigerians have also not done enough to help the growth of Nigerian language. In 1981, the Linguistic Association of Nigeria, wrote some eminent Nigerians who had been known to make extremely generous donations at launching all over the country. The proposal was to study and document the languages and cultures of the peoples of Abuja who were to be uprooted from their original homes to a new site. In some cases, there was a negative reply. In others, there was no reply at all. There was not a single positive reply.

Finally, our civil service has been part of our problem. No matter who is in power, he will need the cooperation of the civil servant to succeed. Unfortunately, the combination of selfishness and a lack of education are preventing the Civil Service from rendering to its nation the kind of service required from it. Take the case of language: there are proposal and proposals flowing into the ministries from all over the country. To the extent that if the proposals do not fit the civil servants' interest they are swept aside. Sometimes they are swept aside because the civil servant does not know what they are all about. Now if the posting of the civil servant to service various arms of the ministries were such as to make the civil servants training relevant to his duties, some of the wastage would be avoided.

Proposals

I would like to end this short write up by putting forward a set of proposals. Little will be new in these proposals (see Bamgbose 1982 (b), 1983; and Amayo 1984). One suggestion which is new I will strongly urge government to consider at once.

(a) Government must set up 'an enlarged and professional Language Center instead of the largely administrative set-up that now exist as a unit of 'Educational Services' in the Federal Ministry of Education (see Bamgbose 1982:12).

The present arrangement has failed because the centre enjoys neither the respect nor the confidence of the language experts in Nigeria. Ministry officials themselves do not regard it as a particularly important set-up because they know exactly the quality and the cadre of the officers there.

- (b) That the language survey which is now being initiated by the Language Centre and which is already taking off on a wrong footing be coordinated by the enlarged National Language Centre, using linguists from all over the country, especially from department of linguistic and (African /Nigeria) Languages.
- (c) That the ministries should always endeavor to find out whether or not the manpower for a given project is available in Nigeria before inviting foreigners to undertake it.
- (d) That Youth Corpers, most of who view the year of service as one for loafing and wasting, be obliged to spend their time in adult literacy work. University and other tertiary-level students can join this exercise in the long vacation (see Bamgbose 1983:25).
- (e) Against the possibility of headcount in future, the National Population Commission be required to include specific questions about language in any national census questionnaire.

This last point has already been made by Bamgbose (1983:25) and the wording is in fact his.

- (f) Department of Linguistics and African/ Nigerian Language should be encouraged to step up the production of graduates in linguistics and Nigerian languages.

My final recommendation is one which I know is totally new and I would strongly urge Government to consider very seriously for immediate implementation.

- (g) Every Nigerian child who goes to University or any other Institution of higher learning to study Linguistics and/or national language which is not his and which he does not already speak should be given a bursary.

In the early 70's, this was done for students going to University to study education. It made a degree in education popular. In these hard times, a bursary to study Hausa, Igbo or Yoruba, with an assurance of a job on graduation, would be a give way to prospective students to opt for Nigerian languages. The Implication of is that a Nigerian whose language is not Hausa, Igbo, or Yoruba, and who also does not already speak any of them would qualify for a bursary once he decide to read any of them. On the other hand, a Yoruba student qualifies only if he opts for Hausa or Igbo. I suspect that, given present trends in Nigeria, Hausa would be greater beneficiary of such program and that in the centuries to come; it may be the one to emerge as our main and national language.

Conclusion

My position in the foregoing may be summarized as follows. It is not the kind of governmental system in operations that matters; it is the way w approach our problems. Unless there is foresight and selfless service, we will always fail. Relating this to language, I say that we need not be scared of language or blame it for the problem of disunity. There are in facts, the way of turning language in to a tool a promoting national unity. I have also pointed out that both the indigenous Nigerian languages and English have a role to play. But I have concentrated on Nigerian languages. I urge Government not to mind the cost of developing Nigerian languages in view of the potential contribution of such development to national development. I have also noted that neither the government, nor the Civil service, nor individuals have approached language in Nigeria with the care and investment it requires. I have put forward a set of proposals, hardly new, which should help Nigerian languages to contribute their proper quota to the national development.

References

Amayo, A. 1983. The search for national integration and national identity in Nigeria since Independence: the linguistic aspect. Paper presented at the National Conference on Nigeria since Independence. A. B. U., Zaria, 28-31 March 1983.

Armstrong, R. 1964. The Study of West African Languages. Ibadan, Nigeria: Ibadan University Press.

Bamgbose, A. (Ed.). 1977. 'Language in Education in Nigeria. ' Proceeding in the Language Symposium. Lagos, Nigeria: National Language Centre.

_____1982a. 'When is language planning not planning?' Paper presented at the Departmental Seminar, Department of Linguistic and Nigerian Languages, University of Ibadan, February 1982

_____1982b. Local Languages Development: policy and practice. In Ikara B. (Ed.) Nigerian Languages and Cultural Development (pp 15-22), Lagos, Nigeria: National Language Centre.

_____1983. Languages and Nation Building. A public enlightenment lecture delivered at the Bendel State University Ekpoma, June 15, 1983.

Das Gupta, J. 1968. Language diversity and national development. In Fishman et al. (Eds.) Language Problems in Developing Nations (pp 17-26). London: Willey and Sons.

Federal Republic of Nigeria. 1979. National Policy on Education. Lagos: Federal Ministry of Information. The Constitution of the Federal Republic of Nigeria. 1979. Lagos: Federal Ministry of Information.

Fishman, J. et al. (Eds.). 1968. Language Problems of Developing Nations. London: Willey and Sons.

Fishman, J. 1968a. "Sociolinguistics and the language problems of developing countries" In Fishman et al. (Eds.) Language Problems in Developing Nations (pp 3-16). London: Willey and Sons.

_____1968b: "Some contrast between linguistically homogenous and linguistically heterogeneous politics. " In Fishman et al. (Eds.) Language Problems in Developing Nations (pp 53-68). London: Willey and Sons.

Greenberg, J. 1963. Languages of Africa. The Hague: Mouton.

Greenberg, E. A. 1970. Kongo-Saharan journal of African Languages.

Hansford, K. et al. 1976. An index of Nigerian Languages. Studies in Nigeria Languages, 5, 1-204.

Ikara, B. 1982. "Towards participatory democracy in Nigeria" In Ikara B. (Ed.) Nigerian Languages and Cultural Development (pp 119-137). Lagos, Nigeria: National Language Centre.

Ikara, B. (Ed.). 1982. Nigerian languages and Cultural Development. Lagos, Nigeria: National Language Centre.

Kelman, H. C. 1971. "Language as an aid and barrier to involvement in the national system' In Rubin, J. & B. Jernudd. Can Language be Planned? (pp. 21-51). Honolulu: University Press of Hawaii. Welmers W. E. 1973. African Language Structures. Los Angeles: University of California Press.

Williamson, K. 1980. "Small languages in primary education. The Rivers Readers project as a case history. " In Bamgbose (Ed.) Language in Education in Nigeria. (pp 81-89). Lagos, Nigeria: National Language Centre

Chapter 4

SWAHILI VERSUS ENGLISH IN TANZANIA: THE WIN-WIN SITUATION

Josephine Dzahene-Quarshie

Introduction

Although it is a fact that of all African languages Swahili is one of the most developed and one that has attained a very reputable status and a strong global presence over several decades, it is also a fact that it has had its fair share of problems and continues to face challenges; the chief of which is its rivalry with English as indicated by works such as *Language Crisis in Tanzania; The Myth of English Versus Education*. Tanzania is one of the few African countries which make use of indigenous languages as both National and official languages in post-colonial Africa[1]. In the face of obvious challenges, Tanzania took the bold step to declare Kiswahili as the National and official language even if in practice the latter was true only to some extent (Whiteley, 1969:99)[2]. Some African countries declared one or more indigenous languages as National languages. Others made no declarations as far as National language was concerned. For example, In Ghana (West Africa) no local languages were or have been declared as National language(s). However, most of other African nations have declared English or French (depending on their colonial masters' language) as Official Language and Medium of Instruction (MOI) at some level of education.

Some African countries declared one or more indigenous languages as National languages. Others made no declarations as far as National language was concerned. In Ghana (in West Africa) for instance, no local languages were or have been declared as National language(s). However, most of them declared English or French (depending on their colonial masters' language) as Official Language and Medium of Instruction at some level of education. In Tanzania the declaration of Swahili as a National and official language was part and parcel of President Nyerere's Policy of *Ujamaa* (socialism) that the TANU (Tanganyika African National Union) put in place on wining the 1961 elections that ushered Tanzania into independence (Whitely 1969). For even before independence,

President Nyerere had already proposed that Swahili should become the National language (Harries 1969:275). The full implementation of Swahili as official language was to be gradual. As far as education was concerned Swahili was declared medium of instruction in primary education and English the medium of instruction in secondary and tertiary education while effort was made towards the implementation of Swahili as medium of instruction at both the secondary and tertiary levels (Bloomeart, 1997:41).

Work was undertaken by various Language Policy Agencies set up by the government, such as the Institute of Kiswahili Research (IKR) and National Swahili Council (NSC) to work out and see to the implementation of Swahili as MOI at the higher and tertiary levels of education. This implementation of Swahili as a medium of instruction was to begin from 1971; however this did not happen (Bloomeart 1997:41). In 1982, the Presidential Commission on Education that was set up by the President recommended that the policy of Swahili as the sole MOI at all levels of Education should be implemented in 1985 as everything had been put in place for the take-off of the policy (Lwaitama & Rugemalira 1990 quoted in Eleuthera Sa 2007:5, Rwezaura 1993:39, Kiango 2005). However, till today this policy has not been implemented and there are indications that it may not see day light for a long time to come. Several factors account for the inability or reluctance on the part of government and policy makers to implement this policy although the necessary preparations seem to have been made.

As a result of the government's inability or reluctance to implement this policy, Tanzania has not seen any significant change in its language policy over forty years after Independence. The Medium of Instruction at the Primary level is still Swahili and that of higher education is still English, contrary to the plans to implement Swahili medium at all levels of education. It is interesting to note that the educational policy spelt out by the Tanzanian Ministry of Education on the National Website alleges that currently the policy being pursued is a bilingual one " which requires children to learn both Kiswahili and English. English is essential, as it is the language which links Tanzania and the rest of the world through technology, commerce and also administration. " (Tanzania National Website, Section on Education) This perhaps is an indication that the plans to switch from English medium to Swahili medium have been abandoned for good.

In the light of the above state of affairs, the paper seeks to demonstrate that the major factors that have led to this dilemma that the Swahili language finds itself in are the retreat from Nyerere's Policy of *Ujamaa* and the move towards a more liberal economy in Tanzania as well as the effects of globalisation. To achieve this, the paper first examines the rivalry that has existed between Swahili and English in Tanzania from the pre-independence period. The paper further recommends the adoption of a language policy that does not see the two languages as languages in opposition or at war, but one that offers a win-win situation, a situation that allows the two languages to exist side by side complementing each other in their unique roles for the benefit of all Tanzanians in the face of the reality of a global world that seems to have come to stay for good.

Background History

The history of the wide spread use of Swahili in East Africa, specifically in present day Tanzania goes back about three centuries. From the latter part of the 1700 to the mid 1800, that is prior to the advent of Europeans to East Africa, Kiswahili which evolved from the coastal area had spread to the interior of East Africa due to the development of trade relations between foreign merchants, the coastal people and the people of the interior. The interior opened up tremendously with the development of trade routes. (Maxon, 1994). The European Missionaries were the first to take concrete steps towards a systematic study of the Swahili language. Within a few years of their arrival, their interest in the language was such that, they began writing down the grammar of the language, and compiled the vocabulary with the intention of producing a dictionary. (Maxon, 1994). By the time the Germans colonialists arrived in East Africa, Swahili had already acquired the status of a lingua franca in East Africa. They took advantage of the language situation and adopted Swahili as the colonial administrative language. They set up training institutions which used Swahili as the medium of instruction to train local people to take up positions of junior administrators within the colonial administration.

The British took over the sphere of influence of the Germans (German East Africa Protectorate) after the Second World War and although they continued to use Swahili more or less as the administrative language, English nevertheless was adopted as the language of communication in the legislature and judiciary and the medium of instruction in the early primary school was either Swahili of vernacular. At the upper primary and higher level, the medium of instruction was English. Swahili was standardized by the British colonial administration in 1930 (Whiteley, 1969). The British administration intended to put measures in place to see to the elevation of the Swahili language to gradually take over some of the functions of the English language both in the colonial administration and in education at a higher level. The British colonial administration demonstrated its commitment to the development of Swahili by commissioning the Inter-territorial (Swahili Language Committee (ILC) to standardise the Swahili language for the purpose of education. However the British administration had to abandon its plan on language planning for Tanzania when shortly after the Second World War nationalist movements were formed by the then emerging educated elite initially to demand for increased African participation in government and consequently self government (Whiteley, 1969:78).

During this era of Nationalism and struggle for self-government, the Swahili language which was still the lingua-franca had become a very important tool for the Nationalists and Politicians. Recognizing that proficiency in English was linked to the few educated elite, coupled with the desire to identify with the masses Swahili was used extensively as a medium for communicating nationalists' ideas, and also for political campaigns. Tanganyika eventually gained independence in December 1963 under the TANU party led by the late President Nyerere. Given the vital role that Swahili had played in the fight for independence, it was seen as a tool for the unification of the people. The TANU government therefore capitalized on the achievements of the language as a tool of communication and took concrete steps to consolidate the position of the Swahili language in Tanzania as a symbol of national unity. It was declared the national and official language as well as established as medium of instruction in primary education. (Whiteley, 1969)

The State of the English Language in Tanzania: Past and Present

As mentioned above, the presence of English in Tanzania dates back to the era of British presence in East Africa. The very first British who arrived in East Africa were mostly missionaries whose main agenda was to convert East African people to Christianity. It was hoped that the conversion of Africans to Christianity would lead to the eventual abolition of the Slave Trade; a trade which was seen an affront to God but was still being practised in East Africa, long after its official abolition by the British government. And one way of achieving this objective was through education. Because the Swahili language was already wide spread in East Africa, they took advantage of it. They learnt the language and used it to communicate with the people. By the very nature of missionary work, educational institutions were established by them to facilitate their task of converting East Africans to Christianity. The first training school was established by the German missionaries (Maxon, 1994). By the close of the first half of the twentieth century, the colonial government had begun to take interest in the education of the people of East Africa. A task that was until then undertaken solely by the missionaries. In collaboration with the missionaries, the colonial administration began to put measures in place in order to ensure that East Africans receive formal education. Unlike the Germans who pursued a Swahili only policy, Britain introduced the English language to the Africans and promoted it considerably even as they saw it important to promote the Swahili language. Several conferences were held to discuss issues on language and education, especially the choice of medium of instruction. The options were, local languages, vernacular, Swahili and English. The debate went on for some time, but eventually Swahili was established as the medium of instruction in primary education. In 1929 the ILC Inter-territorial (Swahili) language Committee) was established first of all to standardize the Swahili language for the purpose of education and secondly to ensure that the standard was adhered to by especially publishers of formal Educational material (Whiteley, 1969 & Mbaabu, 1991).

Although most administrative materials were written in English, the colonial administration was more or less carried out in Swahili. When Britain took over from Germany, Swahili was preserved as the medium of instruction at the lower primary (that is first five years), but at upper primary that is last two years and also at the secondary school, the medium of instruction was English. Presently at the secondary school the language of instruction is English. However it is noted that the transition from Swahili medium to English medium is not smooth, therefore the tendency for both students and teachers (who themselves may not be very comfortable using English) to explain issues in Swahili is usually high. This situation also occurs in some private English medium primary schools too (Rugemalira, 2005). Even at the tertiary level, it is observed that for most students communication in English is very difficult and uncomfortable. On the university campus the language spoken outside the lecture room is inevitably Swahili except when communication is between local students and foreign students. Although Swahili supposedly is the official language of Tanzania this has been only partially true because documentations in most state institutions such as the law courts and banks are still done in English. Swahili is used as the medium of communication only in oral communication. Most official documents exist in English and translations of official documents into Swahili are undertaken from time to time.

The primary courts use Swahili in their entire proceedings, both oral and written. Tanzania court of appeal (amendment of rule 3A) Rules, 1985 provides that:

> "3A the language of the court shall be either English or Kiswahili as the chief justice or as the court may be. The presiding Judge holding such court shall direct. But the judgment, order, or decision shall be in English. In the magistrate court, proceedings can be in Swahili but, the magistrate must write the court records as well as the judgment in English. " (cited in Rwezaura 1993:32)

At the high court level, the judge writes all proceedings in English and all written submissions are to be in English. Kiswahili has been used in parliamentary debates since 1962 and the proceedings of the house have been published in Swahili, but Bills are still drafted in English. The state constitution of 1977 however was drafted and published in Swahili (Rwezaura 1993:37). In the case where a parliamentarian is not proficient in English (there could be several such), they are short changed when bills are drafted in English but debated in Swahili. In state institutions such as banks oral communication is in Swahili but, written documentation is in English.

The Place of Swahili within the Policy of *Ujamaa*

It is worth noting that prior to the struggle for self rule and independence in Africa, that is, shortly after the Second World War; nationalist movements arose, mainly to agitate for more African representation in the colonial administration. In Tanzania, the TAA, a nationalist movement was formed, with the late President Nyerere as its leader. It was during the campaigns of the TAA that Swahili became a symbol of national unity. Later when the TAA was transformed into a political party having experienced how indispensable Swahili had become as a tool to the TAA, Swahili became entrenched as the medium through which the political ideology of the party would be communicated to the people. Indeed the party leaders resolved to adopt Swahili as the medium of communication within the party and with the masses. Upon winning the elections to form the first independent government of Tanganyika, the use of the Swahili language became a government policy. The whole ideology of the party was projected by the use of Swahili as a unifying force and 'a symbol of The Tanzanian Nation'

(Legère 2006:176). Nyerere's political ideology, the Policy of *Ujamaa* sought to achieve a totally self-reliant classless and egalitarian society with a common language where all institutions are owned by the state. The policy of *Ujamaa* also consciously pursued national integration and sought to substitute national for tribal loyalties. (Maxon 1994)

The move towards ensuring total self-reliance was driven by the fact that although Tanzania was independent, it still relied heavily on foreign aid from Britain and America. Nyerere wanted to move way from relying on foreign aid which first was not helping the development of Tanzania. In order to achieve total self-reliance, Nyerere put forward a blueprint for self- reliance and this was outdoored as part of the famous Arusha Declaration in 1967 (Bloomeart, 1994 & Maxon, 1994). Nyerere is said to have claimed that he was not following European Marxism but rather the socialism that has been part of Africa's own past social and economic system (Maxon, 1994). By the declaration, all private banks, major food processing companies, insurance companies, and major export and import companies were taken over by the state. Also, estates and settler farms were taken over by the government. As soon as the TANU came into power, the party's position on Swahili became a government policy.

The Swahili language became central to all government policy concerning Education for Self-Reliance. Swahili was declared the national language and later the official language as well. The focus of education changed. Agriculture was now to form an important aspect of primary education. Much attention was not given to higher education. After all at this point in time only a relatively small percentage of pupils were expected to continue to the secondary level of education (Kiango, 2005:160). Under *Ujamaa* special institutions and agencies such as IKR and NSC were set up by the government to promote the Swahili language. Also at one point the special position of a Promoter was created and at another time the position of The Director of Culture and National language were created to see to the promotion of Swahili. It must be noted that the quest for the promotion of Swahili apart from indicating freedom from language imperialism and demonstrating national identity, most importantly it forestalled the problems of tribal and ethnic divisions which other independence countries were struggling with. For this purpose its promotion was deemed paramount to the building of the new socialist state in which the spirit of oneness was of utmost importance (Topan, 2008: 258).

This was an obvious conscious effort by the government to promote the Swahili language while nothing was done to promote the English language (Harries, 1969:275). While the British colonial government created the impression that English was a higher language than Swahili, the TANU government created the opposite impression. Its leaders made the people understand that Swahili was the most important language for Tanzanians for the sake of national integration and unity. Ultimately as Stated by Harries (1969:276), *"The strongest argument for the promotion of Swahili as a national language was a political one. "* Looking at the socialist's ideal where Tanzania would be totally independent and self-reliant, indeed all Tanzanians would need to communicate in Swahili. *Ujamaa* villages were created; these were communities that were put in place to engage in communal agriculture. Under the policy, agriculture was to be strengthened. The promotion of Swahili went down well with the people and they came to believe that Swahili was a symbol of nationalism while English was a symbol of colonialism (Harries, 1969). Looking at the policy of *Ujamaa* then, it is clear that the language policy adopted by the government was very suitable for the dictates of Nyerere's socialism and more especially the policy of Education for Self-Reliance, ' although Harries (1969:275), reports Nyerere as stating in an interview that the "ultimate aim was that every citizen of Tanzania should be bilingual in the sense that they could speak Swahili and English. " It does not seem that the effort that was made towards the promotion of Swahili at the time was extended to English. After all only a small percentage of pupils were expected to continue to the secondary school (Kiango, 2005:160; Topan, 2008:259) where competence in English would matter since it was the MOI.

Although Topan (2008:262) and others state that Nyerere in fact had a vision of a bilingual Tanzania, it seems either this vision may not have been communicated effectively or may not have been emphasised enough. Clearly apart from Nyerere's rejection of the 1982 Presidential Commission for Educations' recommendation to implement Swahili as MOI in secondary schools and his acceptance of the English Language Teaching Support Project (1987-91) funded by Overseas Development Agency (ODA) of the British government, not much was done in the way of promoting the English language. Rubagumya (1991) states that *'in the 60s and 70s nationalistic sentiments were so high in Tanzania that people who spoke English in Public were accused of ... 'colonial hangover'* (pg. 70).

Retreat from *Ujamaa* and its Impact on the Swahili Language

In the 1980s, the economic situation in Tanzania became very bad. However with the IMF and the World Bank policies, Tanzania could not be helped until certain conditions such as structural adjustment, devaluation of currency and opening up to foreign investors and privatization of state owned institutions among other things were met. This period marks the beginning of a phenomenal boost in the value of English in Tanzania (Rubagumya, 1991:75). The pressure was so much that in order not to appear to have failed as a socialist, Nyerere stepped down as president of Tanzania and was succeeded by Ali Hassan Mwinyi in 1985 (Maxon, 1994). Soon after the take over, Mwinyi had no option but to succumb to IMF and World Bank policies yielding to the conditions attached. This marked the beginning of the unannounced retreat from *Ujamaa*. Although Nyerere was not in agreement with this move, Mwinyi saw it as the only option for Tanzania. The World Bank/IMF conditions obviously conflicted with the extreme socialist ideologies of *Ujamaa*. *Ujamaa* clearly had collapsed.

The importance of the English language came to play with the yielding of Tanzania to IMF/ World Bank policies and conditions as well as other international organizations and donors. Continually English became the medium through which these policies, agreements and so on were transacted. Under *Ujamaa*, Swahili was supposed to become the MOI in secondary schools but that had not happened. Nyerere himself was said to have admitted to the fact that the English language was as important as Swahili and without it, Tanzania would not be able to communicate with the outside world. He is also said to have explained elsewhere that English is in fact is the Kiswahili of the world. Again he is said to have recommended the maintenance of English as medium of instruction at the secondary level (Bloomeart, 1997). By 1990 the Directorate of culture and National Language had translated all secondary school text books into Swahili (Kiango, 2005). There was supposed to be a programme put in place by the government that would see to the gradual replacement of English by Swahili in secondary schools by 1971 and the only courses that would be taught in Swahili would be civic/political education (Bloomeart, 1997:41). Ironically, Nyerere's acceptance of the ODA English Language Project also meant the acceptance of the condition of English remaining as the MOI in secondary education. In a way this could be viewed as one of the symptoms of the fall of *Ujamaa*. With the retreat from *Ujamaa* and the move towards a liberal economy in Tanzania, as manifested by the IMF and World Bank policies and a heavy presence of foreign investors and companies as well as privatization of state owned institution, the Tanzanian society that for sometime now time was sheltered by *Ujamaa*, began to become more and more aware of the encroachment of globalization in the Tanzanian economy and this has affected the ordinary Tanzanian's view of the Swahili Language vis-à-vis the English Language.

Tanzania has evolved considerably and one now needs more than Swahili to survive economically and hold ones own in the Tanzanian economy. Competition for jobs is becoming keener and foreigners are competing with Tanzanians for them. Competence in English is an advantage in this competition. Many Tanzanians are therefore doing everything possible to acquire English Medium education at least for their children, as they see this as the only way to ensure that they come at par with their counterparts elsewhere (Rubagumya, 2002). The average Tanzanian parent, wants their children to have English medium education, and would do everything possible within their means to achieve this either by sending them to local English medium private schools, or by sending them to neighbouring countries like Uganda and Kenya or better still by sending them to Europe or America (Rugemalira, 2005:68). Although in one way or the other the rivalry or competition between Swahili and English has existed since the colonial era, the fresh evidence of this competition between Swahili and English: are the ongoing debates on Language and Education Policy and more evidently the mushrooming of Private English Medium Schools in Tanzania as a preferred choice to Swahili medium schools among some Tanzanians, especially the elite in the society.

The Place of Globalization in the Competition between Swahili and English

The imposition of English on various British Colonies during the British Colonial Rule and its aftermath was referred to as 'Linguistic Imperialism'. The implications of this imposition are manifest in Ansre's (1979:12-13, cited in Phillipson 1992:56) definition of the term:

> The phenomenon in which the minds and lives of the speakers of a language are dominated by another language to the point where they believe that they can and should use only the foreign language when it comes to transactions dealing with the more advanced aspects of life such as education, philosophy, literature, governments, the administration of justice etc....

As much as language imperialism is detested and condemned by various factions, it is also a reality that it is part of life, a colonial legacy that will be with Africa for a long time.

However in the case of Tanzania, we see that although it was affected by the phenomenon, it was on a relatively minimum scale in the sense that even during British rule, the Swahili language was very dominant despite the elevation of the English language by the colonists. Secondly the language of primary education and government administration upon independence was switched from English to Swahili. Swahili literature although influenced by English literature remained written in Swahili not English. The language of the higher courts is predominantly English while that of the lower courts is predominantly Swahili. As stated above, it was by the efforts of the TANU that Tanzania was shielded to some extent from language imperialism. In recent times the dominance of the English language has heightened again and on a much larger scale affecting the entire globe Crystal (1997) and this time its dominance is attributed to the Globalization phenomenon.

Tabb (2006) defines globalization as a 'comprehensive term for the emergence of a global society in which economic, political, environmental, and cultural events in one part of the world quickly come to have significance for people in other parts of the world. ' He goes on to explain that 'Globalization is the result of advances in communication, transportation and information technologies. ' What Tabb did not add is the fact that the advances in these three areas have indeed turned the world into a global village in which English is the language of communication. As a result of globalisation English has become relevant to even countries such as China in which English was not regarded. Today Tanzania has become like any of its compatriots. Privatization of State Institutions and the influx of multinational companies representing foreign investment is the order of the day. One can say that the situation where almost every person one meets on the street spoke Swahili is gradually changing. More foreigners have migrated to Tanzania as a result of the influx of multinational companies. Globalization then can be blamed to some extent for the 'new linguistic market' in which English finds itself in Tanzania and other countries such as China. English has become the international language that links the world together. Nyerere's words "English is the Swahili of the world" remains a reality.

Debates on Language Policy in Tanzania

The mere fact that for over twenty years, the initial plan of the Tanzanian government to switch the MOI secondary and tertiary education to has not been implemented is an indication that the matter is not an easy straight forward one. Also if it was not implemented in the eighties and nineties when the necessary preparations for the switch over had be completed, then it will be more difficult to do so in this age of globalization where the English language is gaining more grounds and becoming more and more powerful as a global language; the language that links the nations of the world. Contrary to the impression that is usually given about the late President Nyerere's view on the promotion of Swahili by a Swahili only policy in education, Nyerere it seems had always held the view that bilingualism is the best for Tanzania, and envisaged a balanced bilingual Tanzanian society with respect to Swahili and English, especially, as *Ujamaa* declined and the pressure to succumb to World Bank /IMF assistance mounted. Although we take cognizance of the fact that before he passed away he is said to have changed his mind again and registered his regrets for not pursuing a Swahili only MOI, his earlier view of a bilingual Tanzania was a healthier and forward looking one.

That there are problems in the educational set up is evident in the magnitude of research that have been conducted targeted at exposing the problems and challenges of the educational system, especially the high levels of failures in the education system and suggestions to resolve the problems. Such researches have involved soliciting opinions from individuals, language policy agencies, Government officials, language policy implementers, observing real classroom situation etc. From the findings and recommendation of most researchers, there seem to be the general recommendation that the current policy is problematic, that is to put it mildly, and has been the source or cause of the problems and therefore not the best for Tanzania and that the best policy for Tanzania is a Swahili only medium throughout the educational system. Research has also shown that there are counter views to the quest for a Swahili only policy although it is often indicated that this represents a minority group. The mushrooming of private English medium schools and the enrolment of pupils in these schools at a fast rate indicate the desire of a cross section of the society for proficiency in English, notwithstanding the underperformance rate and the failure of some of these schools to achieve the desired results. This problem of non-performance of some schools has been used as grounds to condemn English Medium Schools. Nevertheless, in so far as some parents believe that English is essential at all cost, bogus English medium schools will continue to increase and more and more parents will be unduly exploited and short-changed because they will not get the desired outcome for their children from these schools.

It is also a fact that dissatisfaction with the outcome of the present Education policy has created this Linguistic Market for English in

Tanzania (Rubagumya, 2002). It is interesting to note from Brock-Utne (2002), the blame game that stakeholders play where the choice of language in education policy is concerned. In the various interviews that were conducted, the impression that the interviewees create most of the time is that they prefer and advocate for a Swahili only model but others (that are not there to answer for themselves) are against it. One issue that if investigated would be interesting is the kinds of schools that children of the policy makers and implementers, opinion leaders and advocators of a Swahili only policy attend. Perhaps that would reflect the real situation on the ground and answer the question whether or not a Swahili only policy is the real desire of the majority of Tanzanians and not an imposition.

In Europe and the Scandinavia where the indigenous languages are used throughout all levels of education, the teaching of English is also relatively very effective, but these are economically powerful countries (often) with populations of a few millions. The African situation is different and also complex as a result of colonialism, poverty and the multiplicity of languages in various countries. Of the African countries the Tanzanian situation is unique. Although there are over one hundred indigenous languages in Tanzania, the Swahili language which is one of them is today spoken by over 95% of the population as a first (L1) or second language (L2) For most L2 users of Swahili, Swahili is as good as their L1 if not better. This situation although has its disadvantages such as the threat of language death to other Tanzanian languages (over one hundred), is simpler to deal with than many other African countries. It is all well and good to have a Swahili only policy, but what is the proof that that would be a solution to the problem. Have enough experimentation been done to ascertain for sure that it will do the trick? Does this option prepare the average Tanzanian to meet Tanzania's portion on education in its vision 2025?

> "Be a nation with high quality of education at all levels; a nation which produces the quantity and quality of educated people sufficiently equipped with the requisite knowledge to solve the society's problems, meet the challenges of development and attain competitiveness at regional and global levels."

There is no doubt that in order for Tanzania to achieve its goal of educated citizens who will be sufficiently "equipped with the requisite knowledge to solve the society's problems, meet the challenges of development and attain competitiveness at regional and global levels" a balanced acquisition and proficiency of both Swahili and English is essential. Brock-Utne (2002) alludes to the fact that most parents' desire at least from her research is synonymous with that of Nyerere that their children will be bilingual in the true sense of the word and indeed that should be the target. The fact that the bilingual policy has not chalked up any successes yet does not mean that invariably the policy is not a workable one or one that is not right for Tanzania. There is no doubt that there are serious problems with the existing policy which need to be addressed It is equally important to accept that there is no quick fix solution to the problem. A true bilingual Tanzanian will be able to function effectively both in Tanzania and elsewhere in the global economy as targeted by Vision 2025.

In many British Post-Colonial states, basically two types of language in education policies are practised; either a monolingual model which is often the English Only L2 model where English is used as MOI throughout all levels of education as is practised in Ghana presently, or some form of a bilingual model where both the child's L1 and L2 (English) are used as MOI at different points within the educational ladder. Several varieties of Bilingual models are identified in the literature such as in Krashen (1991). Two models of the Transition Bilingual Education (TBE), Early Exit-TBE and the Late Exit-TBE are commonly used by several countries in Africa. In the early Exit TBE, L1 is used as MOI in the first few years of primary education and English takes over towards the end as was practised in Ghana until 2002. In the Late Exit-TBE, L1 is used as MOI for a longer period and English takes over from there as practised in Tanzania presently. In the case of Ghana, apparent problems with the bilingual approach led to the change to the English Only Policy (in May 2002), but as to whether the change will address the situation is the matter of ongoing debates. Already some scholars and groups have come out to condemn the change in policy and the debate continues. Owu Ewie (2006) argues that the English Only option is not a better option for Ghana.

In response to the current language crisis in Tanzania several scholars (Rubagumya, 1991; Brock-Utne, 2002) as a result of research and investigations have advocated for a monolingual model in which Swahili is the sole MOI throughout the education system as a possible solution. Among other reasons given as justification for this view is the fact that English is not delivering and the fact most Tanzanians would not proceed from Primary level and therefore may not need to use English at all in their lives after school, but the fact that they may be out of school does not mean they may not need English. There has however not been enough evidence to support this view although pockets of research and investigations have been conducted experimenting with a few subjects (Rugemalira, 2005). Others also advocate a monolingual L2 (English Only) model for Tanzania; it is assumed that an early introduction of English as MOI will ensure appreciable proficiency by the secondary school level however, research findings by Rubagumya (2002) and Rugemalira (2005) indicate already that there are serious problems with some of the (relatively) few Private English medium primary schools. A third option, the bilingual model is viewed as a possible compromise by Roy-Campbell (2001), Vavrus (2002), and Sa (2007). Rubagumya (2002:164) suggests that an 'additive bilingualism' would be a more helpful option. Sa (2007) recommends the Swahili only model that allows code-switching between Swahili and English.

Our view however is that in as much as code-switching is becoming increasingly common and acceptable in Tanzania and elsewhere, and will no doubt be employed from time to time, it does not solve the problem. In as much as there are problems with the Language in education policy as it stands in Tanzania as iterated by Campbell (2001), Vavrus (2002), Sa (2007), Rubagumya (1991, 2002:164), changing the medium of instruction in secondary education to Swahili may not solve the problem just as changing it to an English only one may not solve it either. In fact there is no strong evidence to suggest that any of these options will work out better as has been demonstrated by research. The failure of the current policy can be attributed to several factors most of which have been reported by various scholars. As pointed out by Vavrus (2002) harsh economic conditions contributes greatly to the failures in the educational system. The way forward therefore is to take time and analyse the problems that hinder the effectiveness of the current policy and adjust it in a way that will ensure a good balance between Swahili and English, a win –win situation.

The Win-Win Situation

In our view apart from addressing problems that stem from lack of adequate resources in the Teaching of English, poor teaching methods and high levels of incompetence of teachers, the area that needs immediate attention is the model that is used and its implementation. Krashen (1991) demonstrates that a properly balanced bilingual education is no lesser effective than an English only one. Owu-Ewie (2006) argues that the Late-Exit Bilingual model of education can be effective if implemented rightly. Although the Late Exit TBE is supposed to prevent a sharp transition between the two levels so as to produce balanced bilingual students, the Tanzanian policy has not been able to achieve that. According to the model throughout primary education Swahili is used as the MOI while English is taught as a subject and at the secondary level English becomes the MOI for all subjects except, civic education which is taught in Swahili. The Late Exit-Transition bilingual model that Owu-Ewie (2006) proposes for Ghanaian situation promises to yield better results, especially in the Tanzanian situation where although Swahili is L2 for most speakers their proficiency in it is as good if not better than that of their L1. In other words Tanzania could be referred to as a reasonably monolingual society and therefore is easier to deal with than a typically multilingual society like Ghana. He proposes a model based on the late-exit TBE model of Ramirez and Merino (1990) in which:

> "A Ghanaian language is used as the medium of instruction up until the fourth year because by then it is anticipated that the child would have had enough L1 background to help transfer gradually into English. Mathematics and integrated science are taught in the L1 until primary five because they are abstract and need a familiar language for learners to understand and appreciate their value. Environmental studies, physical education, and religious and moral education are instructed in English from Primary 5 because the learners have sufficient background experience in these areas from their community/culture. The study of a second Ghanaian language in the Junior Secondary School is a start towards learners becoming bilingual in Ghanaian languages. " (Owu-Ewie 2006:81)

This model ensures a balance which the current Tanzanian policy lacks. Although the language situations in the two countries are different, the late-exit bilingual model advocated by Owu-Ewie (2006) could be adopted and adjusted to suit the Tanzanian situation. The study of a second Tanzanian language in addition to Swahili at a later stage (the secondary level) could be a positive move towards addressing the current status quo where other Tanzanian languages apart from Swahili are threatened with language death.

We propose a model that would ensure a reasonable balance that will successfully ensure that the average Tanzanian will be a reasonably balanced bilingual after going through primary and secondary education.

Table 1: The proposed Late-exit Transitional Bilingual Education Model

Class	Swahili as MOI	English as MOI
P1	100% (All Subjects including English)	
P2 – P3	90% (All Subjects excluding English)	10%
P4	80% (including Mathematics and science)	20% (English + another subject)
P5	70% (including Mathematics and science)	30%
P6	60% (including Mathematics and science)	40%
P7	50% (including Mathematics and science)	50%
Secondary 1- 4	20% (Swahili + other Tanzanian Language)	80%

Figure 1: Graphic representation of proposed late-exit Transitional Bilingual Education Model

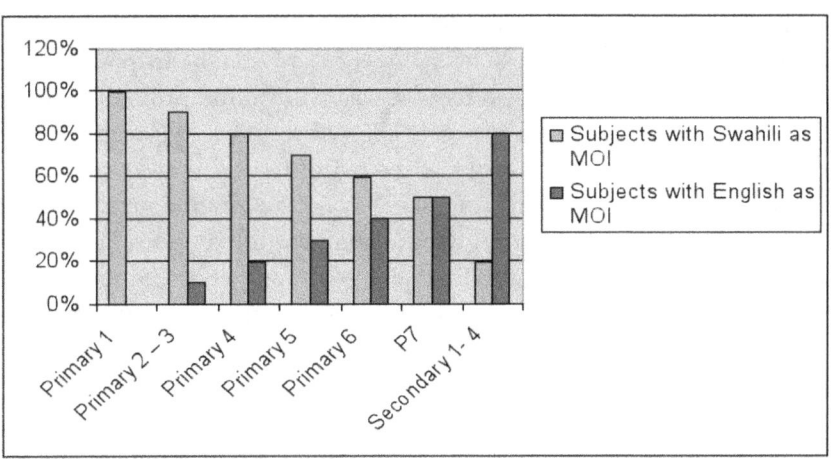

The advantage of this model is the fact that the take over of English as MOI is not as abrupt as it is presently. This model ensures a gradual transition from Swahili as MOI to English as MOI. This model ensures a gradual introduction of English as a MOI gradually, by restricting it to specific subjects and gradually increasing the number of subjects with English as MOI as the students improve on their ability to understand and read, write and communicate in English. Also the subjects which are more abstract in nature like mathematics and Science are taught in L1, in this case Swahili for a longer period because it will help them to understand and relate to the subjects better. By the end of primary 7, approximately 50% of the subjects would be taught in Swahili and 50% in English. At the secondary school, about 80% of subjects would be taught in English and about 20% in Swahili of the 20% taught in Swahili one course will be Swahili language and the other will be a second Tanzanian language. It is expected that the continual use of Swahili as MOI in some subjects will help students in their acquisition of English since a good knowledge of L1 said the old system could be phased out gradually. If implemented successfully it could help bring about the win-win situation for Swahili and English. Also the educational materials that have been prepared in Swahili already could be made available to students as supplementary material.

Conclusion

The paper has attempted to demonstrate that both Swahili and English have had a place in the history of Tanzania, and various governmental policies during the colonial and post colonial period has brought about a rivalry between the two languages. The policy of *Ujamaa* put in place during the post independence era sought to promote the Swahili language while little attention was paid to the promotion of the English language. This turn of events affected seriously the acquisition of the English language. As a result of the fall of *Ujamaa* and globalization, the English language is beginning to receive attention in Tanzania and is competing with Swahili for attention. Given the premise that both languages are important in the Tanzanian economy, the need to promote English cannot be disputed. The proposed long term solution is a bilingual education that is geared towards producing reasonably balanced bilingual Tanzanians who can function satisfactorily in Tanzania and the global world as spelt out by the vision 2025. If Tanzanians are educated properly to understand that both languages are equally important, the situation where either English or Swahili is abhorred would not arrive. Swahili will continue to flourish in the areas in which it is used in Tanzania and the East and Central African regions. It will continue to be the symbol of unity and solidarity and nationalism in Tanzania and a lingua franca in East and Central Africa. It will continue to receive global recognition, be used in international broadcast media, be a subject in higher institutions all over the world and continue to attract research from scholars all over the world.

Notes

1   The other is Ethiopia, where Amharic is both official and national language.

2   English is still used in certain official capacities such as the language of operation in the higher courts; parliamentary bills are drafted in English. (Rwezaura 1993)

References

Blommaert, Jan. 1997. State Ideology and Language: The Politics of Swahili in Tanzania. *LICCA* paper nr. 3. Duisburg: Gerhard Mercator University.

Brock-Utne, Brigit. 2002. The Most Recent Developments Concerning the Debate on Language of Instruction in Tanzania, Presented to *the NETREED Conference from 7th – 9th of January 2002*

Crystal, D. 1997. *English as a Global Language*. Cambridge: Cambridge University Press.

Harries, Lyndon. 1969. Language Policy in Tanzania *Journal of the International African Institute, Vol. 39, No. 3,* July, 1969, pp. 275-280.

Kiango J. G. 2005. Tanzania's Historical Contribution to the Recognition and Promotion of Swahili, *Africa & Asia*, No. 5, pp. 157-166.

Krashen, Stephen D. 1991. Bilingual Education: A Focus on Current Research, NCBE FOCUS: Occasional Papers in Bilingual Education, No. 3, Spring 1991 http://www.ncela.gwu.edu/pubs/focus/focus3.htm

Legère, K. 2006. Formal and Informal Development of the Swahili Language: Focus on Tanzania. In Arasanyin O. F. & Micheal Pemberton (Eds.), *Selected Proceedings of the 36th Annual Conference on African Linguistics: Shifting the Cener of Africanism in Language and Politics and Economic Glibalization*, (pp. 176-183). Somerville, MA: Cascadilla Proceedings Project.

Maxon, Robert M. 1994. *East Africa: An Introductory History*. Virginia: W. Virginia University Press.

Mazrui, A. & Mazrui, A. A. 1993. Ominant Languages in a Plural Society: English and Kiswahili in Post-Colonial East Africa. *International Political Science Review*, Vol. 14, No. 3 pp. 275-292

Mbaabu Ireri. 1991. *Historia ya Usanifishaji wa Kiswahili*. Kenya: Longman

Okello, Benson. 2002. *A History of East Africa*. Kampala, Uganda: Fountain Publishers Ltd.

Owu-Ewie, Charles. 2006. The Language Policy of education on Ghana: A Critical Look at the English-Only Language Policy of Education. In John Mugane et al *(Eds.)*, *Selected Proceedings of the 35th Annual Conference on African Linguistics*, (pp. 76-85). Somerville, MA: Cascadilla Proceedings Project.

Phillipson, Robert. 1992. *Linguistic imperialism*. Oxford: Oxford University Press.

Roy-Campbell, Zaline Makini, & Martha A. S. Qorro. 1997. *Language Crisis in Tanzania. The Myth of English versus Education*. Dar es Salaam: Mkuki na Nyota Publishers.

Roy-Campbell, Zaline Makini. 2001. 'Globalisation, Language and Education: A comparative studies of the United States and Tanzania' *International Review of Education*, Vol. 47, No. 3/4 Globalisation, Language and Education, pp. 267-282.

Rubagumya Casmir M. 2002. English Medium Primary Schools in Tanzania: A New 'Linguistic Market' in Education, 9 pp. A Paper Presented at the Workshop on Language of Instruction in Tanzania and South Africa. April 22 – 24, Morogoro, Tanzania.

_____1991. Language Promotion for Education Purpose: The Example of Tanzania. *Internal Review of Education*, Vol. 37, No. 1 pp. 67-85

Rugemalira J. M. 2005. Theoretical and practical challenges in a Tanzanian English Medium Primary School, *Asia & Africa*, No. 5 pp. 66-84.

Rwezaura, B. 1993. Constraining Factors to the Adoption of Kiswahili as a Language of Law in Tanzania, *Journal of African Law*, Vol. 37, No. 1: 30-45. Sa, E. 2007. Language policy for Education and Development in Tanzania http://www.swarthmore.edu/socsci/linguistics/pPapers/2007/sa-eleuthera.pdf

Tabb, William K. 2006. Globalization, Microsoft Encarta Online Encyclopedia 2006. http://encarta.msn.com/text_1741588397___1/Globalization.html

Tanzania National Website http://www.tanzania.go.tz/human.html

Topan, F. 2008. Tanzania: The Development of Swahili as a National and Official Language. In Simpson, Andrew (Ed.). *Language and National identity in Africa*. U. K: Oxford University Press. Pp. 252-266.

Vavrus, F. 2002. Postcoloniality and English: Exploring Language Policy and Politics of Development in Tanzania. *TESOL Quarterly, Vol. 36, No. 3,* Autumn. pp. 373-397.

Whitely, W. H. 1969. *Swahili: The Rise of a National Language.* London: Methuen

Chapter 5

CONFRONTING THE DIALECTICS OF NIGERIA'S LANGUAGE POLICY LAWS: THE CONSTITUTIONAL SOLUTION

Olaoba F. Arasanyin

Introduction: The Foundation

In 1979, Nigeria shifted politically from the Parliamentary System of governance which by all measure, a failure, to the Presidential system. The shift, by Ehindero's (1991:37) estimation, meant: 'the executive authority' that was once "vested in one person [the President] and exercised by another, [the Prime Minister}" was reconceived with preference for power convergence. What emerged was the collapsing of central authority into a singular portfolio, the Executive Presidency, with authority vested in an individual with elevated constitutional power to control both the offices of Head of State and Head of Government. In this new arrangement, there was a strong need to establish other policy apparatuses to insure both equilibrium and equity in national power configuration in ways that reflect the congenital character of the nation. This became all the more necessary where the majority of the nation's electorate, through partisan politics elects the President who reserves the prerogative to govern through the constitutionally sanctioned zero-sum, winner-takes-all administrative principles. To avoid political autocracy and power personalization, a triangular distribution/separation of power into the Executive, Legislative and Judiciary was established. However to maintain national unity and political cohesion via philosophical consensus that is not only collective but also devoid of group-centered power concentration in the political center, the nation has to settle for a more elaborate political balance vested in institutionally-sanctioned federalization of political participation and social access.

Essentially, the popular contention if not consensus is that Nigeria's capacity to survive politically as a nation lies in the fundamental philosophy that grants all its citizens equal socio-political representation and participation. This idea was, in 1979, molded into constitutional statute and ordained politically as the *Federal Character Policy (FCP)*, which to the political power brokers, holds the key to the survival of Nigeria's federalism. The political goal was to promote this policy as the national magna carta that reins supreme in all legal decisions of consequence at all levels of government. Thus, it became the revered, all-encompassing national law around which all other major federal laws are conceptually configured and interpreted functionally. It is the document that defines the fundamental guarantee of inalienable rights and privileges to Nigerian citizens. Even with this constitutional arrangement in 1979, the nation only survived four years of sustained civilian political management under its terms as it became victim to the customary military interventionism. The abandonment of this arrangement marked the beginning of yet another effort on the persistent constitutional recycling with which the nation has had to struggle since attaining political independence. To the military rulers who replaced the nation's constitution with military decrees, 1995 was an ideal time for the nation to revisit its constitutional enterprise and, for this purpose the National Constitution Drafting Committee (NCDC), was formed. In his inauguration of this body, the then Nigerian head of state Sani Abacha (1995:xi) declared: "We, Government, and you, the people representatives in the Constitutional Conference, have today entered into a sacred partnership on behalf of the nation. "

With this solemn declaration, Abacha went on to offer an operational directive: "You have the mandate to deliberate upon the structure of the Nigerian nation-state and to work out the modalities for ensuring good governance; to devise for our people a system of government guaranteeing equal opportunity, the right to aspire to any public office, irrespective of state of origin, ethnicity or creed, and thus engender a sense of belonging in all citizens". The working order of the framers of the new constitution (1999) could not have been clearer. They were to serve the nation by providing a timeless document with all legal apparatus and power to guarantee "enduring institutional arrangement that can ensure steady consolidation and growth of a democratic nation-state", (Constitution 1995:xi). Three fundamental imperatives stood out of the legal mandate-cum-prerogatives accorded NCDC by the Nigerian state. The body was to decide (or deliberate) on: (i) a working (or effective) political structure; (ii) a mechanism (with finite modalities) for institutional/administrative efficiency (or good governance) and (iii) a constituted system (or government) that insures unadulterated equal social access and political capital to the entire Nigerian citizenry. Abacha's instructional preamble was a philosophical demand constructed not so much on the mandate of the history that instructed Nigeria as a nation-state but on the irony this preamble ipso facto espoused.

For years, the nation's military of which Abacha was a bona fide product has demonstrated nothing but arrant contempt for Nigeria's sovereignty and constitution. [1]Justice Ayoola (2003) observed, "the aberration of the military regime dealt a dangerous blow to the law, because military regimes engendered lawlessness". And furthermore, in his view: "You cannot have law when somebody is above the law. Law must be supreme". Although Abacha was a lawless embodiment of personification of power in the sense reminiscent of [2]France's Louis XIV idea of "L'État, c'est moi", nonetheless, the terms of his instruction, as expected, soon became an ideological promissory note imprinted onto the social psyche and political consciousness of every Nigerian that matters. The promise these terms affirm became the resource as well as a catalyst, as it were, for attitude formulation and social behavior animation in complementary terms. Equity in all spheres of sociopolitical management to the elite and masses alike translated into and understood as a birthright rather than a political dividend that state management exigency dictates. This meant the collective demand not only to promote but also to legislate the principles of mutuality required to neutralize structural hierarchy in group participation and social configuration as a way to achieve political harmony and management cohesion. Where this establishes the normative values and maxims for political consciousness of the Nigerian population, it thus begs the question that any government policy perceived to circumvent these maxims is doomed to failure politically or otherwise. Policies that have consistently failed compliment of Nigerians' religious adherence to the principles of social equity are the nation's language policies that tend to privilege the majority languages over those of the minority groups.

On the failures of these policies, academic scholarships and political discourse abound only to generate earnest concerns that this piece in effect addresses. Consistently until now, the failures in Nigeria's language policies have been blamed on the conceptual ambiguity implanted between the goals of this policy and the principles within which these goals are supposed to be accommodated, (Bamgbose 1991, Sofunke 2004, Ofuokwu 2004). To the extent that this explanation has been used as the basic logic behind Nigeria's language policy failures, this piece constitutes nothing but a conceptual departure. Looking into the reality of the Nigerian language policies, the submission is that it is indeed the clarity, not the ambiguity in Nigerians' understanding and application of the conceptual mismatch between the Federal Language Policy (FLP) laws and the nation's basic federalist principles, i. e. Federal Character Policy (FCP) laws, that generate conditions of failure in the nation's language policies on the level of implementation. Essentially, it is important to acknowledge that the ubiquitous failure of Nigeria's language policies is consistent with national consensus on the conceptual paradox that drives the terms of their overall interpretation. The basic assertion is that the context wherein this consensus is constructed is provided by the nation's constitution, which accommodates serious conceptual inconsistencies in the laws that govern its overall language policy and the modalities designed for its implementation.

Federal Character Policy (FCP) Laws: The Paradox

Going back to the NCDC mandate, one of the conceptual highlights of Abacha's instruction for the national constitution was the notion of 'equal opportunity' for the entire Nigerian citizenry. To avoid the traditional inequity in group political representation and economic participation, the constitution, in his view, had to address "frontally some of the thorny political issues, which tended to divide rather than unite various ethnic groups [of the Nigerian nation]", (Constitution 1999:xiv). The need for constitutional referendum on the persistent national disunity was not so much a prerequisite dictated by the contemporary political dynamics of the day but a philosophical requirement demanded by a history that reminds the nation consistently of the tumultuous years of its young existence when the principle of equal opportunity was abridged with greater regularity and detrimental consequences. To the Nigerian state, these years carry deep political scars from civil war to regular religious strife and ethnic factionalism that continue to threaten the logic of the Nigerian political existence as recently as the 2008 ethno-political debacle in Jos in Northern Nigeria. The 1995 military mandate bequeathed Nigeria's 1999 and current constitution whereto FCP is once again core. What drives both the statutory persistence and conceptual significance of this policy lies in the idea that a nation as ethno-culturally diverse as the Nigerian nation-state and lacking traditional apparatus that guarantees equal social capital to all its peoples, (Fishman 1972), cannot but legislate an Affirmative Action of some sort that locks all governmental activities and agendas into constitutionally-ordained legal obligations.

Although the final draft of the constitution (1999:xiv), promised not to be "a review of any of the earlier constitutions", the policy provisions on the federal character philosophy of the earlier constitution remained unchanged, if anything, it appeared reinforced. With the new mandate, the once de facto federal character philosophy, written into law in the preceding constitution, (1979) was in effect accorded greater institutional prominence and credence. In the 1979 constitution where FCP first surfaced officially, the policy reads simply thus:

> The composite of the Federal Government or any of its agencies, and the conduct of their affairs shall be carried out in such manner as to recognize the federal character of Nigeria and the need to promote national unity and to command national loyalty. (*Chapt. II, sec. 277 (1)*)

The article of this policy was again adopted in the 1999 constitution with an additional clause that concludes:

> There shall be no predominance of persons from a few States or from a few ethnic or other sectional groups in that government or in any of its agencies. (*Chapt. II, sec. 14(3)*)

By this policy, Nigeria's brand of political management was once again realigned with the ideals of federalism predicated on the concepts of equality and justice for all, regardless of ethnicity, language, culture or any other aggregates of social divide for that matter. With the constitutional adoption of the consolidated FCP, the Nigerian nation effectively sanctioned a model of sociopolitical management organism with two distinctive yet converging structural composites: the *nuclear management frame* within which both the national formulae for politics and policy are predicated on FCP and, the *supra-nuclear frame* wherein the national social policies including those pertaining to language, education and media are situated, (Figure 1).

Figure 1: Nigeria's Federalism: The Conceptual Frames

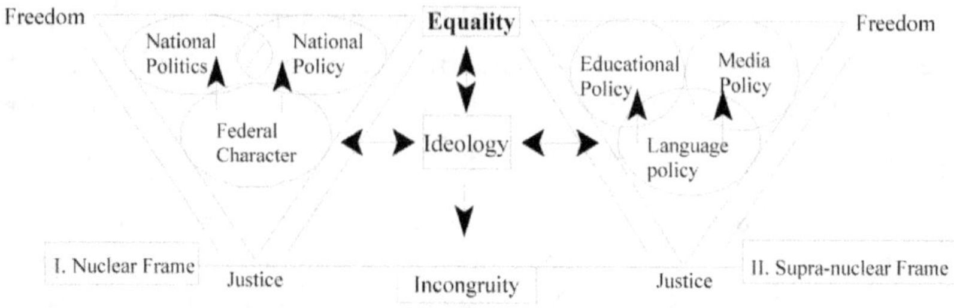

```
Freedom                        Equality                              Freedom
      National      National                  Educational    Media
      Politics      Policy                    Policy         Policy
                 Federal                              Language
                 Character  ◄►  Ideology  ◄►          policy

I. Nuclear Frame                                              II. Supra-nuclear Frame
              Justice      Incongruity       Justice
```

The situational overlap between the two frames is predicated on the paradigm that the national politics and policy are closely interwoven such that the political environment determines policy character/accomplishment and vice versa. Still, uniting the two management frames in more significant ways is the concept of *equity* with multidimensional application to all federal policy agendas regardless of administration or regime. By adopting these structural formulae mediated by the notion of equity, FCP once proposed as a necessary legal umbrella for accommodating fairness in Nigeria's resource allocation and social access, was, by the terms of the constitution, granted the necessary political avenue to evolve into a strong, all-encompassing national ideology. With the support of the constitution and, as indicated in Figure 1, it became and continues to be not only the conceptual center of Nigeria's federalism but also the institutional maxim that drives the nation's collective mindset. Earlier, to many Nigerians, FCP laws did not go far enough in insuring modalities within which the ideals of equity are absolute in federal socio-political management. The advocacy for FCP reinforcement was written to law in the same 1999 constitution that elevated the political status of FCP. The result was the establishment of three basic statutes which to some are needed to grant the necessary political character to FCP itself: (i) the social order laws (founded on ideals of freedom, equality and justice: *sec. 17, (1):1979, and chapt. II, sec. 18(1):1999*); (ii) the economic objective laws (assigned to national wealth distribution: *sec. 16:1979, and chapt. II, sec. 17(2):1999*); and (iii) the educational policy laws (based on the principles of equality of educational opportunity: *sec. 18:1979, and chapt. II, sec. 19(1):1999*). The 1999 constitution represented these ideals thus:

> The State social order is founded on ideals of freedom, Equality and Justice, [and] in furtherance of the social order; every citizen shall have

equality of rights, obligations and opportunities before the law. (*Chapt. II, sec. 18 (1&2a)*)

In the nation's diverse constitutions the language of justice has not changed any. And, what this means in essence is that:

The Federal Republic of Nigeria shall be a State based on the principles of democracy and social justice, (*Chapt. II, sec. 15(1)*)

Judging by the areas of coverage of these laws, three essential government objectives are accommodated: (i) to maintain 'the Social Order of State (SOS) built on the ideals of freedom, equality and justice' [by which] 'every citizen shall have equality of rights, obligations and opportunities before the law'; (ii) to promote 'balanced economic access; free mobility of people, goods and services; and national integration and unity through participatory equity', [and to ensure] 'that the economic system is not operated in such a manner as to permit the concentration of wealth or the means of production in the hands of a few individuals or of a group' (*chapt. II, sec. 17(2c):1999*), [and thus] 'the State shall manage and control the national economy in such manner as to secure the maximum welfare, freedom and happiness of every citizen on the basis of social justice, equality of status and opportunity' (*chapt. II, sec. 17(2b):1999*),; and finally (iii) to ensure 'equality of educational opportunities at all levels along with eradication of illiteracy' [and in this vein] 'government shall promote the learning of indigenous languages'. What is indeed essential to these three conceptual loci within which constitutional credence is rendered to national apparatuses of governance and policy production is in no doubt defined by the ideals of freedom, equality and justice that the principles of FCP guarantee ever so persuasively.

As distinctive legal entities, the FCP laws and the ancillary laws that underpin them seem reasonable as political prerequisite for the Nigerian federalism, particularly, given the objectives that motivate them. But then, it is the collective implementation of all these laws as a policy system or paradigm that tends to generate serious anomaly as the laws themselves converge functionally only to lend credence to paradox. In its goal of achieving equity in participation and resource allocation, FCP has inadvertently encouraged a social atmosphere that is highly conducive to formation, nurturing and fortification of group identities. And, as FCP-oriented identities translate into separate-but-equal mindset and also, as this mindset results in 'us-against-them' attitude in the Nigerian political mainstream, generated as a consequence is a pervasive intergroup intolerance, a psycho-social syndrome, which in Nigeria remains a persistent mental plague that provides the necessary resource for divisive ethno-nationalism, cultural demagoguery and linguistic parochialism. While ideological adherence to FCP principles is no doubt divisive, such adherence is by all measure beneficial as it provides voice to the voiceless in the nation's affairs of management. Still, the fact that the group identity definition that FCP laws support is politically and economically profitable for both majority and minority alike defies absolute merit where it remains core to the working paradox that has so far left Nigeria in perpetual management crisis mode.

To the extent that these laws are profitable is in effect the logic behind their effective exploitation as they become not only the legal sanctuary for ordaining sectarian agendas and ideology that groups consider beneficial, but also the attitudinal constructs these groups resort to in their generation of factional response to national agendas. Where the relationships between FCP and other federal policy laws are co-deterministic, the outcome in one in effect accounts for the output in the other. Essentially, the argument here is that where FCP in the nuclear frame remains core to Nigeria's federalist management, and where it continues to be the ideological tool for identity definition and attitude formulation, the national language policies, which it is supposed to support, cannot be implemented in ways that are indeed consistent with constitutional objectives on the nation's language question. As groups define their identity-oriented socio-economic, culturo-linguistic, political, religious and ideological boundaries under the FCP provisions, they are, in effect, setting the boundary within which any language supported by the constitution is allowed or not allowed to spread. Going by the current linguistic state of affairs in the Nigerian nation, what has no doubt ensued are serious language policy failures arguably brought about by the conceptual mismatch between the principles of FCP and the language policy laws. Regardless of the arguments that have been proposed to halt the trend of these failures, the fact of the matter is that the constitution cannot promote FCP that thrives on the insurance of group equality and identity reinforcement while at the same pushing for language policies designed to neutralize the social divide that such identity reinforcement generates as a matter of course. Even, the constitutionally sanctioned outlets for the implementation of the national language policy, education and media, have within reasonable expectation proved inadequate.

The national educational policy and the media policy were appropriately established not only to create what the government perceived as reliable institutional outlets for the country's language policies but also to promote equality of opportunity for all Nigerians in all the domains aligned with these outlets. As shall be affirmed later, the contention is that these outlets have been ineffective. The ineffectiveness of these outlets is a product of the effectiveness of FCP in formulating the character of the collective psyche of the nation in its open accommodation of cleavage philosophy as its functional norm. Given that the idea of equality is what FCP celebrates and given that education and media under the terms of equality can also be employed as outlets for group identity reinforcement, what the symbiosis between FCP and the federal policies on education and media exposes is conceptual incongruity between the two management frames that undergird the Nigerian federalism. Additionally, the fact that FCP affords the central government the tool for greater political pacification of the masses has not helped the situation any. Since acquiring de jure status, FCP laws have been used by successive Nigerian governments to grant the people, particularly, the minority, greater political voice and autonomy through the creation of states and local governments with direct access to the national political center. The requirement to configure power on three levels, federal-state-local, was defined by the need to generate strong institutional apparatus for equal representation of Nigerians without regard to religion, ethnicity, language or region. This has also meant that each of the new states created by virtue of FCP is, by the terms of the constitution, accorded full right on language policy matters including, selection, choice, standardization and usage allocation.

Accordingly, the states have, as expected, taken advantage of this provision to concentrate their efforts on the development and promotion of only the languages spoken within their administrative borders. Since most of these languages are minority languages, the three majority languages that form the cornerstone of the national language policy have been left to fend for themselves in the states where they are spoken just like any other language. Education and media that were designed as the outlets for federal language policies implementation are now, under the guiding principle of equality, been used to promote all standardized languages where institutional priority emphasized in the constitution and granted to the majority have for all practical purposes been abandoned. The constitutional promotion of the three majority languages to function as national languages has indeed been circumvented by the management requirements that FCP ipso facto engenders. What FCP principles have so far generated is a national obsession with the identity philosophy in all group interactions of consequence. And now that the nation has subscribed to political democratization and judicial liberalization, this obsession has in effect assumed a new height of socio-political significance if not abuse as it drives multidimensional cleavages that undermine the very unity the constitution was charged to seek. Today, this is marked by persistent social animation of the divisive aggregates of ethnicity, culture and religion that have so far left the nation in perpetual crisis of divided identities. With this as the basic output of the FCP interpretation, managing the nation's language policy aimed at achieving some semblance of national cohesion or unity for that matter has been an exercise in futility.

Federal Language Policy (FLP) Laws: The Dialectics

Along with the fundamental conceptual imperatives that FCP generates are the national objectives on language question mentioned earlier. For years, before and after political independence in 1960, Nigeria as a nation has been consumed by the ideals of linguistic nationalism. The nation's intelligentsia and political ideologues have often adopted positions that diverge in form, content and logic on language matters. Still, the need for the nation to adopt clear language policy directives has remained firmly unambiguous. To the linguistic nationalists (Ikara 1987 and Jibril 1990), the path to Nigeria's sovereignty, economic self-reliance and political autonomy cannot be effectively constructed outside the nation's clean departure from the policy that imposes an alien colonial language, English on its peoples. Still, at the other end of the national language dialogue are words of caution from the nation's nationists, no less nationalistic but more pragmatic in what they perceive to be the ideal response to Nigeria's language question (Achebe 1985, Emenanjo 1988 and Odumuh 1993). As the nation debates its concrete options and the policy choices these options offer on the issue of linguistic sovereignty, the government opted for a policy middle-ground in what it perceived as a political compromise thereby creating language policy resolution that no sector of society is ready to embrace or sanction. Indeed what has emerged out of government political compromise is a policy arrangement equipped with built-in imperatives that have so far plunged the nation into a chaotic [3]triglossia of which none is yet to assume responsibility. The first post-independence government position on national language question was articulated in the constitution of 1979; and sanctioned in the subsequent constitutions of 1995 (Draft) and 1999 (Adopted). On the level of legislation, the nation's 1979 language policy simply states:

The business of the National Assembly shall be conducted in English, and in Hausa, Ibo and Yoruba where adequate arrangements have been made therefore, (*Chapt. II, sec. 3 (2)*)

Chapter II, Section 19(4) of the same constitution went on to state that:

Government shall promote the learning of the three main languages namely, Hausa, Ibo and Yoruba in all primary and secondary institutions in Nigeria

On education, the policy reads:

One of the three major languages [Hausa, Ibo and Yoruba] to be taught where the language selected should be the child's mother tongue. The government considers it to be in the interest of the national unity that each child should be encouraged to learn one of the three major languages to be Hausa, Ibo and Yoruba, (*Chapt. II, sec. 3 (2)*)

Looking at these laws in terms of their conceptual constructs and logic, several red flags are raised. The first concerns the question of functional equation assigned to the nation's languages. Given the arrangement the laws suggest, is English, by design, supposed to function at the same level as the [4]Wasobia majority languages, i. e. Hausa, Igbo and Yoruba? In other words, do these laws make Nigeria a nation with a multilingual policy arrangement that allow four languages to function equally in official roles? Or, is there an implicit hierarchy to the nation's linguistic arrangement where one out of the four languages, presumable English functions in official and the other majority languages function as national languages? And where this is the case, does the nation's language policy put languages native to the country at functional disadvantage? Lastly, Chapter II, Section 19(4) of the 1979 constitution did allude to Mother Tongue (MT) education; still, why should only three out of 400 or more languages native to the country be selected for a child to learn in addition to its MT? Does this arrangement condemn the minority languages to social disadvantage is dissonance with the basic principles of FCP? Why should the minority Nigerians learn the languages of the majority where their own languages are by law reduced to position of subordination and limited social benefit and advantage? In what ways does hierarchy on linguistic distribution based on demographic status afford social harmony or unity in a nation known for its intergroup suspicion and conflict?

These are some of the questions this section attempts to answer in ways that reflects serious conceptual oddity in the manner in which Nigerian language policies are framed not only as autonomous document but also as a working derivative of other legal documents that adopt federalism as the nation's political default. Still at this point and, before paying earnest attention to the conceptual ramifications these questions attract, suffice it to affirm that the outcome of the Nigerian language policy laws in terms of their implementation can only be measured in futility. To the extent that this development is not in doubt, the Nigerian government has taken steps to modify the language of its language policy. Yet, on the level of pragmatism the language of the new laws has chosen conceptual open-endedness in place of the ambiguity the old laws accommodate. Now, consider the current legal article on national language management as represented in the 1999 constitution still in a simple statement that reads:

> The business of the national Assembly shall be English. Nigerian languages shall become additional languages of business of the National Assembly as the National Assembly shall by law prescribe (*Chapt. V, sec. 58*)

With the above law, the official position of English relative to other indigenous language is now less than ambiguous. The so-called alien, colonial language henceforth stands alone at the apex of social significance as the law accommodates it as the language that speaks officially for the nation. In the same vein, the majority languages automatically remain as national languages that may or may not share official stage with English. The new functional hierarchy imposed on Nigerian languages has done little to alleviate the concerns, or elevate the socio-linguistic status of the nation's minority groups whose languages remain confined to the lowest social/functional echelon. Melchers and Shaw (2003: 151) captured the *de jure* pyramidal functional distribution of Nigerian languages from top to bottom in Figure 2 below.

Figure 2: Language Pyramid for Nigeria

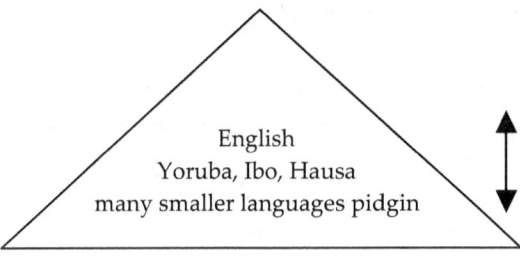

Source: Melchers and Shaw, 2003, p. 151, Fig. 5. 4.

Moreover, the structural modification in language distribution entailed by the new constitution also meant revisitation of other ancillary language policy laws, particularly those dealing with education. As of 2004, the Nigeria's language policy as it applies to the nation's educational guidelines and objectives was forced to undergo major conceptual adjustment. What is now recommended for every Nigerian child in primary education is found in Section 4 (e) & (f) of the National Policy on Education (NPE 2004) that states:

> The medium of instruction in the primary school shall be the language of the environment for the first three years. During this period, English shall be taught as a subject. From the fourth year, English shall progressively be used as a medium of instruction and the language of immediate environment and French shall be taught as subjects. (*Section 4 (e) & (f)*)

On the importance of language to national unity, two complementary policy provisions are advanced:

(a) Government appreciates the importance of language as a means of promoting social interaction and national cohesion; and preserving cultures. Thus every child shall learn the language of the immediate environment. Furthermore, in the interest of national unity it is expedient that every child shall be required to learn one of the three Nigerian languages: Hausa, Igbo and Yoruba.

(b) For smooth interaction with our neighbours, it is desirable for every Nigerian to speak French. Accordingly, French shall be the second official language in Nigeria and it shall be compulsory in primary and Junior Secondary Schools (JSS) but non-vocational elective at the Senior Secondary School (SSS).

Here, once again, these policy provisions however accommodating they may be with regard to minority language concerns, they, by their conceptual design, continue to raise many questions with binding imperatives that are as implicit as they are pragmatic. Now, why should it be in the interest of the child to learn those majority languages that the constitution and education policy ordain as national languages? What are the advantages accrued the child from a minority group for learning these languages? What are the social or educational concessions granted to this child for learning a language other than its own? For the sake of equity and reciprocity would a child from a majority group be required to learn a language spoken by a minority group? Still, why, out of 400 languages available for learning in the country, only three are continually selected? Should group demographic status matter in policy construct in a nation where the central political and constitutional goal is to promote equality for all? Overall, the Nigerian language policies face many questions where it has so far managed to deliver few answers.

Once again, the objective here is not to answer all these questions directly but to employ the logical imperatives these questions generate in lending a new conceptual dimension to domains where potential answers could be sought. The conspicuous change in the language of Nigeria's constitution on language policy in less than three decades, between 1979 and 2004, was not due to a sudden discovery of expressive deficiency or anomaly in the nation's supreme law. Neither was such change founded on the arbitrariness of the actions of the nation's constitutional designers. But rather, it is a perfect reflection of the nation's 'politics of uncertainty' and the social imperatives such politics tend to attract as a matter of course. The change has meant a finite deviation from the strategy of majority language imposition where the Wazobia languages, Hausa, Igbo and Yoruba were singled out for constitutional recognition (Figure 3).

Figure 3: Functional Distribution of Languages by Policy in Nigeria

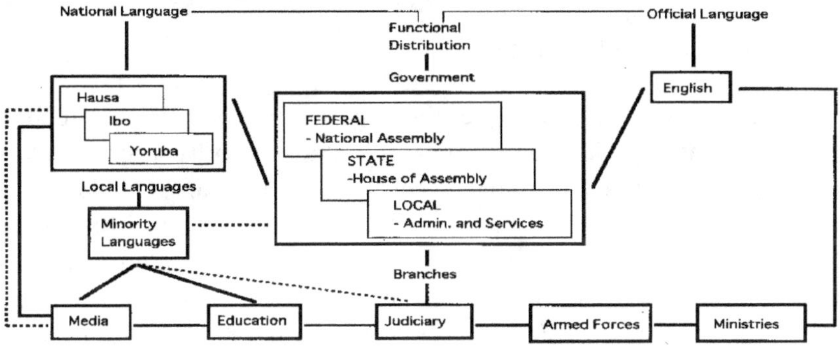

Source: Arasanyin (1995:198), African Study Monograph, 16(4)

In the spirit of federal character and the social equity it demands, 'Nigerian languages' shall by constitutional provisions become only 'additional languages' to be employed in the management of national affairs. The question now is which of the nation's 400 languages will be granted policy credence not only to function nationally but also to operate as the official language where a sector of the nation, which comprises the linguistic nationalists, clamors for language indigenization and self-reliance. Today in Nigeria, English occupies a special functional class unrivaled and, challenged by no other, (Figure 3). It is the language of the officialdom that runs the apparatus of State. Also, it becomes the singular code in which all documents at all levels of government are recorded and disseminated. And apart from being the language of education per the constitutional provision, it is the official language for the nation's judiciary, ministries, armed forces and media. The social/functional net of this language is stretched wide thus rendering inconsequential the social demands for the indigenous languages with which it is, supposedly by law, in competition. While the function and social status of English remains unequivocal; if anything, it gains complementary functional support of French. And for what is worth, what the French did not achieve through colonial conquest and years of imperial intervention, i. e. linguistic infiltration of Nigeria, the national language policy seems to have engendered as government promotes French as the expedient response to the West African regional economic dynamics. That the State did not reduce via FLP the influence of European languages in the nation's social life, but instead took steps to expand it based on State political exigency has plunged the nation into serious arguments that are as contentious as they are pragmatic.

Debating FLP: The War of Ideas

The demographic tapestry of the Nigerian nation divides its peoples into two basic social sectors, majority and minority accommodated differentially by the articles of the constitution. Hausa, Igbo and Yoruba are the three languages of the majority, which according to Jibril (1990) are spoken by over 60. 0 percent of the Nigerian population. That more Nigerians speak these languages than any other set of languages including English and French in effect forces the State to grant greater recognition to the majority in terms of its linguistic ranking and circumstance and, by association, its ethno-cultural status. Essentially, what denominates this recognition is the political belief in some quarters that with time and all things being equal, one of these languages will inevitably out-compete the others and, in so doing, emerge with greater demographic standing to operate as the sole homegrown language with the capacity to relieve English of its official duties. Howbeit, what this recognition seems to promote rather persuasively is a strong paradoxical imperative, the sort that suggests unadulterated conceptual asymmetry between government positions on FLP on the one hand and the principles of FCP and many other federal social policies that the national constitution supports on the other. With the application of the FCP principles, each of the nation's 36 states reserves the constitutional right to manage the linguistic issues and their attendant logistics within its territorial boundary. This has raised the fear of language politicization, a scenario that the linguistic nationalists concede to be a detriment to eventual unification of the country through a singular indigenous language.

Jibril (1990:113) acknowledged the issue of language politicization with regard to the teaching and learning of Other Tongues (OT) as second language (L2). He noted: "Two or more states, for instance, may enter into an agreement to exchange Other Tongue teachers and thus effectively isolate the third major language". Alternatively, in his view, "a state may teach or may not teach a specific Other Tongue in bad faith so as to accelerate or undermine its emergence as a national language". While the ultimate goal is to minimize the number of languages recognized for official functions on national level, the structural disposition of the nation's laws on language inadvertently acknowledges the supremacy of the three majority Wazobia languages Hausa, Igbo and Yoruba, (Elugbe 1990, Sofunke 2004 and Essien 2004), over the remaining

397 or more languages classified as [5]minority languages (Awolowo 1968, Hoffman 1974, Murdock 1975, Gandonu 1978, Otite 1990 and Adegbija 2004). Still, if the Nigerian federalism is indeed driven by the federal character provisions that guarantee at the least ethno-linguistic equality, then what constitutional concessions do these provisions make to accommodate the social concerns of the minority groups whose languages have been denied equal recognition under the federal laws (Wardhaugh 1987, Demoz 1991)? In a nation that continues to struggle with the provision of adequate logistics for the implementation of the terms of the constitution vis-à-vis the functional positioning of the majority languages, the answer to this question is simply, very little.

Under the constitutional terms of FCP should the minority groups retain the prerogative to exercise their linguistic autonomy and demand equal linguistic recognition as a guarantee of equity in their social participation as well as a security against the eventual linguistic domination of their lot by the linguistic majority? In fact, why should they accommodate any of the majority languages with which they maintain little or no traditional affinity or cultural affection in a country where a colonial language, English reigns supreme as the official language and, a Language of Wider Political Access (LWPC) as well as Language of Wider Communication (LWC)? On this question, Adegbija (2004:57) contends that: "When given a choice, most speakers of minority languages would rather learn English than another indigenous Nigerian language (…). To him the obvious reason is that English maintains "[a] higher value exchange rate at the utilitarian level, [and] prestige value [along with] economic and international potency". Still, while the constitution continues to promote statutory privilege of English language via the existential social divide between the majority and the minority Nigerians at one end, it downplays, at the other, the longstanding culturo-political antagonism among the ethnic groups that lay autochthonous claims on those majority languages it elevates.

Where, by the articles of the constitution, there is no legal provision guaranteeing hierarchical functional distribution of the three majority languages, eliminated as a matter of course are the elements of political détente among these languages as they are forced to compete for exclusive socio-political status in the national mainstream. In their quest to out-compete one another, none is ready to lose social/functional ground to another, hence, by default they are forced to cede functional supremacy to English, which per nationalists' designation is a language alien to the country in all respect. Arasanyin (1995:201) cautioned against the cavalier, disdainful dismissal of English as an alien language. He observed, among other variables that "the legislation of English as the sole official language of Nigeria [has] prompted a social response underscored by favorable, and broader applicatory appeal for the language than customary". And reiterating Bamgbose's (1991:74) view that, "a language is like a currency; the more it can buy, the greater value it has"; Arasanyin went on to argue that "preference for English is positively correlated with the kind of the roles to which the language is assigned".

The question the linguistic nationalists are yet to answer is why should English be subjected to arrant attitudinal contempt if the nation's supreme legal instrument, the constitution is ready to elevate it into the apex of national significance? The attitude among the indigenous groups, majority or minority, in the country is that English is an ethnically unmarked language that grants no socio-political advantage, status or prestige to any of the nation's indigenous groups (Fishman 1972). It is in essence an ethnically neutral code to which groups are predisposed to relate without factional or parochial prejudice, or even the feelings of group domination that the social elevation of any one of the majority languages will likely attract. For this reason, the minority groups, particularly those in the elite class, prefer to interact in English not only as a social marker of their collective rejection of constitutionally sanctioned majority language imposition but also as an indirect way of preserving without compromise the integrity of their group identity (Williamson & Van Eerde 1980). Eventually, what is neutralized is the social advantage of the majority languages that are left to function only in less than envisaged social status and prestige as the policy-ordained national languages. With that, Arasanyin (ibid.) concluded, "the Nigerian language legislation inherently has mutated biculturalism in intergroup language acquisition" leaving each of the nation's language to fend for itself mainly within its own ethnic base.

Although English is, by way of institutional tradition that sustains it, a language with relatively low demographic base in Nigeria (Bamgbose 1983, 1991, Heine 1990), it remains, by the laws that support it, a language that wields enormous institutional power given the character of its functional allocation. By the terms of the nation's constitution, it assumes the socio-political status and prestige that can only be contemplated by its closest competitors, the majority languages. To Ammon (1989), status maintains two basic meanings: (i) position within a specific social system; and (ii) rank in social hierarchy. In both scenarios, English by official declaration is located at the structural apex of functional distribution of Nigerian languages. To Achebe (1985) this development is politically predictable. It is nothing but an imperative that evolves within the natural trajectory of the nation's language question and history. In his view: "There [are] not many countries in Africa today where you could abolish the language of the erstwhile colonial powers and still retain the facility for mutual communication", (Achebe 1985:58). To him a major component of Nigeria's political reality is the language on which its *raison d'être* was built in the first place. Yet, Ikara (1987:38) strongly lamented this logic as he wondered whether or not "[it is] a marvelous bondage to become servants to a foreign language for learning sake" with the English language, in his words, "reminding us of our enslavement and bondage (...)". In fact, Ikara (1987:21) took issues with the country's sluggish pursuit of national integration through language policy laws which to him are saddled with conceptual anomalies.

Nigeria, in his view should strive for an uncompromising linguistic homogenization where one of the nation's indigenous languages is selected for official role. As (Ikara ibid.) preached Nigeria's Arusha-like nationalist awakening and national redemption via linguistic self-reliance, he was no less blunt with his functionalist, 'state-first' argument that the nation should "jump directly to selection of only one language, as is the case with most parts of the world where national integration and unity has had to be forced for the purpose of national development". Still, Ikara (1987:25) sharpened his advocacy of linguistic independence and self-reliance as he opined that, "[English in Nigeria] has hindered genuine nationalist concerns and socio-cultural integration, (...)". On this development, he was of the opinion that, policy adjustment permitting, Hausa should evolve as "a language that has the authority of government conferred on it as the lingua franca of all the ethnic groups in the country, as a matter of deliberate choice by the government. [It should be] the official language of the country, which apart from being used in the conduct of government business, cut across the entire strata of society in its use and application". Ikara was never the only voice advocating inward-looking approach to Nigeria's language question and political quest for choice.

Williamson (1977:81) relied on the argument of 'cost effectiveness' while suggesting the need for Nigeria to select a single language, preferably an indigenous language to function in official role as a way to avoid duplicity in linguistic selection. Simpson (1978:1) reiterated the need for Nigeria to "[break clean] with the language(s) imposed by erstwhile slave masters and today's neo-colonialists". Olagoke (1982:199) sees this break as a political choice ingrained in the potential to foster the nation's 'ideals of self-discovery and pride'. These positions and, in particular, Ikara's advocacy of functional centrality of an indigenous language, Hausa in official role, has not gone unnoticed by those who advocate preference for a nationist approach. Osaji (1979:155) dismissed Ikara's proposition as an exercise in wishful thinking, a position that was in effect buttressed by the *Daly Times*, a government Newspaper. In its editorial reproduced in the *New York Times* of May 23, 1991, the paper argued that: "The least luxury we [i. e. Nigerians] can afford is an idealistic experiment in linguistic nationalism, which could cut out our children from the main current of human development". Moreover, the legal recognition of Hausa along with two majority languages is by default an endorsement of functional supremacy of English in national roles. Where, by demographic status, none of the majority languages is superior, encouraged in effect is functional competition not compromise among them. By Jibril's (ibid.) population estimates of these languages, Hausa speakers constitute 22. 04 percent of the nation population where Yoruba and Igbo account for 21. 41 and 17. 49 percents respectively.

Again, where none of these languages is demographically dominant or account for a clear majority, promoting one to the detriment of the others can only create social disharmony with the potential to up the ante of conflict among the ethno-cultural groups aligned with them. More importantly these languages are so territorialized with limited spread beyond the region of group ownership to be effectively introduced and maintained with solid participation of the outgroups. For Hausa, a language spoken predominantly by the Hausa-Fulani ethnic groups in the northern sector of the country to be accepted by the Yoruba speaking people in the western section, strong policy-driven concessions must unequivocally be put in place for such ambitious proposition to take hold. Granted, in the words of Nida and Wonderly (1971), no language in Nigeria is politically neutral, the most basic concession revolves around the idea of reciprocity that should insure the acceptance of Yoruba among the Hausa-Fulani in the North in a *quid pro quo* political arrangement. Now, if the nation's language laws in education subscribe to Emenanjo's (1988:27) 'people-first' idea that, "mass mobilization and education are more meaningful, more effective and more creative, when they are carried out in people's language"; and if the nation's mother tongues provide this basic advantage to the people, and the only logical language of equal advantage at national and emotional levels is none other than

English, why should the people engage in involuntary cross-ethnic language learning where the formula for potential intergroup accommodation is what the laws of the land only suggests and not enforces.

What are indeed the political incentives to reconstitute the minority attitude to align with Hausa or any of the majority languages under the nation's language laws, which they perceive not only as discriminatory but also as assimilative in form and practice? With the minority groups, the basic item of language learning incentive is to ascertain which language behavior yields the "most benefit for the least cost" (Fasold 1990:254). To this end, English serves them better than any other language. Added to this situation are issues of language management logistics that have very little to do with minority suspicion of the language laws that seem to encourage linguistic imposition or assimilation by the majority. That the constitution requires each and every Nigerian child to learn one of the majority languages as L2, means that the nation's educational institutions need to design a workable system of language pedagogy to implement the terms of the constitution. The simple translation here is that the national government has to engage in massive investment in the training of language teachers to accommodate the linguistic needs of the nation's children which by the World Bank's (2000) estimate account for close to half of the population at 46. 5 percent. Still, this situation is not the immediate bête noire in the series of problems the nation has had to navigate to come to terms with the shortcomings of its own constitutional desire and ambition.

The 1988 Report of the Technical Committee on the Production of Teachers for Three Nigerian Languages said it all. Of the total 55, 237 teachers that will be required to carry out the nation's language policy, only 6, 383, i. e. 11. 6 percent teachers are available. This constitutes nothing less than another coup d'arrêt in the political plan for linguistic indigenization that neither the linguistic nationalists nor the government can afford to ignore or dismiss if both are to remain committed to linguistic self-reliance as a marker of Nigeria's national pride and identity. Even where Nigeria succeeds in conquering its linguistic bête noire and procure enough teachers to support its program on cross-ethnic language training, essentially, how will the government counter the existing conceptual paradox in its policy laws? The working asymmetry in both FCP and FLP laws continues to foster social environment and collective attitude that undermine the nation's legislative directives on the national language question. Additionally, the same paradox observed in the FCP-FLP functional symbiosis not only exposes awkwardness in the conceptual configuration of Nigeria's social policy laws, it is arguably the logic behind the inadequacy of three of the avenues the central government considers critical to the accomplishment of its overall language policy agenda. Those three major avenues include: (i) minority empowerment; (ii) educational mandate and (iii) media role, all hereby subjected to critical examination.

Legislating Minority Empowerment

Although the FCP and FLP laws are in complementary terms disharmonious, yet one of the major goals of both laws was to elevate the minority voice into a level where its socio-political aspirations and demands are accorded the apparatus to resonate clearly with the national political center. The primary way in which this voice has been accommodated is through a concerted minority pacification strategy, which in political terms has resulted in the constitutional adoption of a three-tier administrative structure and functional provision for minority languages in education and the media. Where FCP mandates ethnic identity and the utilization of such identity for political participation and economic competition what is often circumvented as a consequence is the incentive for national groups to compromise the conditions of their individual identities for the sake of socio-linguistic harmony. Indeed, what has come to characterize FCP is the reinforcement of those ethnic identities thereby generating intergroup attitudes often made manifest in low accommodation of socio-political and linguistic overtures to outgroups. Where this is the case, the idea of cross-ethnic language learning that Section 3(2)) of the constitution (1999) suggests, offers nothing more than a political contemplation, a philosophical wishful thinking that the nation's political reality clearly undermines. The need for the minority groups to utilize their ethnic identities as political capital for socio-political benefit acquisition is obligated by nothing other than the Articles of the constitution.

Two of these Articles are the ones implanted in *Chapter I, Sections 2 (2-3)* and *3 (1-2)* of the constitution that defines the essence of the Federal Republic of Nigeria (FRN) in the language that states:

> Nigeria shall be a federation consisting of states and the federal capital territory, [and it] shall be governed through a three-tier structure of government namely the Government of the Federation, the State Government and the Local Government, [and] there shall be 30 States in Nigeria, [and] each State shall consist of the Local Government area (...).

Under the terms of this law, the central government reserves the political authority to create states and local government to maintain equilibrium in administrative engineering of the nation. For what it is worth, the minority groups have been the greatest beneficiaries of this law as the power of the central government has been used quite often to create states as part of the political formula designed for minority pacification. As the minority groups who have by tradition been under-represented continue to make demands for greater political capital and equity, more and more states have been created to accommodate their demands. Suffice it to note that six more states have now been created since the adoption of the 1999 constitution that recognizes only 30 states in the Nigerian federation. It is also important to acknowledge the fact that the minority groups clamor for their separate states not just to gain administrative autonomy but to acquire the economic empowerment that such autonomy by law attracts.

The federal government revenue allocation is predicated not so much on population variables but on the number of states and local governments present in the nation. For the minorities to acquire adequate or equitable economic access, the demands for more states abound where such demands are, by the terms of national constitution, justified. On the economic front the law states:

> The State shall manage and control the national economy in such a manner as to secure the maximum welfare, freedom and happiness of every citizen on the basis of social justice, equality of status and opportunity; [and] that the economic system is not operated in such a manner as to permit the concentration of wealth or the means of production and exchange in the hands of few individuals or of a group. (*Chapter II, Section 17(1a & 2c)*)

By this law, the only way the minority could control their own economic aspirations and destiny is through administrative empowerment that state and local government acquisition engenders. Now, where all the aforementioned laws become tricky is when they are conceived in complementary terms with the supplemental language laws that grant policy autonomy to the states on matters concerning language choice. On language policy at state level, *Chapter V, Section 100* of the constitution states:

> The business of [state] House of Assembly shall be conducted in English, but the House may in addition to English conduct the business of the

House in one or more other languages spoken in the State as the House may by resolution approve.

The power the constitution granted the states to control their linguistic destiny, under statute 100, seem, on the surface not to contradict FLP under statute 58. If anything and by government intentions, the two statutes are by design supposed to complement one another. But where FCP principles are interjected between them, the outcome only exposes a major functional asymmetry between them given the factors that define their social implementation. While the central government sees FLP under statute 58 as political compromise and a way to promote social harmony and political unification, the minority groups see it as assimilative and a way of imposing majority linguistic values on the minority. To these groups, statute 100 is seen as a way of countering what Ansre (1976) described as 'indigenous cultural imperialism' as the statute provide legal avenues for them to develop their own languages for administrative and media use and, in essence fortify their individual group identities. The pervasive belief among these groups goes beyond the constitutional recognition of their political capacity to make language choice; it is to them a measure that elevates their political capital into a new height.

The constitutional rights accrued the minority under statute 100 have meant an upsurge in the use of minority languages in the state educational systems, government institutions and media establishments. This has led to concerted standardization of minority languages and the inevitable political demand that minority languages be granted constitutional recognition equal to that granted to the languages of the majority. The minority finds political anchorage for their demands under statute 15, i. e. the FCP maxim. If group equality is indeed the driving force of this maxim, the minority sees no reason why they should not be accorded equity in the constitutional configuration of their languages in relation to those spoken by the majority. What the maxim afforded the minority was a political avenue for a strong voice contesting the notion of subjugating one sector of the nation's population to another through inequity in the nation's language choice. Even before FCP first became law in 1979, the minority groups have been on record in their collective rejection of linguistic inequality. Upon attainment of independence in 1960, the Nigerian nation-state was cloaked in the superficial euphoria of linguistic nationalism. It was a euphoria that espoused the need to elevate a language native to Nigeria, preferably Hausa, to the official language status thus dethroning English, the 'alien language' from its official role. According to Niyi Akinnaso (2006: 2), "The first post-independence attempt to bring Nigerian languages to the table came in November 1961, when a legislator proposed the teaching of Hausa, Igbo, and Yoruba in the nation's schools". In his view, this constituted "preliminary step toward the emergence of an indigenous national language".

No doubt this was immediately perceived as a less than prudent political strategy as the nation seeks unity from 'the fragile coalition of various linguistic nationalities' that form its political structure, (Akinnaso, ibid). Of no particular surprise was the outright rejection of such legislative intervention in the course of language policy evolution in the country. The rejection and the eventual defeat of the 1961 language bill were led by Chief Anthony Enahoro, himself, a minority parliamentarian. In his famous parliamentary speech, he argued: "As one who comes from a minority tribe, I deplore the continuing evidence in this country that people wish to impose their customs, their languages, and even more their way of life upon the smaller tribes (…). How can they now, because the British brought us together, wish to impose their language on us?" On behalf of the minority group, he went on to assert: "we have not fought the imperialist in order to establish a new imperialism in the country". Whereas the 1961 language bill was never enacted into law, it however evaded complete political death, where 26 years later it was reactivated from its legislative dormancy and reformulated as the conceptual nexus of the 1977 National Policy on Education (NPE). Still, the minority groups continue to stand in opposition to any form of linguistic homogenization that grants undue social privileges to any of the majority languages. In 1981, two years after FLP was enacted, the president of the Nigeria's senate in the third republic, Joseph Wayas, a minority, was once quoted as affirming that he will, under no circumstances, be forced to speak any of the majority languages in the nation's upper house, the Senate, and that the only way to make him reverse course is over his dead body. Here, the minority linguistic contestability is based on the understanding of the parameters of the federal character laws that grant them equality in all social spheres. The persistent push for linguistic equality has had a remarkable effect on the central government position on language issues.

Brann (1989) noted that the minority demands for linguistic equality have led to the elevation of some of their languages into higher social status as these languages are assigned new institutional roles. He also observed that by these demands, the government has had to make provision as of 1989, ten years after the 1979 constitution, for the adoption of any minority language spoken by one million or more people into the status of a Networks language to be used in all nationally owned media establishments. Nine of the minority languages fall in this category and are now being used nationally in broadcasting and newsprint, (Table 1). Overall, the minority groups have relied on FCP laws to guarantee decentralization of power apparatus and equity in group representation, particularly, in the domain of administration, states/local government creation and revenue allocation. Howbeit, the minority linguistic empowerment that FCP guarantees only occurs to the detriment of majority language spread.

Table 1: Selected Nigerian Language Population in Descending Order

	Majority			Minority					
Language	Speakers (N)	%	Gp	Language	Speakers (N)	%	Gp	Language	Speakers (N)	%
Hausa	23,233,000	22.04	1)	Fulfulde	9,538,000	9.05	2)	Edo	1,904,000	1.81
Yoruba	22,571,000	21.41		Kanuri	4,498,000	4.27		Nupe	1,314,000	1.25
Igbo	18,434,000	17.49		Ibibio	3,999,000	3.79		Urhobo	1,274,000	1.21
				Tiv	2,779,000	2.64		Igala	1,160,000	1.10
				Ijaw/Izon	2,171,000	2.06				
Total	64,238,000	60.94		Total	22,985,000	21.81		Total	5,652,000	5.27

Source: Munzali Jibril 1990, pp111-117; Arasanyin 1996, p. 16.

In fact, it has managed to halt the territorial gains majority languages have traditionally enjoyed in minority areas. The need for the minority political elite to connect with their political base has also promoted the establishment of local newspapers in local languages thereby elevating the local languages (Groups—Gp 1/2) socially as competitors that challenge the social supremacy of the majority languages. Where the minority groups feel rewarded politically and economically for their demographic status via federal affirmative action that FCP represents, there is little or no incentive for them to adopt federal linguistic guidelines which by and large they consider a detrimental imperative in the way of their political benefit if not advantage. This inevitably begs the question of the level of success of FLP on the level of implementation.

Language Policy: The Media Role

The democratic doctrine of 'government of the people by the people for the people' is well preserved in *Chapter II, Section 15(2a)* of the 1999 constitution that states: "Sovereignty belongs to the people of Nigeria from whom government through [the] constitution derives all its powers and authority". This was supported by *Section 15(2c)* that states simply:

"the participation of the people in their government shall be ensured in accordance with the provision of [the] constitution". By acknowledging the Nigerian sovereignty, the constitution in essence promotes a bottom-up power construct that in turn suggests the idea that the supreme power over the Nigeria's body politic lies with the people, the citizenry. And if the nation's supreme law subscribes to the autonomous, unalienable power of the socio-political base, i. e. the people; then the Nigerian government, under this law, is by all measure forced to derive working resource from the citizenry whose power the constitution holds supreme. This policy stemmed from one of the guidelines provided by the Military Government (September 1975) to NCDC that drafted the 1979 constitution. This guideline requires the incoming civilian regime to evolve a political system that will "[6]discourage institutionalized opposition to the government in power and instead develop consensus politics and government based on a community of all interests rather than the interest of sections of the country".

Of great importance to this guideline is the need for constitutional provision for power decentralization as the means for diffusing the traditional socio-political tension among the diverse ethno-linguistic groups that constitute the Nigerian nation-state. As the need to maintain Nigeria's federalism through socio-political equity evolved into national preoccupation and constitutional obligation, of consequence is the fundamental desire of the nation's political stakeholders to implant federal social policies that generate collective ideological consensus on the need for broad participation of the masses in the affairs of government. In the 1999 constitution, Nigerians are encouraged to pledge to the idea of living together "in unity and harmony as one indivisible, indissoluble, democratic sovereign nation under God and, to promote a constitution for the purpose of promoting good government and welfare of all persons in the country on the principle of freedom, equality and justice" (Constitution 1999:1). For this pledge to be brought to pragmatic fruition, government deemed it a prerequisite that the masses maintain a well-defined broad access to the affairs of state and the primary avenue of achieving this proposition is via efficient information traffic between government and the people. The preservation of national sovereignty that the constitution advocates is, from government perspective, better served through the media that enjoy constitutionally sanctioned freedom to serve the masses and government in complementary terms. The roles of Nigeria's mass media that have changed very little since the days of the nation's struggle for independence was reformulated in the current (1999) constitution that states:

> The press, radio, television and other agencies of mass media shall at all times be free to uphold the [nation's] fundamental objectives and highlight the responsibility and accountability of the government to the people. (*Chapt. II, sec. 23*)

In *Chapter IV, Section 40*, the constitution presents the 'right to freedom of expression and the press' thus:

> (1) Every person shall be entitled to freedom of expression including freedom to hold opinions and to receive and impart ideas and information without interference

This law is complemented by two provisions of great conceptual consequence to the claims made in this study. These provisions are contained in the following statutes:

> (2) Without prejudice (...), every person shall within the provisions of any Act of the National Assembly in that regard be entitled to own, establish and operate any medium for the dissemination of information, ideas and opinions. (*Chapt. IV, sec. 40(2)*)

> (3) The print, electronic and other agencies of the mass media shall at all times uphold the provisions of [the] Constitution and in giving coverage to any news or programme ensure the responsibility and accountability of the government to the people and the people to the government. (*Chapt. IV, sec. 40(3)*)

While the domains not covered by these provisions include non-governmental operation of television or any wireless broadcasting stations; they nonetheless affirm private press ownership in accordance with the constitutional provisions with modus operandi in the federal character principles. But then, since the philosophy that drives the terms of these policy laws did not start with the 1999 constitution, a pip at media history is at this point necessary to lend logic to the interpretation this philosophy in effect generates. The 1976 establishment of the News Agency of Nigeria (NAN) by military decrees brought the country's media under specific operational guidelines. Two [7]provisions of the guidelines, (a) and (c) out of six stood out in direct discord with the popular modus operandi of the contemporary national media. Provision (a) charged NAN with the authority "to uphold the integrity of the

Federal Republic of Nigeria and promote harmonious relationship among the different groups in Nigeria". The (c) provision charged the Agency "[to] positively influence public opinion and constitute the evolution and formation of correct national policies". For the national media to truly uphold the integrity of the country and serve in support of national cohesion, it should in effect, assist in the promotion of government agendas designed to achieve these national objectives and these include the nation's language policies. With just these two provisions, the role of the media in Nigerian society can be evaluated in three basic ways: (i) *accountability*; (ii) *education* and (iii) *choice*. On the level of accountability the nation's media must make few choices: (a) it must choose between being accountable to the government or to the people; (b) it must decide between *nigerianization* and *regionalization*; in other words the media could serve the interest of the nation as a whole or reserve preference for serving various sections of the nation; (c) it must make a concerted choice between partisanship and bipartisanship, whether to be parochial or not and, much more.

With education provision, the media should serve as the apparatus of information dissemination designed not only to inform but also to educate the citizenry about the policies and agendas of state. In this role, the media can ascertain a two-way connection between government and the citizenry. And finally, without indulging in linguistic ideology, the media should serve in the identification and promotion of the language that best serves the long-term national interest; in other words, the media should help the nation make effective language choice. Here again, the problem facing the Nigerian national media is none other than that dictated by the attendant principles of FCP. The stringent application of these principles in the nation's political life has done a lot more than any other factor in creating an environment that bolsters sectarian politics of which the media has had to become the inevitable institutional conduit. In its assumed role as parochial politics driver and equalizer granted the effects of FCP, the media seems to have chosen sectarian accountability over broad national representation and, in doing so it has inadvertently undermined the social latitude required for inter-group attitude fusion, the sort that generates positive collective response to government policy including that pertaining to language.

In an Internet-based consumption survey designed to gauge the attitude of Nigerians vis-à-vis newsprint establishments in the country, the Inter-news Organization (2001) found that more than 75. 0 percent of Nigerians prefer to read newspapers printed in their region of origin.

More than 80. 0 percent Yoruba Nigerians from the Western sector of the country prefer to acquire news information from the *Daily Sketch* and the *Nigerian Tribune*, printed in the West than relying on any other source including the *Daily Star* and the *Champion* from the East and *The New Nigerian* and *The Reporter* from the North. All the non-Western newspapers boast of less than 10. 0 percent Yoruba readership. The same attitude is true to the readerships from the Eastern and the Northern sectors where they have the option of choosing between papers printed in their own respective regions and those from the other parts of the country. They too overwhelmingly preferred to read news papers from their respective regions. But then, this was not where the real issue lied. In the same survey, the subjects were asked which of the Nigerian newspapers they trust on several levels where the values include familiarity, objectivity and truthfulness among others. On all the values, the readerships accorded the highest scores, over 70. 0 percent to newspapers that identify with their individual places of origin. The regional outlook that most of the nation's newspaper outlets have assumed seems to resonate in politically significant manner with the constituencies whose interests they claim to represent.

Now, where the real problems lie is that the news that constitutes objectivity and truthfulness in one section of the country is often considered subjective and questionable in another. Altogether, this is nothing but a recipe for intergroup mistrust and conflict that run in direct dissonance with the nation's desire for social cohesion. But these problems are not confined to the newsprint sector alone. With regards to the newscast establishments, i. e. the radio and television, what has traditionally prevailed is the excessive influence of non-native programming. UNESCO (1974:15) in a worldwide survey found that only 27. 0 percent of transmitted program hours are devoted to locally produced programs in Nigeria. And this has changed very little more than three decades later in Nigeria of today. The preponderance of foreign programming has left very little avenue for the nation to promote its own language policies and cultural values. Another electronic medium, the radio, seems to take cues from its counterpart, the television. For instance, [8]Radio Nigeria-Two (RN-2) AM-FM devotes more than 70. 0 percent of its airtime to popular music produced outside the country. Where the primary audience is between ages 15-25, mainly the school age constituency, the radio provides very little in molding the minds of the youth where the goal is cultural renaissance and linguistic self-reliance. How can these networks promote indigenous cultures and the languages that instruct them in their programming where those same languages are granted peripheral recognition in these news outlets?

If indeed it was the political wish of the government to bestow high functional values on the indigenous languages through constitutional credence, why has it become so difficult for the government to garner effective outcomes from the nation's most potent public instrument, the media? Based on national policy, English continues to be used for more that 70. 0 percent of television programming at state and federal levels. This has led to the enactment of laws that limit foreign programming to less than 10. 0 percent of the overall programming time of these media outfits. In fact, it has prompted government take over or nationalization of most the nation's television establishments. To this extent, the national television broadcasting was centralized under the management of the Nigerian Television Authority (NTA) via a military decree later upheld in the 1979 constitution. NTA was commissioned "to restore a sense of national destiny and propagate common cultural bonds (...) among all the ethnic groups in Nigeria", (Uche 1989: 66). As a government-controlled institution, it was divided into six operational zones as a measure designed to effectively ensure that the distinctive regional interests in terms of people, language and culture are well served through selective programming. The adoption of the zoning strategy was, according to Uche (1989:69) dictated by "similarities in linguistic and cultural affinity and the factor of geographical contiguity".

This division is equally designed to accommodate the 1988 policy recognition of twelve indigenous languages: Hausa, Igbo, Yoruba, Fulfude, Kanuri, Ibibio, Tiv, Izon, Edo, Nupe, Urhobo and Igala in Table 1 to function as networks languages in ways that diminish the minority perception of linguistic hegemony in the constitutional affirmation of the Wazobia language group, (Brann 1989). However, government actions have done very little to transform the longstanding programming culture of these establishments. If foreign programming forced the Nigerian government to take over television establishments in the country more than three decades ago, and if the need for cultural renaissance constitutes the main justification for this takeover, the question that must be raised therefore is why the government has not, to any degree of effectiveness managed to hold these outfits to the principles that underpin their raison d'être and functional obligations. All things considered, it appears that the liberalized policy, the national government has so far accorded the national media has done every little to advance the national language policy agenda, but instead it has helped engendered the environment where the influence of the media has become so proliferated by its sheer number, (Table 2).

In today's Nigeria, almost all the states and in some cases, local governments have established their own television and radio stations, newspapers and newsletters of some sort. According to the Bureau of Democracy, Human Rights and Labor (February 2001), Nigeria currently boasts of more than 60 television stations (federal, state and private), more than 65 Daily newspapers and more than 20 weekly and bi-weekly magazines and periodicals. Adegbija (2004) even put the numbers higher by another 5. 0 percent. The general belief is that the state political agenda cannot be better transmitted if it relies absolutely on media largesse of the federal government. Yet what the ubiquity in media establishment has so far accomplished, again compliment of the FCP laws, is the national proliferation of sectarian politics. With these laws, state-owned television outfits are caught in the politics of indigenization that privileges ethnic parochialism in programming over obligations that centralize national agenda. The inward-looking strategies such programming adopts have done very little to enhance the national social cohesion that the constitution contemplates. Media freedom and power have only meant legitimacy for outlets guided by divisive ideologies wherefrom the benefit of social cohesion through linguistic homogenization cannot be harvested

Table 2: Media Outlets in Nigeria

Media Establishment	Numbers	Patronage (in millions)	Circulation (per 1000 persons)
Daily Newspapers	67	3.9	36
Magazines	26	1.7	21
Television Stations	64	5.0	58
Radio	72	34.9	372
Satellite Outlets	6	0.8	23

As the media political orientations reinforce group ideology and interest constellations, the need for inter-group linguistic alignment diminishes as groups erect ideological frontiers and fortify them politically. And as news reporting becomes parochial in content and outlet, the readership fractured to reflect divided solidarity in the public orientations vis-à-vis issues of national importance. Where the need for media objectivity is in conflict with the need for media obligation and dedication to factional political and ideological courses, nurturing media news consumption with broad national subscription can only be desired. To Uche (1989:100), it is nothing short of irony that "the press that brought colonial rule to an end in Nigeria became parochial and lost the nationalist orientation it had earned". But, as groups employed state established broadcasting systems to bolster their ethnolinguistic identities and group solidarity, loyalty to national policy of cultural inter-permeation is inevitably replaced by ethno-cultural fortification as a strategy of managing group legitimacy, which indeed is needed for group competitiveness at the national level. While the media systems promote political parochialism as they claim the need to represent their ethnic base; they are doing so in English, not in the languages native to this base. But, judging by the terms of FCP, the shift in media mission and language appear predictable.

What the mission engenders is the articulation of the public interest and people's social agendas to the political center. Where the language of that center is English by national policy, the choice of language in the nation's media establishment is indeed preordained compliment of the national policy itself. Here again, Nida and Wonderly (1971:65) observation that: "In Nigeria, there is simply no politically neutral language" is germane. To bolster group competitiveness and viability, media outlets are often established in English as the nation's official language. The desire for mass communication in English is justified by the fact that no particular group is disadvantaged by the choice of this language where the group political agenda is intra-national rather than intra-ethnic. That the nation's media are forced through intra-national political circumstances to disseminate their news in English only reinforces the social significance of this language in ways that are detrimental to the social competitiveness of the indigenous languages. While the nation's media promotes English as part of the existing elitist culture, the actual prognosis of the media language choice is the ethno-cultural divide it reinforces.

Where national news in local languages only attracts divergent, ethnic-based audiences with certain degree of proficiency in these languages, the same news in English afford these audiences to converge in a singular language. Also, while the social divide fostered through the use of indigenous languages is regional or group-based, that of English is education or class-driven. That English transcends the nation's regional and ethno-cultural divide has been heralded by the elite as the condition for achieving the hitherto elusive national unity. In fact, some even doubt the viable existence of Nigeria without this language. The main point here is that the media is part of the problem, not the solution. English, the Language of Wider Communication (LWC) constitutionally legislated to unite the diverse ethnic groups in Nigeria maintains the potential to divide as it becomes the instrument of sentiment peddling and social conduit of group agendas through the media. The battle over ethnonationalism is now being fought in the nation's media where English serves as the trans-ethnic outreach language. English has not only served the media in their newly acquired parochial roles but also aided the ideological forces for ethno-cultural partisanship in the nation. And, to the extent that such partisanship persists, any policy designed to promote any of the majority languages beyond its region of application becomes suspect with the prospect of broad rejection. But, where the media has so far failed to live up to its constitutional obligation, perhaps the nation's educational systems, identified as a complementary outlet for national policy on language will suffice.

Language Policy: Education Role

In this section the simple question to answer is whether or not the Nigerian educational systems can serve as viable resource and outlet for the nation's language policy agenda. In other words, will this agenda materialize here where other situations have amounted to nothing more than questionable strategic choices? To make sense of this question, the basic assumption is that education can provide a conceptually feasible environment not only for implanting the terms of national language policy but also for accommodating the objectives contained in those terms. Howbeit, the submission here is that the Nigeria's constitutional laws designed to achieve the nation's language policy goals on the back of its educational systems is nothing but a national experiment in conceptual mismatch. From the ambitious provision of the 1979 constitution that declared: "The business of the National Assembly shall be conducted in English, and in Hausa, Ibo and Yoruba" (*Chapt. II, sec. 3 (2)*) to a more pragmatic linguistic meltdown of this provision in the language of the 1999 constitution that states: "The business of the national Assembly shall be conducted in English. "; and the added ex post facto provision that that says: "Nigerian languages shall become additional languages of business of the National Assembly as the National Assembly shall by law prescribe"; it seems Nigeria's language policy have taken the trial and error route to come to terms with the pragmatics of the nation's real character. The drastic change in the language of the constitution may have been reality-driven, still, it exposes areas and factors that affirm unassailable weak link between the nation's language agendas and the educational programs procured by policy to fulfill them.

Six factors raise serious concerns about the effectiveness of education to serve as a major resource in the implementation of FLP per the terms of the constitution and, they include: (i) *standardization*; (ii) *system*; (iii) *duration*; (iv) *logistics*; (v) *pragmatics* and (vi) *attitude*. On the level of *standardization*, many Nigerian languages close to 60 have been standardized. Brann (1979) acknowledged that, based on certain variables which he reduced to quantitative indices, some languages are more developed than others. To acquire these indices, he considered four basic features: (i) scientific study of language (orthography, grammar and dictionary); (ii) language use in mass media (newspapers, magazines, radio and television); (iii) use in publications (educational, literary and translations) and (iv) application in pedagogy (primary, secondary and tertiary instructions). Each of these features was assigned numerical values, which were allocated to languages based on their individual level of linguistic development. Brann managed to quantify the developmental levels of 51 Nigerian languages where the three majority languages, Yoruba at 26, Hausa at 25 and Igbo at 23. 5 maintain the highest and rather close indices of functional development. And, even where this is the case, the interest of Nigerians to acquire any level of second language proficiency in these languages continues to diminish with time and, in effect, reflected in the lowering of policy expectation in regard to national language objectives specified in the 1999 constitution.

But then, the standardization of 60 or less languages in a country of 400 or more language, only accounts for less than 20. 0 percent standardization rate. With such low rate in language development, how then does the nation fulfill its constitutional requirement that obliges its children to be educated in their first language (L1), i. e. their Mother Tongue (MT)? Where the Nigerian National Policy on Education (NNPE: 2004) states that: "The medium of instruction in the primary school shall be the language of the environment for the first three years", (*Section 4 (e) & (f)*), the logical conclusion this generates is that many Nigerian children, largely in the minority class, whose MT's are yet to be standardized are being educated in languages other than those spoken in their immediate environment. Often, this forces the children from minority groups to make linguistic choice contrary to FCP principles so early in their educational career. And here, the choice of language of instruction tends to favor one of the majority languages customarily used as the lingua franca in the minority areas. NNPE (ibid.) also asserts that during the three years period of a child's education in his/her MT, the child "shall be taught English as a subject. " What this mandate requires is a *system* that entails that: "From the fourth year, English shall progressively be used as a medium of instruction and the language of immediate environment and French shall be taught as subjects", *(Section 4 (e) & (f))*.

Advocated in this regard is a clumsy and rather awkward language role reversal that is not only confusing but also impractical. First, that the child learns English as a subject does not guarantee sufficient proficiency for this language to be used effectively as language of instruction at the end of the third year of learning it. Second, the system only affords a narrow temporal window for the child's first language to develop effectively before transiting to another; in other words, the child's formal competence in his/her MT is bound to diminish as the role associated with it becomes subordinated to those of Other Tongues (OT's), English and French. The three-way progressive language acquisition seems to maintain all the ingredients of achieving what Mackey (1989:162) describe as "partial bilingualism" at each stage of the child's language acquisition. This means the length of time, i. e. *duration* or period assigned to either MT or OT's are suspect in the policy scheme designed to promote both. In fact many studies (Simpson 1978, Awoniyi 1987), have blamed the mass failure of young school-age Nigerians in the language sections of the national standardized tests on the inadequacy of time devoted to preparing these Nigerians for the skills required to excel in these tests. In Table 3 below, more Nigerians take the Senior Secondary Certificate (SSC) examination in English than they do in all the Nigerian majority languages combined.

Table 3: Performance in the Major Languages: SSC Examination (1988-90)

Language	1988			1989			1990		
	Total Sitting	Credit Pass	%	Total Sitting	Credit Pass	%	Total Sitting	Credit Pass	%
English	92,529	7,022	7.7	91,665	8,213	9.0	195,840	12,382	6.3
Hausa	33,194	6,151	18.5	38,826	13,520	34.8	46,848	11,398	24.3
Igbo	26,833	11,989	44.7	25,845	15,504	60.0	45,245	18,539	41.0
Yoruba	230	156	67.8	568	261	46.0	30,907	10,951	35.4
Arabic	609	248	40.8	479	421	87.9	758	361	47.6
French	376	140	37.2	304	99	32.6	394	115	29.2

Source: West African Examination Council, Yaba; Senior School Certificate Examinations, June 1988 and Nov. /Dec. 1988-90. Nigeria Statistics of Entries and Results; cited in Akere 1995:195.

Where 92, 529 students took the English SSC examination between 1988 and 1990, about 60, 257 students sat for the same examination in Hausa, Igbo and Yoruba combined in the same period. While many more Nigerians took this examination in English, less than 10. 0 percent boast of a Credit-Pass in this language each time. This is a testament to language policy failure predicated on system failure. By and large, Nigeria is not producing students with mastery of English, its official language and neither is it managing an educational environment capable of producing students with advanced literacy in their own native languages. Table 3 shows that in 1988, less than 50. 0 percent of students who sat for the final secondary school standardized test in Igbo received the required Credit-Pass in this national language. Students who took Hausa in the same examination faired much more poorly with only 18. 0 percent Credit-Pass. Those in Yoruba did much better with over 67. 0 percent Credit-Pass rate. The two years that followed, 1989 and 1990, did not show a reversal of fortune in student Credit-Pass rate. In fact in 1990, the highest percentage of Credit-Pass in the three national languages was 41. 0 percent recorded for Igbo.

Consistently, Nigerian students have performed poorly in the standardized examinations designed to test student competence and mastery in the languages the constitution ordains for official and national functions. More significant however, is the observation of great preference for English due to what might be attributed to the *pragmatic* values it commands. As the official language of the nation, it is the language of education, occupation, employment, law, media and international relations (Figure 3). For these reasons Nigerians perceive it as the language of unrivaled benefit and advantage. This drives the overall attitude of Nigerians towards this language, which many consider as the primary instrument of their social survival regardless of the great difficulty they encounter in their collective endeavor to gain its mastery. Today, most Nigerian students see English not only as a ticket out of functional illiteracy, but also regard it as the sole linguistic aggregate of their career development and professional competitiveness. And where this happens to be the case, what other incentive is left for these children to align themselves with any of the majority languages that lack comparable status and functional power?

The conditions that underpin FLP laws and the circumstances the laws engender in Nigeria's socio-political life makes the answer to this question as complex as it is predictable. By the terms of these laws the choice favors English than it does any of the national languages. The laws deny these languages their competitiveness given their subordination to secondary roles in the Nigerian language policy and hence society. These languages are now faced with permanent status abdication to English given the enormity of the functional privileges it commands. Moreover, the fact that the federal education laws recognize Mother Tongue (MT) education does not advance the terms of FLP any. Indeed, this fact raises three fundamental questions. Why should children from the minority groups learn or align with any of the majority languages if by fortifying their own individual linguistic identity they are, under the law, better situated for greater political and economic reward? And, what advantages, political or otherwise, will they enjoy by learning three majority languages where the law requires all Nigerians to learn one language, English as the supreme code of both official and social engagements in the country? Also, why should they continue to accommodate those languages which they consider as the instrument by which their ethno-cultural identities have traditionally been subjugated if not violated? Thus, the idea that the minority groups and their children will gravitate towards the continued social supremacy of the Wazobia linguistic group is more otiose than it seems.

Conclusion

In Nigeria of today, there is a tempered validity to the question of whether the absence of constitutionally-sanction language policy should in effect constitute the policy Nigeria as a nation ought to pursue instead of institutional investment in language policies that have created nothing but social chaos and confusion. In other words, is the negative premium of the present state of language policy too high in Nigeria as it struggles to navigate itself out of the persistent fragility of its political disposition? These are questions designed for the Nigerian political and policy stakeholders to answer. So far, finding answers to these questions have not only been driven by political exigency but also have been reduced, by the stakeholders, to an enterprise devoid of great political dividend. Most of them have relied absolutely on the national laws to provide answers to these questions. Yet, as demonstrated in this piece, the three sectors where these laws are supposed to be tested or implemented with marked objectives, (i) majority-minority socio-linguistic coalescence, (ii) media mediation of government-people symbiosis and (iii) language-policy-implementation interface via education have been predisposed to imperatives that circumvent the conceptual logic that motivates them. What has transpired is a consistent national struggle with these imperatives. Where the primary goal is to achieve majority-minority sociolinguistic harmony through balance of power predicated on the centralization of the FCP laws, the result has been a paradox. With FCP, the voice of the silent minority was activated and elevated into a new height of socio-political resonation.

The nation's newest federalist constitution has so far led the minority groups along the path where it is so much easier for them to contemplate the perceived socio-cultural tyranny of the majority as a historical experience they are apt to reject. The need for minority rejection of hierarchy in national social structure under FCP laws has inevitably set the limit on how majority languages are given political leeway to spread within the territorial domains whereto the minority lays autochthonous claims. The minority political indulgence in inward-looking linguistic identity and assertion has made this spread virtually impossible. As the laws designed to counter the zero-sum, winner-takes-all management principles that have for years underscored the national political culture, FCP was readily adopted by the minority groups as the legal modality for addressing and redressing their traditional disenfranchisement based on four basic concepts ingrained with legal connotations: (i) *accountability*; (ii) *compatibility*, (iii) *contestability*; and (iv) *acceptability*. Here, *Accountability* is predicated on the letters of the law to the degree that the nation's citizenry serve as the political agency that holds the law and those who manage it accountable to the people.

Where the managers of the law who indeed are policy makers underperform or operate outside the functional allowance of the law, the people maintain the socio-political capital and rights granted by the same law, to invest in actions, behaviors and attitudes designed to counter the activities of the law managers. Thus, the voice of the people tends to serve as what Ogowewo (2005:39) described as a "competitive threat" to the absoluteness of policy laws, social or otherwise. Where the minority political elite in Nigeria find the language policy laws less accountable to their political base, they counter the terms of these laws by not readily subscribing to their primary objectives. Their suspicion of these laws has been well articulated in the media they control and the educational system wherein they participate. The conceptual domain of *compatibility* in relation to federal statutes on FCP and FLP raises a simple question on the functional congruity of the two statutes. Essentially, as social management instruments, are the two statutes executable with a sense of logical mutuality or doomed by operational asymmetry where one, i. e. FCP occupies the functional center and the other, i. e. FLP is condemned to the periphery with indirect subordination to the center. Where FCP in no uncertain terms endorses group equality in all its socio-political dimensions including culture and language, FLP seems to suggest linguistic subordination of the minority groups to the majority.

To these groups this is tantamount to transgression of their ethno-cultural rights, which the principles of FCP legally guarantee. Emerging from the clarity of policy contradiction built into the national constitution is a collective understanding of FCP that has so far rendered the federal language legislation ineffective. Still, on a conceptually complementary level are the ideals of pragmatism and fairness that tend to underpin the notions of *contestability* and *acceptability* in relation to the application of the FCP and FLP laws. While accountability is ipso facto socio-politically regulatory, with focus on the modalities by which the principles of the law are dispensed, both contestability and acceptability concern choices, political or otherwise, that people or groups are predisposed to accommodate as a result of the terms dictated by the law. In Nigeria where FCP assumes absolute political potency in group decision-making, the social response of the masses to federal language policies has been benign or look-warn at best. If FCP indeed constitutes the nation's affirmative action law and, in a layperson's understanding, a redressive measure designed to elevate minority status via socio-political equity, this law ought to be held accountable in achieving just that. Now, if the minority groups constitute a major stakeholder in the principles that motivate and drive Nigeria's affirmative policy law, why should these groups, in spite of their sizable demographic representation, succumb to or accept other laws that dictate their linguistic marginalization and eventual social assimilation?

The philosophical contradiction between the legal imperatives of FCP and FLP laws exposes unambiguous conceptual mismatch that serves as grounds for minority collective contestation or rejection of the language policy laws. This has led to the failures associated with nation's language policies. Simply, these failures can now be acknowledged in two fundamental ways. First is the illogical support that the constitution, saddled with the principles of federal character, renders to the terms and implementation of the language policies. Second is the inadequacy of the institutions designed for the implementation of these policies at national level. The two most prominent institutions that this piece examines are the media establishments, at one hand and, nation's education system at the other. The two have so far failed to accomplish the goals of the Nigeria's language policies. The role of the media as a para-public establishment for mobilizing national consciousness and executing the government's plan of action has been diminished by government's social affirmative policy designed to accommodate the nation's diverse cultural groups with a certain degree of equity. In searching for equity through political legislation, the nation's policy makers may have paved the way for greater socio-political fracture and linguistic disharmony.

The federal character principle and all the social policies it denominates: education, media and language, provide divergent answers to the same question, i. e. national cohesion. When all is said and done, when all the knots and bolts of the nation's social management laws are put in place, what cannot but be subjected to earnest conceptual scrutiny is the question about the logic that drives their overall operational chemistry. What FCP lends to national political consciousness is a sound sense of group worth. But then, the essence of this situation is one that is marked by cleavage-driven social divide and political parochialism whence group-cum-sectarian mobilization emanates only to drive ethnic competition and eventually, ideological conflict that has in more ways than one left the nation's search for socio-political cohesion in perpetual state of transitivity. Given Nigeria's political preoccupation with national unity, effective goal-driven language policy cannot be envisaged outside a functionalist political construct, and for that matter, neither can the nation's collective sense of purpose and constitutional survival be subordinated to group-driven political agendas.

The employment of the media to promote group agendas have of late evolved into institutional investment in dysfunctional political enterprise, which *ipso facto* is predisposed to generating modal asymmetry between national language policy agenda and citizen's collective attitude. It has provided the avenue for reconstituting the traditional ethnically-driven political disharmony and religious antagonism. Politically, the novel national shift to a democratic mode of governance has been a mixed blessing. Democracy has not only translated to the lifting of military sanctions on free speech, but has also elevated the media into a new level of political significance as all its branches become potential apparatuses of socio-cultural factionalism. The avenue for parochial politics has been the media. Often, this has destabilized the center and contributed to its inability to pursue programs, particularly, those pertaining to language designed to harness political cohesion. For the Nigerian nation to deviate from its persistent state of recycled social chaos, perhaps this is the time for it to cut its linguistic losses and opt, as a practical resolution, for the nationist approach that gives permanent functional premium to the language, English, without which the Nigerian nation as we know it would not have come into political existence in the first place. After more than forty five years into its political independence, the Nigerian nation-state ought to have outgrown its growing pains of linguistic nationalism and settle for a language policy approach that is as logical as is pragmatic.

Notes

[1] Cited in Ogowewo, Tunde (2005:39) based on the interview of Justice Ayoola with Funke Aboyade of THISDAY newspaper, 30 November 2003.

[2] King of France from 1643 and patron of the arts, the 'Sun King' who established absolute monarchy and waged several wars to bolster his belief in totalitarianism.

[3] A three distribution of language by function; Nigeria's triglossia include English as the Official Language (OL); majority languages: Hausa, Igbo and Yoruba as National Languages (NL), and the minority languages as Local Languages (LL).

[4] A three way reference to the English verb >come= in the three majority languages: Yoruba, Hausa and Igbo in that order. It is coined to describe both a linguistic category and possible coalescence of the three ethno-politically distinct languages

5   Actual number remains uncertain as the mapping of the languages native to Nigeria continues to work in progress. No uniform figure adopted by government or scholars; the number currently ranges between 51 and 400. See Otite 1990, pp.44-57 and Adegbija 2004, pp.40-45 for more comprehensive documentations.

6   See Ehindero 1999, p.38

7   See Uche, 1989, p.113

8   See Uche, ibid, p.87

References

Abacha, Sani. 1995. National Constitution Drafting Committee (NCDC) Mandate. In *The Constitution of the Federal Republic of Nigeria*. Abuja (1999): Federal Ministry of Information.

Achebe, Chinua 1985. English and the African Writer, in Mazrui, A, (Ed.). Transition. Reprinted from Transition 4:18 (1965), Appendix, pp. 216-223.

Adegbija, E. 2004. Multilingualism: A Nigerian Case Study. Trenton, NJ: Africa World Press.

Ammon, U. 1989. Towards a Descriptive Framework for the Status/Function (Social Position) of a Language within a Country, In Ammon, U. (Ed.). Status and Function of Languages and Language Varieties. Berlin: Walter de Gruyter, pp. 21-106.

Ansre, G., 1976. National Development and Language. 12th West African Language Congress, Ile-Ife: University of Ife.

Arasanyin, F. O. 1996. Utility, Status and Languages in Competition in Middle Belt Nigeria. Kyoto, Japan: African Studies Monographs. 16(4). Pp. 195-223

Arasanyin, F. O. 1996. Learning from India's Experience: The Quest for Unilangue in Nigeria. Journal of the Third World Spetrum Vol. 3(2), pp. 1-34.

Awolowo, O. 1968. The People's Republic. Ibadan, Nigeria: Oxford University Press.

Awoniyi, A. 1987. Evaluation of the Annual WAEC Examinations 1983-1985 Results. In Dada, A. (Ed.). 1987. Mass Failure in Public Examinations (Causes & Problems), pp. 3-24. Ibadan: Heinemann Educational Books (Nigeria) Ltd.

Ayida, A. 1990. Rise and Fall of Nigeria. Oxford: Malthouse Press Limited.

Bamgbose, Ayo, 1983. Language and National Building: A Public Enlightenment Lecture delivered at Bendel State University, June 5, 1983, Epoma.

_____1991. Language the Nation: The question of Language in sub-Saharan Africa. Edinburgh: University Press.

Brann, C. M. B. 1979. Mother Tongue, Other Tongue and Further Tongue. University of Maiduguri: Inaugural Lecture. 1979. Maiduguri.

_____1989. Lingua Minor, Franca & Nationalis. In U. Ammon, ed. Status and Function of Languages And Language Varieties. Berlin: Walter de Gruyter, pp. 372-385.

Bureau of Democracy, Human Rights and Labor. 2001. Internet-based Survey of the Nigerian Media News Consumption.

Demoz, A. 1991. Report on Ethiopia. Les Langues en Afrique a l'Horizon 2000, Symposium, Brussel, 7-9 December 1989. pp. 141-163

Ehindero, S. G. 1991. The Constitutional Development of Nigeria. Jos, Nigeria: Ehindero Publishing House, Limited.

Elugbe, B. O. 1990. National Language and National Development. In Emenanjo, E. N. (ed.) (1990) Multilingualism, Minority Languages and Language Policy in Nigeria. pp. 10-19.

Emenanjo, E. N. 1988. Linguistics, Language and the Nation. University of Port Harcourt Inaugural Lectures, 1987 – 88, Port Harcourt.

Enahoro, A. 1961. 'Legislative Speech on National Lingua Franca. ' In Aborisade, O. & Mundt, R. J. (ed.) (1961), Politics in Nigeria. p. 86.

Essien, O. E. 2004. The Future of Minority Languages, in E. N. Emenanjo (Ed.) (2004), Multiculturalism Minority Languages and Language Polici in Nigeria, Agbor: Central Book Ltd, pp. 155-168.

Fasold, Ralph, 1990. The Sociolinguistics of Society. Oxford: Basil Blackwell.

Federal Republic of Nigeria. 1979. The Constitution of the Federal Republic of Nigeria. Lagos: Federal Ministry of Information.

_____1999. The Constitution of the Federal Republic of Nigeria. Abuja: Federal Ministry of Information.

_____1977. National Policy on Education. Lagos: Federal Government Press.

Federal Republic of Nigeria. 2004. National Policy on Education. Yaba, Lagos: NERDC Press.

Fishman, Joshua, 1972. Language and Nationalism: Two Integrative Essays. Rowley: Newbury House.

Gandonu, A. 1978. Nigeria's 250 Ethnic Groups: Realities and Assumptions. In Holloman R. and Arutiunov, S. (Eds.). Perspectives on Ethnicity, The Hague: Mouton, pp. 247-279.

Heine, Bernd. 1990. Language Policy in Africa. In Weinstein, Brian (Ed.) Language Policy and Political Development, pp. 167-184, Norwood, NJ: Ablex Publishing Corporation.

Hoffman, Carl. 1974. The Languages of Nigeria by Language Families. Mimeograph. Ibadan, Nigeria: University of Ibadan.

Ikara, Bashir. 1987. Minority Languages and Lingua Francas in Nigeria. University of Maiduguri Public Lecture Series, 1987, Maiduguri

Jibril, M. M. 1990. Minority Languages and Lingua Francas in Nigeria Education. In Emenanjo, E. N. (Ed.) (1990). Multilingualism, Minority Languages and language Policy in Nigeria, Agbor: Central Books Limited. pp. 109-117.

Mackey, W. 1989. Determining the Status and Function of Languages in Multinational Societies in Ammon, U. (Ed.) (1989), Status and Function of Languages and Language Varieties. Walter de Berlin: Gruyter, pp. 3-20.

Murdock, G. P. 1975. Outline of World Cultures. New Haven: Human Relations Area Files Inc.

Nida, E. and Wonderly, W. L. 1971. Communication roles of Languages in Multicultural Societies. In W. H. Whiteley (ed.) (1971), Language Use and Social Change, London: OUP for the International African Institute, pp. 57-74.

Odumuh, A. 1993. Sociolinguistics and Nigerian English. Ibadan: Sam Bookman.

Ofuokwu, D. 2004. Ethnolinguistic Vitality and Language Planning: The Nigeria Situation, in E. N. Emenanjo (Ed.) (2004), Multiculturalism Minority Languages and Language Policy in Nigeria, Agbor: Central Book Limited, pp. 73 – 81.

Ogowewo T. I. 2005. Self-inflicted Constraints on Judicial Government in Nigeria. Journal of African Law Vol. 49. No. 1, Cambridge University Press, pp. 39-53.

Olagoke, D. O. 1982. Choosing a National Language for Nigeria. Journal of the Linguistic Association of Nigeria, No. 1: 197-206.

Osaji, B. 1979. Language Survey in Nigeria. Quebec: International Centre for Research on Bilingualism.

Otite, Onigu 1990. Ethnic Pluralism and Ethnicity in Nigeria. Shaneson C. I. Ltd., Ibadan. Report of the Technical Committee on the Production of Teachers for the Three Major Nigerian Languages, 1988. Main Report. Vol. 1. Lagos: Federal Government Information.

Simpson, E. 1978. Babel: Perspective fro Nigeria. Quebec: International Centre for Research on Bilingualism.

Sofunke, E. 2004, National Language Policy for Democratic Nigeria, in E. N. Emenanjo (ed.) (2004), Multiculturalism Minority Languages and Language Policy in Nigeria, Agbor: Central Book Limited, pp. 31-49.

Uche, Luke Uka. 1989. Mass Media, People and Politics in Nigeria. New Delhi: Concept Publishing Company.

UNESCO. 1974. Television, a one way street? Mass Communication Reports & Papers, #70, Paris, p. 12.

Wardhaugh, Ronald 1987. Languages in Competition. Basil Blackwell, New York.

Williamson, R. C. & J. A. Van Eerde. 1980. Subcultural Factors in the Survival of Secondary Languages: A Cross-national Sample. International Journal of the Sociology of Language, The Hague: Mouton Publishers, 25:59-83.

World Bank Africa Database. 2000. African Development Indicators. Washington, D. C: The World Bank.

Chapter 6

LANGUAGE-BASED PROBLEMS AND NATIONAL DEVELOPMENT IN NIGERIA

Akinloyè Òjó

Introduction

The return to democratic rule in Nigeria has been a positive development for the Nigerian populace. It has brought about the push for and the steady establishment of democratic traditions in the country. The 2005 national conference on political reforms despite its numerous shortcomings, illustrated the growing understanding for public discourse within the Nigerian polity. In addition, various national debates, such as the national allocation quota and the crisis in the Niger Delta area, have increasingly included non-traditional voices without the well-known political establishment in the country. Many Nigerians were part of the debate in 2006 that raged in the country's legislative houses over the issue of constitutional reform that would have allowed a maximum third term for political offices. The second set elections in Nigeria's latest attempt at entrenching democratic rule recently occurred in 2007. Unfortunately, the electoral process was considered marred by both local and international observers. The general consensus appeared to be that the elections were smeared with widespread malpractices and fraud. While the legal wrangling continues in the Nigerian judiciary, May 29, 2007 saw the inauguration of Nigeria's thirteenth head of state but only the fourth elected President. Historically, this marked the first ever hand over of government between two democratically elected civilian governments.

These exhilarating developments in the politics and political discourse of the country have however exposed an enduring challenge of national integration and popular participation in the political and economic development of the country. This is in addition to the prevalent political corruption. A significant number of Nigerians were not effectively part of the national debate due to two enduring challenges: language use and language in education. These two challenges, in our opinion, are decidedly linked and have continually contributed to the demise of various development plans and national integration efforts in the country. The majority of Nigerians, due to their low level or lack of (western) education (often translating into identical low level or lack of economic opportunities) have incessantly lacked the means for full participation in the social, economic and political development of the country. This challenge has continually been complicated by the multi-lingual nature of the Nigerian federation, the dominance of the English language (one of the least widely spoken language in the country) in official domains and the ineffective role of the government in implementing the viable language in education policy.

Language in education embraces the wider questions of the languages taught and learnt in the educational system, and the languages used for educating at various levels and sectors of a national system (Obanya, 1992). The failure of the Nigerian educational system to effectively educate the population either in the exoteric official languages of English and French or in the three national languages of Hausa, Igbo and Hausa or in the over three hundred and fifty other local languages have excluded many citizens from full participation in the system and as acted as one of the major stumbling blocks to national integration and development in Nigeria. In addition, there are vast challenges about the contents and the implementation of language policy stated in the Nigerian National Policy on Education (henceforth NPE). This PRESENTATION considers some of the language related issues in Nigeria's quest for development and national integration. The paper suggests that a major problem to be fixed is the language policy as contained in the Nigerian **National Policy on Education** (NPE) and its flawed implementation. Drawing illustrations from the challenges encountered in the implementation of the language policy at various levels of education, the paper provides some recommendations on how language planning and the effective implementation of the language policy can contribute to the goal of national integration and development in Nigeria.

A Sociolinguistic Profile of Nigeria and Issues Arising

A sociolinguistic profile of Nigeria will reveal the county's multi-ethnic and multi-lingual composition. The Nigerian multi-ethnic character is reflected in the population of over one hundred and forty million (according to the 2006 census) that is made up of over one hundred and twenty distinct ethnic groups. The colonial history of the country and the post-colonial developmental and political activities in the country has also brought in other residents from other African countries,

Europe and the Middle East. This multiplicity of cultures (religions and perspectives) has brought its own developmental challenges and it might actually be argued that this multi-ethnic character is the major bane to national integration in Nigeria. However, this multi-cultural environment has greatly enriched the Nigerian identity and the Nigerian educational system, through cross-cultural exchanges, has been better for it. Particularly since independence from Britain in 1960, the Nigerian educational system has been the arena for teaching tolerance and creating awareness about this diversity of people and worldviews. Arguably, this has been crucial to the continued survival of the Nigerian federation, despite all the political and economic struggles (such as the 1967-1970 civil war) that at various times have threatened to obliterate the country.

This multi-ethnic situation is further convoluted by the multi-lingual situation in Nigeria. Nigeria, indubitably, is the most linguistically diverse country in Africa and definitely one of the most diverse in the world. There are various estimates on the number of languages spoken in country, ranging from three hundred and fifty to five hundred and fifteen (Crozier and Blench, 1976, 1992 and Gordon, 2005). These languages are variously categorized within the educational and political systems with the three biggest –in terms of speakers and spread: Hausa, Igbo and Yoruba serving as national languages. Correspondingly, Nigeria's colonial history and the post-colonial developmental and political activities have also brought about the incidences of foreign languages such as English, French and Arabic (Nigerian and Lebanese) in the country. Of all these other languages, the English language is the most dominant in the country, particularly in education. It has served as the official language for the country since 1960 (joined in 1998 by French, at least legislatively) and has been the de-facto language of instruction at various levels of education in Nigeria.

English has a significant status and plays an important role in Nigeria. It has had a great influence on content and structure of Nigerian languages. It has also greatly affected the cultural and religious practices of Nigerians. Its dominance in several important and official domains of communication in Nigeria has been well discussed in the literature (Jowitt, 1991; Bamgbose, Banjo & Thomas, 1995; Schaefer & Egbokhare, 1999; Oyetade, 2001, Igboanusi, 2001, 2005 and Ojo, 1996 among others) but an indication of its importance in the Nigerian polity is the evolution or emergence of various forms of the language in the country. In addition to the variety of English spoken by Europeans (and North Americans), that is British and American English, there is Standard Nigerian English.

This is used mostly by educated Nigerian elites and is often the actual language of instruction in education. There is also a creolized Nigerian Pidgin English that is spoken, natively, in areas such as the Niger Delta area of Nigeria. Nigerian Pidgin English (NPE) There is also the least structured form, Broken English, used by mostly uneducated speakers of various Nigerian local languages (Awonusi, 1985).

In connecting the multi-ethnic and multi-lingual elements in the formation of the contemporary Nigerian identity, there are two possible opinions. Ironically, the opinions share a common starting point that one of the primary markers of ethnic identity is language and that in Nigeria, as in many other multi-ethnic and multi-lingual societies, variation in the language is a foremost demarcation of variable (local and national) identities. Nigerians, due to the multiple elements of the country, have both local and national identities. This is where the two opinions begin to differ, especially in the construction of these identities in relation to the task of nation building. Critically therefore, at the ethnic level (on the stage of local identity), language is a unifying force whereas at the national level (on the stage of national identity) it may or may not be perceived as a considerable foe for national unity. For the Nigerian government and proponents of the 'National Character, ' strengthening the influence of the three national languages in the three geo-political regions of the country is and has historically being the best route to ensuring national consciousness and integration.

However, the differing opinion suggests that strengthening local identities within the multitudes of ethnic groups is the most viable route and that historical manipulations, ever since the colonial era, are responsible for the perceived regional identities that are socio-politically masked as local identities. As noted by Garuba (2001), "through a collusion between missionaries, the colonial government and local politicians, these (language) differences were glossed over by the creation of standard languages and the deployment of common myths of origin. Languages that were hardly mutually comprehensible were declared dialects o f a common tongue, and ethnic identity became fixed on the basis of this language. Variations in identity on the basis of variations in language were foreclosed, and a national ethno-linguistic identity was imposed. " Using examples of the three national languages (Yoruba, Igbo and Hausa), he demonstrated that "clans and communities possess a local identity which is self-generated and has a symbolic value for the people themselves. National ethno-linguistic identities were therefore constructed to dispel the pull of these more authentic local identities and to serve as tools for mobilization in the contest for political power and the struggle over limited resources. In this process, national identities created the myth of a homogeneous whole, which was then assumed to be fixed and rendered invariable. Access to multiple identities on the basis of actual language spoken was therefore blocked. "

The Nigerian National Language Policy

A fascinating sociolinguistic profile as the above, especially with the large number of languages, the preponderance of English in the official life of the country and the varying socio-linguistic opinions on national and local identities, will suggest that Nigeria would be fully committed to an organized, deliberate, and effective policy on the use of language in the country, particularly language in Education. This is incredibly not the case and it is a rather curious task to try and present the Nigerian National language policy for two reasons. First is the lack of an explicit national language policy for the country. Second is the presumed national policy for languages in education as stated in the NPE. These POINTS WERE BETTER by Emenanjo (1992) in his discussion of languages and the NPE (1977, revised 1981, 1998 and 2004):

> It is common knowledge that Nigeria does not have a well- articulated and explicit national language policy that can be found in one document. But it is also common knowledge that Nigeria does have a national policy for languages in education and, by default and implication, in the polity. Emenanjo (1992)

He went on to identify sections of the various Nigerian government documents that included statements on language in education. The main document was the National Policy on Education released by the Federal Ministry of Information in 1977 and later revised in 1981. The NPE was further revised in 1998 and 2004. The Federal government published the revisions through the National Educational Research and Development Council. Significantly, each NPE revision contained what can be considered 'a statement of language policy' only slightly different from the preceding revision. The specific sections of the NPE in which this (national language) policy, according to Emenanjo (1992) is 'sometimes, explicitly and, sometimes obliquely, stated" along with the types or levels of education specified are:

Section 1: Philosophy of Nigerian Education

2: Paragraphs 9 and 11, for Pre-Primary Education

3: Paragraphs 14 and. 15(4) for primary Education

4: Paragraphs 18, 19(4) and 27 for Secondary Education

5: Paragraphs 32 and 37 for Higher Education, including professional Education

6: Technical Education

7: Paragraphs 51 and 52: Adult and Non-formal Education.

The actual statements relating to the de-facto National Policy on language (in Education) as contained in the revisions of the NPE are presented below in Table 1. The other supporting documents identified by Emenanjo (1992) are:

(a) Chapter X 'Special Issues in Nigerian Politics' Paragraphs 270 - 272, pp. 62 - 63 entitled: 'National Language' of the Government Views and Comments on the Findings of Recommendations of the Political Bureau (1987).

(b) Sections 19(4); 21; 53; and 95 of the Constitution of the Federal Republic of Nigeria (1989).

(c) The Cultural Policy for Nigeria (1988: 16-17).

Table 1: Nigeria Language Policy as contained in the NPE: Policy Statements

1977 (revised 1981)	"In addition to appreciating the importance of language in the educational process and as a means of preserving the people's culture, the Government considers it to be in the interest of national unity that each child should be encouraged to learn one of the three major languages, other than his own mother-tongue subject to the availability of teachers. In this connection, the Government considers the three major languages in Nigeria to be Hausa, Ibo and Yoruba. "
1998	"Government appreciates the importance of language as a means of promoting social interaction and national cohesion; and preserving cultures. Thus every child shall learn the language of the immediate environment. Furthermore, in the interest of national unity it is expedient that every child shall be required to learn one of the three Nigerian languages; Hausa, Igbo and Yoruba. For smooth interaction with our neighbors, it is desirable for every Nigerian to speak French. Accordingly, French shall be the second official language in Nigerian and it shall be compulsory in schools. "
2004	Government appreciates the importance of language as a means of promoting social interaction and national cohesion, and preserving cultures. Thus, every child shall learn the language of the immediate environment. Furthermore, in the interest of national unity, it is expedient that every child shall be required to learn one of the three Nigerian languages: Hausa, Igbo and Yoruba. For smooth interaction with our neighbors, it is desirable for every Nigerian to speak French, Accordingly, French shall be the second official language in Nigeria, and it shall be compulsory in primary and Junior Secondary Schools but non-vocational elective at the Senior Secondary School.

The Goals and Provisions of the Implicit Policy

The discussions in the above section highlight what has become the accepted outline of the de facto national policy on languages (in Education). From the policy statements presented in Table 1 and contents of the various documents, it is possible to identify the sociolinguistic philosophy and provisions of the policy as well as some of the presumed goals of the policy.

The Goals of the Policy

Prior to the 1998 revision, it is evident that the concern for language in the educational system was its use as a 'means for preserving the people's culture' and for ensuring the 'interest of national unity. ' This was continually expanded and by the 1998 and 2004 revisions, it was as a 'means of promoting social interaction and national cohesion; and preserving cultures. ' In the 1977 statement and the 1981 revision, the targets of the proposed preservation are the cultures associated with the three national languages (identified by the government). This corresponds to the opinion of those seeking the strengthening of the Nigerian national identity over several segmented local identities. Interestingly in 1998, the other opinion about the importance of local identities seem to have been added to legislative pondering as the Nigerian government stated its appreciation of the fact that in addition to preserving cultures, language is also a tool for social interaction and national cohesion. Therefore, while the learning of the national languages was still expedient for the goal of national unity, learning the language of the immediate environment is prescribed as 'a means of promoting social interaction and national cohesion (lest we forget); preserving cultures. '

A well intended but controversial goal was introduced in 1998 and this was the use of language (specifically French language) for 'smooth interaction with our neighbors. ' To achieve this goal, French was declared the second official language in Nigeria and made compulsory in schools. The 2004 revision retained this goal but the compulsory teaching of French was limited to the primary and Junior Secondary schools making it a non-vocational elective at the Senior Secondary school. For those opposed to this development, the country does not require another exoteric official language especially since there are limited successes with the use of English. To them, the national languages should be better developed to challenge English and eventually emerge as the official languages of the country.

An analytical examination of the goals of language learning outlined in the NPE shows that there are three primary functions for language in Nigerian Education. The functions are making Nigerians capable of acquiring knowledge, skills and attitudes that will make Nigeria a highly developed nation ("the importance of language in the educational process"); making Nigerians capable of preserving and positively utilizing their cultures ("a means of preserving people's culture"); and making Nigeria become a virile and united nation ("in the interest of national unity") (Afolayan, 1990:5-6). An additional function can be added to the list based on the later revisions of the NPE. This will be making Nigerians gracious regional citizens within the West African region ("for smooth interaction with our neighbors, it is desirable for every Nigerian to speak French").

However as noted by Afolayan (1990) and echoed in Emenanjo (1992), in terms of actual school, four specific roles are mapped out for language in Nigerian education:

(i) Educational process: school subject

(ii) Educational process: a medium of instruction

(iii) Preservation of culture: a means of additive communication as a first target.

(iv) Promotion of unity: a means of integrative communication as a second target.

Essentially, the major goals of the national policy on language (in Education) include the following:

(a) promotion of multilingualism through the acquisition of the national languages and the language of the immediate environment

(b) preservation of Nigerian cultures

(c) promotion of national unity and integration

(d) recognition (and promotion) of a Nigerian national identity

(e) recognition of regional and national identities

(f) promotion of socio-economic development through the use of language

(g) increasing regional cooperation and interaction with Francophone West Africa

The Provisions of the Policy

There have been numerous considerations of the provisions of the Nigerian national language policy (Obanya, 1992; Bamgbose 1992, 2000; Arohunmolase, 1998, 2006; Emenanjo, 1990, Egbokhare, 2004, and Ojo, 2006 among others). As Emenanjo (1990) noted, 'this policy recognizes the multidimensional, multi-lingual three tier political-polity which tries to capture the multi-ethnic and, ipso facto, multi-lingual polity which Berlin and the British have hammered into a rough-hewn existence. ' Indeed, this is a reference to the challenges of multi-ethnic and multi-lingual within the Nigerian polity that we discussed above. Critically viewed, the goals of the policy are attainable because of the provisions of the policy. These provisions include the following:

(i) Mother-Tongue (MT) and/or Language of the immediate community (LIC) as the Language of initial literacy at the pre-primary and junior, primary levels, and of adult and non-formal education.

(ii) The three major (national) Languages - Hausa, Igbo and Yoruba at L2 as the languages of national culture and integration.

(iii) English - the official language - as the language of formal literacy, the bureaucracy, secondary and higher education, the law courts, etc.

(iv) Selected foreign languages especially, French, and Arabic, as the languages of international communication and discourse. These are the languages for which language villages have been set up.

In terms of unstated policy, the NPE policy on languages:

(i) Advocates multilingualism as the national goal.

(ii) Recognizes English as the de facto official language in the bureaucracy and all tiers of formal education.

(iii) Treats Hausa, Igbo and Yoruba as potential national languages which are to be developed and used as LO and L2 all through the formal educational system.

(iv) All Nigerian languages as meaningful media of instruction in initial literacy, and in life-long and non-formal education. Tables 1 and 2 below schematically present what should be the facts of languages in Nigerian education with respect to literacy and formal education. (ref: Emenanjo, 1990).

A closer look at all the provisions of the NPE reveals that the use of any Nigerian language as a medium of instruction is limited to the primary and pre-primary levels (paragraph 11:3) p. 10; and paragraph 15 (4), p. 13). Therefore, the goal of medium of instruction in the educational process is irrelevant to the teaching of Nigerian languages at the JSS level. Again of the three relevant for the teaching of Nigerian languages at the JSS level, the designers of the NPE had at the back of their minds the preservation of culture and promotion of Nigerian unity as crucial to the JSS. Otherwise all the languages English, French, Arabic, taught as school subjects at the JSS have intellectual relevance.

Challenges with the Contents and Implementation of the Policy

The constant revisions of the language policy statement in the NPE (1977, revised 1981, 1998 and 2004) is an indication that it is an evolving guiding principle about language in education in Nigeria. This notwithstanding, the explicit languages' aspect of the NPE has come under great criticism both in terms of the contents and implementation of the policy. These criticisms can be divided into those that are about the contents of the policy and those that are about the challenges for the implementation of the policy. Yet there are two concerns that are primarily shared by most of the critics of the policy. The first of the shared concerns is the fact that the statement on language in the NPE merely constitutes just a statement of intent rather than a serious program for implementation. Connected to this concern is the abstractness of the objectives of the policy. There are no clear concrete steps identified for the attainment of the goals stated in the policy.

Another principal concern about the policy is the lack of established patterns or objectives for the periodic policy reviews. In fact, some critics worry about what appears to be the frequent and unmethodical review of the NPE and consequently, the language policy. These continue to have negative impact on the successful implementation of what could be considered practical policies. An examination of the policy statement from 1998 and 2004 in which there was only a minimal change in terms of the level of education where French would be compulsory is a good illustration of this fact. Some of the criticism can be found in works by Bamgbose (1972, 2000); Banjo (1975); Ahmed (1982); Babalola (1982); Brann (1977; 1980; 1982), Emenanjo (1985, 1990, 2001), Jibril (1986), Obanya (1996), Egbokhare (2004) and Arohunmolase (1998, 2006) just to name a few.

Challenges with the Contents of the Policy

The initial challenges with the contents of the policy particularly in the latest revision are the inclusion of French language as the second official language and the exclusion of Nigerian Pidgin which has grown into one of the major languages in the country. In including French (another language to vie for programming attention) in the implementation of the policy as an official language is compounding the challenges of language in Education in Nigeria and increasing the number of languages that students in the Junior Secondary Schools (JSS) has to work on. It is laudable that implementing the policy is about the spirit of regional cooperation in West Africa and a practical provision for Nigeria that is surrounded by Francophone nations but the limited success of educating the population in English, the first official language is enough proof that adding another 'unfamiliar' language is going to be a vital challenge for the policy. Omoniyi (2003) provides a critical appraisal of the political ideology underlying the decision of an additional official language for the country.

Another challenge with the contents of the policy has to do with the issue of mother tongue. As Emenanjo (1990) noted, there are two critical concerns. First, if the mother tongue (MT) or the language of the immediate community is considered so important at the pre-primary level as an integral part of the child's culture and the link between the home and the school, why should it be "principal" and not "solely" used at this level? Also, if the mother tongue or the language of the immediate community is considered a very important medium for achieving initial and permanent literacy and numeracy, why should it be only used 'initially' and not throughout the whole of primary education. It further noted that the Ife Six Year Primary education Project (SYPP) and "experimental" MT project in Niger Republic have confirmed that those who have their total primary education in MT who had turned to technical pursuit have proved more resourceful than their counterparts from other schools when they met on the technical plane.

The Ife SYPP children have demonstrated greater manipulative ability, manual dexterity and mechanical comprehension. In their relationship to their colleagues the project children have demonstrated a great sense of maturity, tolerance and other affective qualities that make them integrate easily and readily with those they come in contact with" (Fafunwa et al. 1989: 141). It can be added also that in addition to changes in when and how long the MT is used, the policy also needs to make provision for the transition from primary school to secondary level of education and beyond. The pronouncements, in the policy statements, about the three major languages are additional challenges with the contents. To the critics, these statements are vague and effeminate. The critics note that phrases that 'encourage (students) to learn' or that make it expedient to study one of the national languages suggest that the choice of language is optional and left to the child to choose or not to choose Common sense dictates that if learning a major national language is a national responsibility then its learning cannot be optional. It has to be compulsory (Emenanjo, 1990).

Challenges with the Implementation of the Policy

As noted above, the challenges with the policy is not only about the contents but also in terms of implementation. Initially, the implementation of this potentially practical policy is hampered by the frequent and unmethodical review of the NPE in which it is contained. Beyond this challenge, there are others that continually seem to hamper the smooth implementation of the policy. Some of these are related to implementing the provisions of the policy as it relates to the choices of languages in education. It is not clear how the language(s) of the immediate community will be identified in pluralistic settings like urban centers or international communities like university campuses. Even then, there is the pedagogical challenge of engaging over three hundred and fifty languages for education since all Nigerian languages can be used as mother-tongue or language(s) of immediate communities.

These types of challenges also relate to the selection and pedagogical utility of the three national languages. In terms of selection, there is no clear indication of who makes the selection of the language. Will the decision be made by the government and if so, what level of the government – federal, state or local government. Tied to this is the lack of information about the level of education at which this selection will be made. Moreover, there is the practical problem of having three national languages adequately serving the educational needs of a multi-ethnic society as Nigeria. There is also the elemental concern of how these national languages can serve to preserve the cultures of the multiple ethnic groups in the group. The contention is that that having these three languages available as second languages will help promote the goal of unity but it is not clear how three years of second language instruction at junior secondary school will be enough for the cultural immersion and political unity envisaged. From the policy statements, it is clear that the Nigerian government considers the learning of these three national languages by every Nigerian child as critical for national unity and integration but there is no articulated national implementation plan nor any mechanism suggested that will sanction any defaulting level or agent of government.

Another set of challenges with the implementation of the policy are related to language teachers and teacher preparation. The 1981 revision of the NPE noted that the implementation of the language provisions is subject to the availability of teachers. Emenanjo (1990) refers to this provision as 'cautious 'escape' phraseology. ' It is undeniably non-committal as regards to the implementation of this provision especially if we consider the fact that the shortage of trained qualified language teachers is a daunting challenge for the policy's implementation. This is a problem that is real for both the teaching of the national languages as a first language (L1) as well as a second language (L2) across the country. Junaidu and Ihebuzor (1993) point to the fact that, the problem of the supply of teachers in Nigerian languages represents one of the greatest problems facing the curriculum development efforts in Nigeria.

The introduction of Nigerian languages (Hausa, Igbo, and Yoruba) as L2 at the JSS level worsened the compounded problem of the supply of trained teachers. In 1988, the country had only about 12% of the needed teachers available to teach the three national languages. The situation is improved today largely to the efforts of the various Colleges of Education in the country. These institutions have greatly helped to improve the situation by producing significantly increased number L1 teachers of these languages in the last decade. It is in these colleges that the best curricula developed by federal agencies (such as NERDC) for the teaching and learning of the three national languages are being applied. The National Commission for Colleges of Education's (NCCE) has also produced the *Minimum Standards for Colleges of Education for teaching the three national languages*. However, in spite of these laudable efforts at the college of education level, there is still a shortfall of both L1 and L2 teachers of Nigerian languages.

To address this shortfall, especially with the production of teachers of these languages as L2, the Nigerian government established the National Institute for Nigerian Languages (NINLAN), Aba to train teachers of Nigerian languages as L2 in 1993. Unfortunately the institute for the first twelve years of its existence did not admit any candidate. The situation has not been helped by the conventional universities as none of these tertiary institutions is producing L2 teachers of the Nigerian languages (Arohunmolase, 2006). A painful illustration of this for most Yoruba nationalists is the fact that none of the eight federal universities in the South-West offers a Yoruba as L2 program. The challenge of inadequate L2 scholars has therefore translated into inadequate textbooks for the teaching and the learning of these languages as L2 in the secondary schools and in the Colleges of Education. The resulting situation now includes the adaptation of L1 teaching and learning methodologies in the teaching of Nigerian languages as L2.

Addressing the Challenges with Contents and Implementation of the Policy

The above noted challenges in terms of the contents and implementation of the policy are merely some of the many that critics of the policy have identified over the last three plus decades. The paramount recommendation for addressing this multitude of challenges will be in the area of policy reform, particularly in revamping the abstract objectives. There has to be an established pattern and precise objectives for any review of the policy. In addition, the central government has to also establish concrete mechanisms for the full implementation of the policy at all levels as well as well defined and legally binding mechanisms for sanctioning government agencies and other levels of governments that fail to effectively fulfill the provisions of the policy.

There must also be a qualitative and quantitative increase in texts of all descriptions available in Nigerian languages. All these resources collectively provide the wherewithal for effectively teaching, discussing, writing, examining, typing, typewriting and printing the major Nigerian languages among others (Emenanjo, 1990). Of highest priority in the material development endeavour must be the development of metalanguage materials in Nigerian languages. A practical consideration that is tied to education and material development is the enforcement of the Mother Tongue Education at all levels beginning from kindergarten. At the lower levels, it will be fairly easy to provide resource materials for teaching and language learning will become part of the average Nigerian child's educational experience. The present condition that applies with the present policy contents and its implementation does not really allow for much emphasis on language learning.

The efforts by the various government agency and tertiary institutions to increase language teachers for the teaching of Nigerian languages as both L1 and L2 must also become concerted and increased. These must include two different institutions that need to make more contributions to the success of the language policy. These are the Nigerian universities and the National Institute for Nigerian Languages (NINLAN) in Aba. Nigerian universities must increase their investment in the teaching and learning of Nigerian languages by either offering Nigerian languages or by increasing the number of available Nigerian languages. They should also consider creating programs in the teaching and learning of these languages as L2.

It is rather appalling to have a condition in which various foreign languages are available for study as L2 in various Nigerian universities whereas the opportunities to learn the Nigerian languages as L2 are not available for Nigerian. Just as English is a critical requirement for University admission, proficiency in a Nigerian should become an admission requirement as well as a requirement for the compulsory General Education Studies. The ailing National Institute for Nigerian Languages (NINLAN) in Aba must begin to attain the federal government's objectives for its establishment by producing teachers for the teaching of Nigerian languages as L2.

The English language presently enjoys an elevated status in Nigeria largely due to Nigerian language policy and this status has translated into socio-economic benefits for its users, especially in terms of employment. The status of the Nigerian languages could also be improved with added benefits for those who are proficient in them. Employment to government positions at all levels should include some level of literacy in local languages with employment at the state and federal level actually having this as requirement for employment. The media is a powerful vector of development. Associating a language with any media is a powerful way of enhancing the vitality of such a language, promoting its use and ensuring positive attitudes towards such a language. Towards this end, Egbokhare (2004) suggests the establishment of community radio services that will be regulated to broadcast only in the languages of their catchment areas. This will promote the use of local languages, preserve them, and promote participation and information dissemination.

The cumulative effects of all these efforts and resources will be felt in various areas of the society even beyond education. These will include a general awareness about the role of indigenous languages in initial literacy, mass literacy, mass mobilization and adult literacy; priority position given to the recruitment of language inspectors of education; recognition of the need to have specialist language teachers and educators; increase in course offerings in languages in tertiary institutions; more air-time in the electronic media for languages; more print-space in the print media for languages; and more proficient numeracy and literacy in languages used in the country. It is interesting to note that these efforts supporting centrality of language to the teaching-learning process, the importance of Nigerian languages to the protection, preservation and promotion of Nigeria cultures and the enhancement of human dignity, and the necessity of learning a major language for purposes of promoting national unity and integration already have constitutional backing in the Constitution of the Republic of Nigeria and the educational justification in the NPE (Emenanjo, 1990).

As Egbokhare (2004) noted, a "language policy should give citizens access to information in the language which they understand and in which they have the greatest facility. " In essence, the Nigerian language policy should give the Nigerian freedom of choice and expression and provide the best option for the individual in terms of the development of natural capacities, psychological and cultural experience. Furthermore, a viable Nigerian language policy will utilize not only prescriptive legislative and constitutional means within Nigeria, but also employ indirect means by integrating languages with local and global economic order. A way of doing this to ensure that at the various levels of the socioeconomic order in the country various Nigerian languages employed are assigned preeminence.

Finally, it is a paradox that the works of critics have variously contributed to the improvements achieved in the development and implementation of the national language policy in Nigeria. Of specific note was the seminar on the implementation of the language provisions of the NPE that was organized by the Language Development Center of the NERDC at Ota, Ogun State in October 1991. The objective of the seminar, that featured the minister of education, was the comprehensive review of the implementation procedures for realizing the objectives of the language provisions of the NPE. The issues that the seminar dealt with are indications that it was organized as a response to all the critiques of the language provisions of NPE over the years. The seminar dealt specifically with, among others:

- General problems of implementation of the language provisions of the NPE;
- Programs for the training of teachers for Nigerian languages as L1 and L2, English and Foreign Languages;
- Curricula and Syllabuses for Nigerian Languages as L1 and L2;
- Teaching of major Nigerian languages;
- The teaching of non-major (minority) Nigerian Languages;
- Review of curricular, syllabuses and pedagogy of English and Foreign languages in the educational system;
- Research requirements for the implementation of the language provision of the NPE.

The Ota Seminar came out with sixteen recommendations on language policy and curricula objectives; sixteen recommendations on the training of language teachers, six recommendations on language research, three recommendations on evaluation and three general recommendations. For a detailed report of the seminar, the summary of the recommendations and other related discussions see Emenanjo's (1992). In fact, Emenanjo's (1992) discussion of the strategies for the implementation of the policy stands out as the most comprehensive. It is remarkable because it provides a far reaching outline for the better implementation of the policy including recommendations and suggestions for all (possible) concerned parties including the Federal Government and its agencies; the state governments and their agencies; Linguists and language educators; language associations; institutions of higher learning and the average Nigerians. The work is a clear indication that addressing the challenges with the policy is primarily the duty of the government at various levels but also involves contribution from various other professional groups as well as the average Nigerian citizens. An extract of Emenanjo's discussions of the seminar, courtesy the Fafunwa Foundation Internet Journal of Education, is appended to the end of this work.

Conclusion

Educational policies, like all issues in education, are dynamic and continuously changing and responding to new realities in the light of new information and expanding visits and horizons. Education is not about languages, teaching language or teaching in languages. It is about responsible and responsive citizenship. It is about the acquisition of skills. All these can be taught and learnt in any language but best in the language in which the teachers and their students are more at home. And that is their mother tongue. (Emenanjo, 1990). These were the revelations of the Ife Six Year Yoruba Project as recorded by Fafunwa et al. (1989:141). If the challenges with the contents and implementation of the language policy are addressed and the recommendations of the experts (as presented in the Ota Seminar) are incorporated in a revision of the current NPE in matters of language, Nigeria would get into the 21st century strong, virile, creative multilingual state which accords all the languages in the polity their respective but complementary statuses, functions and contexts.

Development is about people. Any development process must create opportunities for participation; otherwise it will exclude sections of the populace and create a privileged group. Such a process must also provide for structure and processes of accountability in order to maintain a balance and to check abuse and exploitation. Where no accountability exists, or where processes and structures for this fail, the process is subverted and groups that feel short-changed may revolt or surrender and become a liability as is the case in Nigeria where the manifestation has been a false piety and recourse to prayers. Contemporary Nigeria is faced with three primary problems: problem of values, problem of information flow and communication; and problem of leadership and governance. We may reduce these to the issue of access if we focus on the socioeconomic dynamics. (Egbokhare (2004).

Access to and utilization of information is right at the heart of development. Prah (2001) draws a crucial connection between language, culture and development. According to him, "in Africa, the cultural base of mass society which is in reality premised on African languages provides the only credible condition for the development of a society which involves the masses and uplifts them socio-culturally and economically from where they are, on the basis of what they have (p18). " Whatever policies and planning we enunciate must facilitate access to information and information infrastructure, promote communication and integration and enhance the preservation of African heritage and knowledge base. National integration is attained with the citizens feeling involved, owning resources and having access. The best tool for achieving these goals in a multi-ethnic and multi-lingual setting as Nigeria is language and linguistic development. Language is an instrument of integration and exclusion and addressing our language and language based problems will go a long way in addressing the seemingly elusive national unity and development.

As Prah (1999:2) noted, An African renaissance is not conceivable without the use of African Languages. " Development is driven by culture and is itself a cultural process. "If Africa is to move forward educationally and developmentally, the culture of the masses would need to be brought in from the cold. Educational and the mass media must reach the urban and rural millions in ways which culturally speak to them, in forms which do not dismiss their historical and cultural heritage; but rather recognizing these, constructs education, knowledge and the use of the media on the basis of what people already know and the cultural institutions to which they primarily respond. " Definitively, our consideration of the language related issues in Nigeria's quest for development and national integration has revealed that addressing the inherent challenges of language policy as contained in the Nigerian NPE and its flawed implementation will contribute to the goal of national integration and development in Nigeria.

APPENDIX 1

EXTRACT FROM EMENANJO'S (1992) DISCUSSION ON THE 1991 NERDC SEMINAR IN OTA

Courtesy: Fafunwa Foundation Internet Journal of Education
(http://fafunwafoundation.tripod.com/fafunwafoundation/index.html)

Teachers, government officials, publishers, writers among all those engaged in the enterprise of teaching, evaluation, and propagating languages must never fail to realize the centrality of their subject to their mission. And plan accordingly for language education and language in education. It is against the foregoing problems and with an eye Federal Government funded the "Seminar on the implementation of the Language provisions of the National Policy on Education. The Seminar which was organized by the Language Development Centre of the NERDC held at the Gateway International Hotel, Ota, from October 6-10, 1991. The specific objective of the Seminar was "Comprehensive review of the implementation procedures for realizing the objectives of the language provisions of the NPE". The Federal Minister of Education and Youth Development was there. So was the Chairman Implementation Committee of the NPE. And so were seventeen specialists in the different but complementary areas of Nigerian linguistics, language education, educational planning and curriculum development. The Ota Seminar dealt specifically with, among others;

(i) General problems of implementation of the language provisions of the NPE;

(ii) Programs for the training of teachers for Nigerian languages as L1 and L2, English and Foreign Languages;

(iii) Curricula and Syllabuses for Nigerian Languages as L1 and L2;

(iv) Teaching of major Nigerian languages;

(v) The teaching of non-major (minority) Nigerian Languages;

(vi) Review of curricular, syllabuses and pedagogy of English and Foreign languages in the educational system;

(vii) Research requirements for the implementation of the language provision of the NPE.

The Ota Seminar came out with sixteen recommendations on language policy and curricula objectives; sixteen recommendations on the training of language teachers, six recommendations on language research, three recommendations on evaluation and three general recommendations. Below is presented verbatim a summary of the recommendation of the seminar. They are ten in number but only nine are relevant for our presentation.

(i) "Government should continue with its policy of multilingualism".

(ii) Government should review and restate in a clearer form the language provisions of the NPE".

(iii) "Government should provide active encouragement to the implementation of the MT/LIC medium of instruction policy at the primary school level".

(iv) "Government should give active encouragement to the training employment of all categories of teachers of (Nigerian) languages.

(v) "Appropriate curricula agencies should review and\or design more functional curricula for (Nigeria) languages.

(vi) "Government should fund research into all aspects of language and language teaching in Nigeria and support such activities through grants to Departments of Linguistics and Nigerian/African Languages in tertiary institutions".

(vii) "Government should provide adequate funding for the survey of Nigerian languages project with a view to ensuring its immediate implementation, language planning, language development and language use purposes".

(viii) "Government should involve linguists and language specialists in all policy matters involving language in this country".

(ix) "The language provisions of the NPE and their implementation should be constantly monitored and evaluated".

References

Afolayan, A. 1976. 'The Six - Year Primary Project in Nigeria'. In A. Bamgbose (Ed.) 1976: 113-134.

Ahmed, U. B. 1982. 'The Promotion of Nigerian Languages within the New Educational System.' *Nigerian Educational Forum 5. 1:97-102*.

Arohunmolase, Oyewole. 1998. *Nigerian Languages for National Development and Unity*. Ibadan, Nigeria: Lolyem Communications.

Arohunmolase, Oyewole. 2006. Globalization and the Prospects of Teaching Yoruba as a Second Language (L_2) in Nigeria. In Arasanyin, Olaoba and Pemberton, Michael (Eds.) *Shifting the Center of Africanism: Language, Economic Regionalism, and Globalization; Proceedings of the 36th Annual Conference on African Linguistics*.

Awobuluyi, Oladele. 1992 'Language Education in Nigeria: Theory, Policy and Practice' In B. Ipaye (Ed.) *Education in Nigeria: Past, Present and Future* (Publication in honor of Prof. A. B Fafunwa). Lagos, Nigeria: Macmillan. pp. 205-214.

Awonusi, V. O. 1985. Sociolinguistic Variation in Nigerian English. Ph. D. Dissertation, University of London.

Awonusi, S and E. A Babalola. (Eds.). 2004. *The Domestication of English in Nigeria: A Festschrift in Honour of Abiodun Adetugbo*. Lagos: University of Lagos Press.

Bamgbose Ayo. 1992. *Speaking in Tongues: Implications of multilingualism for Language Policy in Nigeria*. Kaduna, Nigeria: Award Winner's lecture, Nigerian National Merit Award.

_____2000. Language and Exclusion: The Consequences of Language Policies in Africa. Hamburg: LIT Verlag.

_____2004. English and Inequality: An African Perspective. In Awonusi & Babalola (Eds.). The Domestication of English in Nigeria: A Festschrift in Honour of Abiodun Adetugbo. Lagos: University of Lagos Press.

Bamgbose Ayo, Funso Akere and Noel Ihebuzor (1992). (Eds). *Implementation Strategies for the Language Provisions of the National Policy on Education*. Abuja: Language Development Centre.

Bamgbose, Ayo, Ayo Banjo & Andrew Thomas (Eds.). 1995. *New Englishes: A West African Perspective*. Ibadan, Nigeria: Mosuro.

Banjo, A. 1975. 'Language Policy in Nigeria' In D. Smock and K. Bentsi-Enchill (Eds.). *The Search for National Integration in Africa.* New York: Freedom Press

Brann, C. M. B. 1982. 'Language Politics and language planning in Sub-Saharan Africa' (mimeo).

_____1989. 'Lingua Minor, Franca and Nationals' in U. Ammon (ed.) Status and Function of Languages and Language Varieties. Berlin: Walter de Cruyter. pp 372 - 385.

Constitution of the Federal Republic of Nigeria. 1999.

Crozier, D. H. and Blench R. M. (Eds.) 1976. *An Index of Nigerian Languages.* 1st Ed. Dallas, TX: SIL Inc.

Crozier, D. H. and Blench R. M. (Eds.) 1992. *An Index of Nigerian Languages.* 2nd Ed. Dallas, TX: SIL Inc.

Egbokhare F. O. and S. O. Oyetade (Eds) (2002). *Harmonisation and Standardization of Nigerian Languages.* CASAS Book Series No 19. Cape Town: South Africa.

Egbokhare, Francis. O. 2004. *Breaking Barriers: ICT, Language Policy and Development.* Ibadan, Nigeria: Univeristy of Ibadan Post Graduate School.

Emenanjo, N. E. 1985. 'Nigerian language policy: Perspective and Prospective. *JOLAN* 3:123 – 134.

Emenanjo, N. E. (Ed.). 1990. *Multilingualism, Minority languages and Language policy in Nigeria.* Agbor, Nigeria: Central Books Limited.

Emenanjo. N. E. 1992. Languages and the National Policy on Education: Implications and Prospects. In B. Ipaye (Ed.) *Education in Nigeria: Past, Present and Future* (Publication in honor of Prof. A. B Fafunwa). Lagos, Nigeria: Macmillan. pp. 215-224.

Fafunwa A. B., Macauley J. I. and J. A. Funso Sokoya. (Eds). 1989. *Education in Mother Tongue.* Ibadan: Ibadan University Press.

Fafunwa Foundation Internet Journal of Education http://fafunwafoun dation.tripod.com/fafunwafoundation/index.html)

Federal Republic of Nigeria. 1977. *National Policy on Education.* Lagos: NERDC Press.

_____1981. *National Policy on Education* (Revised). Lagos: NERDC Press.

_____1998. *National Policy on Education* (Revised). Lagos: NERDC Press.

Federal Republic of Nigeria. 1988. *Cultural Policy for Nigeria.* Lagos: Federal Government Printer.

_____2004. *National Policy on Education* (Revised). Lagos: NERDC Press.

Garuba, Harry. 2001. Language and Identity in Nigeria. In *Shifting African Identities.* Simon Bekker, Martine Dodds and Menshack Khosa (Eds.). Pretoria: Human Sciences Research Council: 7-20.

Gordon, Raymond G., Jr. (Ed.), 2005. Ethnologue: Languages of the World, Fifteenth edition. Dallas, Tex.: SIL International. Online version: http://www.ethnologue.com/.

Igboanusi, Herbert (Ed.). 2001 Language attitude and Language conflict in West Africa. Ibadan, Nigeria: Enicrownfit

Igboanusi, Herbert & Lothar Peter. 2005. Languages in Competition: The Struggle for Supremacy among Nigeria's Major Languages, English and Pidgin. New York: Peter Lang.

Ivowi, U. M. O. (Ed.). 1993. *Curriculum Development in Nigeria.* Ibadan, Nigeria: Sam Bookman Educational and Communication Services.

Jibril, M. 1986. Minority Languages and Lingua Francas in Nigerian Education. In Emenanjo N. E. (Ed.). *Multilingualism, Minority languages and Language policy in Nigeria.* Agbor, Nigeria: Central Books Limited. pp. 109 – 117.

Jowitt, D. 1991. *Nigerian English Usage: An Introduction.* Lagos, Nigeria: Heinemann

Junaidu, I. & Ihebuzor, Noel. 1993. Developing Curricula: Nigerian Languages. In Ivowi, U. M. O. (Ed.) *Curriculum Development in Nigeria.* Ibadan, Nigeria: Sam Bookman Educational and Communication Services. pp. 28-38.

Obanya, Pai. 1992. Language Education in Africa: Lessons for and from Nigeria. In B. Ipaye (Ed.). *Education in Nigeria: Past, Present and Future* (Publication in honor of Prof. A. B Fafunwa). Lagos, Nigeria: Macmillan. pp. 195-204.

Òjó, Akinlọyè. 1997. Incorporation of English Words in Yoruba: A Sociolinguistic and Phonological Analysis. M. A. Thesis, Department of Modern Languages and Linguistics (DMLL), Cornell University, Ithaca, New York.

Òjó, Akinloyè. 2006. A Global Evaluation of the Teaching and Learning of Yoruba Language as a Second or Foreign Language. In Arasanyin, Olaoba and Pemberton, Michael (editors) *Shifting the Center of Africanism: Language, Economic Regionalism, and Globalization; Proceedings of the 36th Annual Conference on African Linguistics.*

Omoniyi, Tope. 2003. Language ideology and politics: a critical appraisal of French as second official language in Nigeria. *Africa and Applied Linguistics 16, 13-25.*

Oyetade, S. Oluwole. 2001. Attitude to foreign languages and indigenous language use in Nigeria. In Herbert Igboanusi (Ed.). *Language attitude and language conflict in West Africa.* pp 14–29. Ibadan, Nigeria: Enicrownfit

Prah K. K. 1999. Workshop Working Paper on the Harmonization and Standardization of Nigerian Languages. Lagos, Nigeria. October 1999.

_____2001. "The idea of an African Renaissance, the languages of the Renaissance and the challenges of the 21st Century. Eisei Kurimoto (Ed). *JCAS Symposium Series 14.* JCAS, Osaka, Japan.

Prah K. K. and Ivonne King. 1998. *Tongues: African Languages and the Challenges of Development.* CASAS Monograph Series (II), Cape Town, South Africa.

Schaefer, Ronald P & Francis O. Egbokhare. 1999. English and the pace of endangerment in Nigeria. *Word Englishes* 18 (3), 381-391.

Chapter 7

LANGUAGE PLANNING: THE BANE OF YORUBA LANGUAGE EDUCATION IN SOUTHWEST NIGERIA

B. A. Amoloye

Introduction

Nigeria is characterized by dense multilingualism and multi-dialectism (Adegbija, 2004). It is also a fact that no single language is predominant throughout the entire country. However, there are regionally and locally dominant languages and Yoruba language happens to be of one of such languages. It is predominant in the southwestern states of the country. As a matter of fact, since the introduction of formal western education in Nigeria, Yoruba language has always had a place in the educational system of most of Yoruba speaking areas of the country, comprising Lagos, Ogun, Ondo, Ekiti, Oyo, Osun and some parts of Kwara and Kogi states (Amoloye, 2006).

The importance of language planning in a country like Nigeria cannot be over emphasized. The role of education in language planning in this instance cannot be underscored too. Education is considered the most effective means of entrenching the activities of language planning because it is the chief medium of the official spread of the different languages in the country; using the language as a medium of instruction or its being taught as a subject in the schools directly or indirectly spreads and entrenches the language. Furthermore, the secondary school level of education has been acknowledged (Adegbija 2004) as the most effective and wide spread organ for formal language spread in Nigeria. Adegbija opined that a larger number of students attend secondary schools than the universities because many of them drop out of schooling at the secondary level. For this, proficiency in language for most Nigerians seems to crystallize at this level, except for those who go on to tertiary institution. In addition, students from many parts of Nigeria study the indigenous languages like Hausa, Igbo and Yoruba etc. as subjects at this level of education.

Ironically, the language provisions as contained in the National Policy on Education which is supposed to promote the selected indigenous languages in each state to be co-official languages with English has been doing more harm than good to the status of all the indigenous languages including Yoruba language even in its language environment. It is our studied opinion that the provisions has actually created a setback in its effective teaching and learning such that if care is not taken, Yoruba language will become an endangered language in its language environment. The focus of this paper is the assessment of the situation through the evaluation of the Yoruba language curriculum at the senior secondary school. This work is the outcome of a postgraduate research carried out at the University of Ilorin, Ilorin, Nigeria. It was carried out in the senior secondary schools in Oyo state. The choice Oyo state to represent the southwestern states was based on the homogeneity of the people of the state in terms of language variety and also the fact that the state commenced effective use of the curriculum as far back as 1985.

Language Planning and Policy in Nigeria

Language planning and policy are viewed as the preparation and implementation of a carefully worked out strategy for the cultural use of languages in various ranges of action in the life or lives of the people of a country and or a state within a federation (Adekunle, 1997). There is no gainsaying in the fact that there is need for language planning and policies in multilingual nation like Nigeria parading over 450 languages (Adegbija, 2004) that are unevenly distributed with uneven number of speakers. The various implications of multilingualism in a polity such as language loyalties, medium of instruction in schools, official or national functions as well as interaction amongst various ethnic groups in the country are well documented.

However, language planning and policies have rarely been documented in Nigeria (Bamgbose, 2001) though elements of planning can be seen in such situations as language use in education, legislation or in the media. Adegbija (2004) has also observed that there is no document that may be referred to as language planning legislation document, but the National Policy on Education (NPE) contains very important provisions, which may be regarded as the most comprehensive provisions available anywhere on language planning and policies in Nigeria.

The NPE was prepared by the Federal Government of Nigeria. It was first published in 1977 and revised in 1981, 1985 and 2004. It was the first major response to the calls for the formulation of a language policy for Nigeria, especially with respect to the domain of education. Consequent upon this, sections 51 and 91 of the 1979 constitution of the Federal

Republic of Nigeria stipulates that English shall be used as official language in Nigeria; Hausa, Igbo and Yoruba are to be used as co-official languages. They are also to be used in both states (of their language environment) and national assemblies. In addition, the use of indigenous languages in initial education and English at a later stage was also implied.

The language provisions as contained in the NPE are as follows:

Section 1: 10a:
In addition to appreciating the importance of language in educational process and as a means of preserving the people's culture, the government considers it to be in the interest of national unity that each child should be encouraged to learn one of the three major languages other than his mother tongue. In this connection, government considers the three major languages to be Hausa, Igbo and Yoruba (NPE, 2004:5).

Section 2: 14c:
Government shall ensure that medium of instruction will be principally the mother tongue or the language of the immediate community and to this end will: (a) develop the orthography for many more Nigerian languages, and (b) produce textbooks in Nigerian languages. (NPE, 2004:7)

Section 4: 19e & f:
The medium of instruction in the primary schools shall be the language of the environment for the first three years. During this period English shall be taught as a subject. From the fourth year, English shall progressively be used as a medium of instruction and the language of the immediate environment and French shall be taught as subjects (NPE, 2004:10-11).

The NPE also made pronouncements on languages at both junior and senior secondary schools, but there are no direct policies. Students at the Junior Secondary School (JSS) are supposed to study two Nigerian languages one of which should be the Language of Immediate environment (LIE) in addition to the identified three main Nigerian languages subject to the availability of teachers (NPE, 2004:4). At the Senior Secondary School (SSS) which is the focus of this study, the students are expected to offer one Nigerian language. The policy was however vague as to which language to be learnt. Thus, is it the MT or the LIE or one of the three main languages (L2)?

The issue was later resolved by the National Council on Education, the highest ruling body on education that it is the L2 that is to be learnt not the MT or LIE. This particular provision has created a major setback in the teaching and learning of Yoruba language in its language environment at SSS level of education. Many principals hide under this provision to discourage the effective teaching and learning of Yoruba language even when there are no teachers to teach the L2. The pertinent question is how then do we produce teachers to undertake the teaching of Yoruba as both L1 and L2 since the senior secondary school was supposed to prepare students for higher studies in their various fields, if the subject is not learnt at this level of education?

The implementation of these various provisions necessitated the production of curriculum in the different subject areas. In the case of the three main Nigerian languages, a single curriculum was produced by the Federal Ministry of Education. It contained contents both in the areas of language and literature. Two syllabi were later produced from the curriculum for the Yoruba language and Yoruba literature as two separate subjects. The language attains a core subject status while the literature becomes optional. This is an innovation in the teaching and learning of Yoruba language which used to be learnt as a single subject. It is our opinion this is not in the best interest of the learner considering the fact that literature establishes literacy in the language and also sustain the vitality of the language. Even in second language teaching, integrative curriculum is being advocated in the language arts, where a piece in literature can be used to teach aspects of the language.

Moreover, competence in Yoruba language requires the study of its culture which constitutes a major part of its literature. There are many expressions in Yoruba, which would be ordinarily unintelligible to those who are ignorant of the cultural or historical basis of such experiences (Abiri, 1981). For example,

> Akini n je akini
> Afinihan n je afinihan
> Ewo ni, pele o, ara Ibadan
> Lojude Sodeke.

Translation:

> *A courteous person differs from a betrayer*
> *What is, how do you do, Ibadan man*
> *At the front of Sodeke's house.*

This proverb is derived from the historical fact that Sodeke was the warlord of the Egbas during their war against the Ibadan people, hence an Ibadan man was in serious danger if found around Sodeke's house.

The implication of this innovation ushered in by the implementation of the language provisions of NPE is hereby addressed in this study. Yoruba language teachers' opinions were sought as par the implication of the innovation on the effective teaching and learning of the language. The following research questions were raised for the purpose of the study:

1. What are the opinions of the teachers on whether the needs of the learners have been identified in the senior secondary school Yoruba language curriculum?

2. What are the opinions of the teachers on whether the objectives reflect the identified needs of the learner?

3. What are the opinions of the teachers on whether the objectives are clearly stated?

4. What are the opinions of the teachers on the adequacy of the curriculums contents for the achievement of the stated objectives?

5. What are the opinions of the teachers on the adequacy of the instructional materials for the implementation of the curriculum?

6. What are the opinions of the teacher on the adequacy of the quality and quantity of Yoruba language teachers?

7. What are the opinions of the teachers on the optional learning of Yoruba literature?

8. What is the trend of students' performance in the senior school certificate examination in Yoruba language?

Methodology

The study adopted descriptive research of the survey type. The target population was the Yoruba language teachers at the senior secondary level. The evaluation was based on the adapted version of CIPP evaluation model formulated by Stufflebeam and his Associates in 1971. Data were gathered on the opinions and preferences of teachers on all aspects of the senior secondary school Yoruba language curriculum. Two research instruments were used. They were a researcher designed questionnaire and the West African Senior Secondary Certificate Examination (WASSCE) results in Yoruba language from 1996 to 2003.

The questionnaire items cover such areas of learners' needs, objectives of the curriculum and the issue of the relevance of Yoruba literature in the learning of the language. On the context variables, questions were asked on the needs and objectives of the curriculum while questions on input variable were on the quality and quantity of teachers, learning activities as well as other instructional materials that were available. On the other hand, questions on process variable were on the actual implementation of the curriculum in the school system. In the case of product variable, the WASSCE Yoruba language results from 1996 – 2003 were analyzed to assess the trend of the student's performance in the language. The data were analyzed using frequency counts and percentage distribution. Responses to the questionnaire items were based on a modified form of Likert's measurement scale. Purposive sampling technique was used to select all the 631 Yoruba language teachers teaching at the senior secondary level. 700 copies of questionnaire were produced and distributed, 631 were duly completed and returne

Results

Table 2 and Table 3 below show the number, qualification and areas of specialization of the Yoruba language teachers at the senior secondary school as at the time of the study.

Table 2: Percentage Distribution of Respondent based on their Qualification

Qualification	No	%
NCE	284	45.0
B. Ed	67	10.6
B. A (Ed)	255	40.4
B. A	13	2.1
B. A + PGDE	12	1.9
Total	631	100

The table above shows that 284 respondents representing 45. 0% of the total respondents were holders of National Certificate in Education (NCE). This is contrary to the federal government policy (1985) which stipulates that holders of NCE are not qualified to teach at the senior secondary level.

Table 3: Percentage Distribution of Respondent based on their area of Specialization

Area of Specialization	No	%
Language	514	81.5
Linguistics	39	6.2
Others	78	12.4
Total	631	100

The table above shows that the number and area of specialization of the Yoruba language teachers at the senior secondary. 78 respondents, representing 12. 4% of the total population, specialized in other fields not relevant to both language and linguistics such as in the science and social science.

Table 4: Identification of Learner's Language needs in the Curriculum

Learners' language need	SA	%	A	%	D	%	SD	%	TOTAL	%
Listening needs	145	23.0	349	55.3	97	15.4	40	6.3	631	100
Speaking needs	170	26.9	320	50.7	112	17.7	29	4.6	631	100
Reading skills	168	26.6	264	41.8	139	22.0	60	9.5	631	100
Writing skills	144	22.8	297	47.1	129	20.4	61	9.7	631	100
Cultural needs	121	19.2	243	39.5	185	29.3	82	13.0	631	100
Literary needs	81	12.8	315	49.9	181	28.7	54	8.6	631	100

To avoid tedium, 'strongly agreed' (SA) and 'agreed' (A) responses were collapsed to represent 'Agreement'. Similarly, 'disagreed' and 'strongly disagree' (SD) were collapsed to signify 'disagreement'. Henceforth, comments would be based on the collapsed responses accordingly. Therefore, table 4 indicates that majority of the respondents agreed that all the language needs of the learners were identified in the curriculum.

Table 5: Adequacy and clarity of curriculum objectives

Questionnaire item	SA	%	A	%	D	%	SD	%	TOTAL	%
Clarity of the objectives	147	23.3	330	52.3	110	17.4	44	7.0	631	100
Do the objectives reflect the identified needs of the learners?	126	20.0	313	49.6	114	22.8	48	7.6	631	100

Table 5 above shows that 477 respondents, representing 75. 6, agreed that the objectives of the curriculum were clearly stated while 439 (69. 6%) respondents opined that the objectives of the curriculum reflected the identified needs of the learners. Opinions of the respondent were sought on the adequacy of curriculum content and learning activities for the achievements of the curriculum law objectives. Majority of the respondents agreed to the adequacy of the curriculum contents and learning activities as indicated on Table 6.

Table 6: Adequacy of the Curriculum Contents and Learning Activities

Questionnaire item	SA	%	A	%	D	%	SD	%	TOTAL	%
Adequacy of the Curriculum content	124	19.7	305	48.3	156	24.7	46	7.3	631	100
Adequacy of learning activities	102	16.2	339	53.7	136	21.5	54	8.6	631	100

As indicated below in Table 7, majority of the respondents agreed that there were no standard language laboratories, the library were not well equipped and that students did not possess relevant textbooks in the two subjects. But majority of the respondents agreed that there were adequate textbooks on both the language and the literature in the market. Majority of them also opined that there were no funds for the procurement of necessary teaching aids.

Table 7: Adequacy of Instructional Materials

Adequacy of Instructional materials	SA	%	A	%	D	%	SD	%	TOTAL	%
Standard languages laboratory	68	10.8	58	9.2	117	18.5	388	61.5	631	100
Well-equipped library	50	7.9	98	15.5	207	32.8	276	43.7	631	100
Relevant text for Yoruba language	50	7.9	141	22.3	228	36.2	212	33.6	631	100
Relevant text for Yoruba literature	56	8.9	137	21.7	208	33.0	230	36.4	631	100
Adequate text for Yoruba language in the market	199	31.5	248	39.3	92	14.6	92	14.6	631	100
Adequate text for Yoruba literature in the market	190	30.1	251	39.8	111	17.6	79	12.5	631	100
Funds for the procurement of teaching aids	57	9.0	188	29.8	210	33.3	176	27.9	631	100

Table 8: Adequacy of Yoruba Language Teachers

	SA	%	A	%	D	%	SD	%	TOTAL	%
Need to employ more teacher	184	29.2	198	30.6	110	17.4	144	22.8	631	100

Table 8 above shows that majority of the respondents were of the opinion that the number of teachers were inadequate and that there is need to employ more qualified teachers for the effective implementation of the curriculum.

Table 9: Suitability of the Methods used in Separating Yoruba Language from the Literature

	SA	%	A	%	D	%	SD	%	TOTAL	%
Suitability of the erstwhile method of combined teaching of language and the literature	125	19.8	255	40.4	128	20.3	123	19.5	631	100
Separation of the two has enhanced the teaching of the language	112	17.7	225	35.7	15.9	25.2	135	21.4	631	100
Adequacy of the number of period for the teaching of the language	106	16.8	207	32.8	168	26.6	150	23.8	631	100

As shown in Table 9, 380 respondents representing 60.2% of the total population agreed that the erstwhile practice of teaching Yoruba language and literature as a single subject can better achieve the objectives of the curriculum. On the other hand 337 (53.4%) agreed that the separation has enhanced the teaching and learning of the language, while 194 (46.6%) claimed otherwise.

Key (for Table 4 – Table 9):

    SA   - Strongly Agreed

    A   - Agreed

    SD   - Strongly disagreed

    D   - Disagre

Table 10: Analysis of Students Performance in Yoruba Language at WASSCE 1996-2003 in Oyo State

Year	No of entries	A1–C6	%	D7–E8	%	F9	%
1996	33, 919	18530	54.63	6353	18.72	7499	22.10
1997	28, 088	14893	53.02	6500	23.14	6811	24.24
1998	38, 126	21045	55.19	8170	21.42	8443	22.14
1999	39, 537	14592	36.90	9939	25.13	12853	32.50
2000	49, 946	20927	41.89	12058	24.14	16934	33.90
2001	53, 209	28242	53.07	11554	21.71	12587	23.50
2002	42, 511	13798	32.45	11959	28.13	13762	32.39
2003	39, 707	9180	23.11	23017	57.96	4557	11.47

Table 10 shows that students' performances in Yoruba language have not been encouraging. The table presents a fluctuating performance. For instance, the best performance was recorded in 1998 when 21, 045 candidates representing 55. 19% of the total entries had credit passes, while 27. 42% had pass grades and 22. 14% failed. The poorest performance was in the year 2003. Out of the total entries of 39, 707 only 9, 180 candidates constituting 23. 11% of the total had credit passes, while 57. 9% had pass grades and 11. 47% failed. These findings, has presented in the tables will hereby be discussed.

Discussions and Conclusion

The findings of this study have so far justified the statement that the language provisions of the NPE were just mere statement of intentions. As can be deduced from the findings, the implementation of the policies lacks the necessary support both on the part of the policy makers and the society in general. The essence of the language provisions in the NPE was to evolve trilingual solution to the national language question. It was the belief that the use of the three major languages, if every pupil in addition to his MT learns one of them or community language will spread among the entire population within one generation and in future presumably the languages would be declared federal and so the national language question would be given a trilingual solution (Brann, 1977). The findings of this study which was carried out after over two decades of implementation of the language provisions as far as the first language learner of Yoruba concerned were not favourable to this position.

The findings showed that the curriculum for the first language learner (Li) was adequate, it was the implementation that was faulty. The instructional materials, both human and non-human were insufficient.

The separate teaching of both Yoruba language and literature was considered not in the best interest of the Li learners. As a matter of fact, this issue of separation has been reviewed. It is now back to a combined teaching and learning of the two as a single subject. It was effected in 2005.

Language teaching and learning at this level of education are very crucial to the success or otherwise of any language planning or policy in Nigeria. This is because the secondary school level is supposed to be the preparation for higher studies. Therefore, in order to have adequate teachers to undertake the teaching of this language as both L1 and L2, there is the need to have highly motivated and well trained products that will later proceed to the universities or colleges of education to build on a solid foundation. However, this is still a mirage considering the trends of performance as shown by the analysis of the WASSCE results for the past twenty years.

Learners need to be highly motivated in order to be able to learn. In addition, the selection of contents must be well graded according to the level and age of the learner. For instance, Adeyemi (1991) criticized the inclusion of phonological aspect of Yoruba language at the junior secondary school.

Similarly, Amoloye (2003) considered the inclusion of phonological topics which hitherto used to be taught at post secondary level as too ambitious and irrelevant for L1 learners at senior secondary level. She argued that since the majority of the learners are native speakers, the production of the sounds is automatic. She opined that this aspect should then be left till the tertiary level for those who wish to specialize in the language. The main objective for the teaching of Yoruba at secondary school level should be to expand the pupils' experiences through language, develop his personality and his sensibilities (Wilkins, 1972).

People now advocate for the necessary legislation and articulation of enabling policies for effective language planning. However, arising from the findings of this study, there is the need for sincerity of purpose and political will from both the government and the people who are entrusted to implement the policies. It is high time for the 'educated elite club' to realize that it is national development and not self interest, that is, in the long run, in the best interest of all and sundry. This probably will create a change in the attitude towards Nigerian languages in general. As it were, the students were poorly motivated and they did not consider any Nigerian language worth of study. In fact, Yoruba language has become a second language in many of our educated elite homes. Some even take pride in the fact that their children cannot speak Yoruba and then act as simultaneous interpreter for their children in interaction with illiterate family and friends. This attitude constitutes a clog in the progress of language planning in Nigeria. We therefore conclude with this paraphrased word of Mann (1996) that until those who have used the esteemed position of English to attain elite status are sympathetic to a change any attempt in language planning will not be fruitful.

References

Abiri, J. O. O. 1981. *Learning and Teaching Yoruba in Post Primary Institutions.* Lagos, Nigeria: Macmillan Nigeria Publishers Ltd.

Adegbija, E. 2004. Language policy and planning in Nigeria. *Current Issues in Language Planning,* Vol. 5, No. 3.

Adekunle, M. A. 1997. National language policy and planning: The Nigeria situation. *West African Journal of Modern Languages* 4, 21-30.

Adeyemi, O. (1991). Teachers' Assessment of the Adequacy of the junior secondary school Yoruba Language curriculum. Unpublished M. Ed project, University of Ilorin.

Amoloye, B. A. 2006. An Evaluation of the Senior Secondary school Yoruba Language Curriculum in Oyo State, Nigeria. Unpublished Ph. D. Dissertation. University of Ilorin, Nigeria.

____2000. The place of phonology in the learning of mother tongue: A review of the phonological aspect of Yoruba language curriculum at the secondary level. *Journal of Method, Language and Literature,* School of language, Oro, CEO 1 (2).

____1999. Mother Tongue in Education: A tool for national development. In *JOSIL: A publication of the school of languages, Ilorin* COE. 1(1), 28-36.

Awoniyi, T. A. 1978. *Yoruba Language in Education 1846–1974: A Historical Survey.* Oxford University Press.

Bamgbose, A, Akere, E & Ihebuzor, N. 1992. Implementation strategies for the language provisions of the National Policy on Education. Abuja, Nigeria: Language development centre. pp 25-37.

Bamgbose, A. 2001. Language Policy in Nigeria: challenges, opportunities and constraints. A paper presented at the Nigerian Millennium Sociolinguistics conference, University of Lagos, 16-18 August.

Brann, C. M. B. 1977. Language planning for Education in Nigeria: Some demographic, linguistics and areal factors. In Bamgbose, A. (Ed.). *Language in Education in Nigeria*. Lagos, Nigeria: The National Language Centre, FMOE, p. 47-61.

_____1980. The Role of language in Nigeria's educational policy. *The Nigeria Language Teacher Journa, 3(11) 5-1*.

Fafunwa, A. B. 1997. Our Educational Problems. News article in the *National Concord*. 6th July, p3.

Federal Republic of Nigerian. 1977. National Policy on Education. Lagos: Government Press. (Reprints: 1981, 1987, 1998, 2000, and 2004).

Jinadu, I. & Ihebzor, N. 1993. Developing Curriculum: Nigeria Languages. In Ivowi, N. M. (Ed). Curriculum Development in Nigeria. Ibadan, Nigeria: Sam Bookman Education Services.

Mann, C. C. (1996). Anglo-Nigerian Pidgin in Nigerian Education: A survey of policy, practice and attitudes. In T. Hickey and J. Willians (Eds.). Language, Education and Society in a changing World. Clevedon: Multilingual pp. 93-106.

Stufflebeam, D. L. et al. 1971. Educational Evaluation and Decision Making. Ithaca, Illinois: F. E. Peacock.

Wilkins, D. A. 1972. Linguistics and Language Teaching. London: Richard Clay (The Chaucer Press) Limited.

Chapter 8

KANGA CAPTIONS: SOCIAL AND POLITICAL COMMUNICATION WITH APPLICATION TO KISWAHILI LANGUAGE TEACHING AND LEARNING

Alwiya S. Omar

Introduction

'Kanga', also referred to as 'leso', is an important piece of cloth worn by women in East Africa. It is used as a vehicle of indirect communication in socio-cultural as well as socio-political domains. It is the cloth that speaks (Zawawi 2005), and a vehicle that conveys ambiguous signs (Beck 2001), women's messages (Linnebuhr, 1997), women's voices (Yahya-Othman, 1997), and women's statements (Cohen 2005). 'Kanga' is also linked to different aspects of a woman's life cycle (Hamid, 1995; Zawawi 2005). In this paper, we will first provide a brief history of the kanga and how it is used in indirect communication in the socio-cultural domain. For the political aspect, we will discuss the history of politics in Tanzania focusing on symbols and 'kanga' captions used to convey political messages. We will also discuss how the 'kanga' can be used to reinforce the 5 Cs of the National Foreign Language Standards (Communication, Cultures, Comparisons, Connections, and Community). Data used for this paper come from newspaper articles, web resources, as well as from previous literature on the kanga, the author's 'kanga' collection, and her personal experience and personal communication (pc). [1]

History of the Kanga

In May 1995, there was a one-week symposium held in Dar Es Salaam, Tanzania on the history and uses of 'kanga'. The symposium was organized by a non-governmental organization called Tanzania Media Women's Association (TAMWA). The proceedings from the symposium were published in the Jukwaa newspaper of Zanzibar as a series of articles that provided a detailed description of the history of 'kanga' and its use in indirect communication. According to Hamid, one of the writers of these articles, women in the rural areas of Zanzibar used to wear a black cotton wrapper called 'kaniki'. Indian cloth merchants of Zanzibar decided to transform the 'kaniki' by adding white spots on it. As a result, the wrapper took the appearance of the guinea fowl, black with white spots. The transformed 'kaniki' became 'kanga', the Kiswahili name for *guinea fowl*.

Figure 1: Guinea fowl

Parallel to the use of 'kaniki' and 'kanga' worn by women in the rural areas, was the use of colorful Portuguese silk scarves 'leso' by wealthy women of Zanzibar town and Mombasa. Six scarves were combined to form a 'leso' of the same size as the 'kanga'. The 'leso' was expensive and only rich town women could afford to buy. Indian merchants decided to make two transformations to the cotton 'kanga': colorize it and make it affordable for all women to purchase. They also added captions to the 'kanga' that later on became the source of indirect communication. The 'kanga' became a colorful cotton wrapper that comes in 'doti' *pair*. It has 'pindo', *border*, 'mji', *town*, and 'jina', *name*. The words 'kanga' and 'leso' are now used interchangeably; 'kanga' mainly used in Tanzania and 'leso' in Kenya, Comoros and other areas.

Names or captions first appeared on the 'kanga' in the Arabic script. Even though most of the women who used the 'kanga' did not know Arabic, they were literate in the Arabic script. They could read the Qur'an, and also read and write their native language, Kiswahili, using the Arabic script. With the arrival of the Germans and the British in the

19th Century, and introduction to Christianity and western education, the Latin script was introduced and kanga captions started to appear in the Latin script. It is very rare these days to find 'kanga' messages written in the Arabic script but it is possible to find one or two like the following 'kanga' that the author purchased in Zanzibar in 2006.

Figure 2: Kanga with caption in Arabic script

1. 'Sitomwacha mume wangu kwa mnon'gono wa mtaani'
I won't leave my husband because of the rumors in the neighborhood

Even though the use of 'kanga' started on the coast of East Africa, it is widely used by women in eastern and central Africa, the islands of Comoro and Madagascar, Middle Eastern countries like Oman and Dubai, and even in some parts of West Africa. Hamid (1995) says this about the wide spread use of the 'kanga':

"Siku hizi kanga imetoa mikia ya pweza na imetawala mpaka sehemu za ndani za Afrika na kwengineko duniani."

These days 'kanga' has spread octopus tentacles to inland areas of Africa and to other parts of the world"

A Peace Corps volunteer and a friend of the author, Abbie Hantgan, while working as a Peace Corps Volunteer in Mali, visited Cameroon and bought a kanga there (pc). The caption of Hantgan's 'kanga' is:

2. Nimenusurika
I am saved

'Kanga' captions also appear in Shingazija, a variety of Kiswahili spoken in the Ngazija Island of the Comoro Archipelago as in Example 3 from the author's collection.

3. Hayiri karibou
Better welcome/come in

Socio-cultural uses of the Kanga

The use of the 'kanga' developed and became an integral part of the culture and traditions of the Waswahili. It is typical for a woman to have dozens of 'kanga' in her cupboard and it is possible that she received training on how to take care of the kanga from the time she reached puberty. Maintaining the 'kanga' is an art: great care is taken when washing the kanga, when lining it up to dry, when folding it, and when placing it in the cupboard. The order in which a 'kanga' is used is very important. It is discouraged to wash a 'kanga' one day and use it the next day as Hamid (1995) points out:

> 'Ni vizuri kuweka kwa mpango kama vile kanga zilizofuliwa mwisho kuwekwa juu na unapotaka kutumia kuchukua za chini. Mpango huu huleta duru ya mzunguko wa sawa na huepusha kurudia kanga mapema kabla zamu yake. Kwa hali yo yote ile kanga ikitunzwa vizuri hupendeza.'

> *'It is better to have a plan like recently washed kanga to be kept on top and to take ones from the bottom to use. This plan brings equal rotation and avoids early use of kanga before its turn. By any means if a kanga is taken good care of it will always be attractive.'*

It is not uncommon for an older woman to reprimand a younger one when the latter does not follow the right procedures in 'kanga' care.

Kanga and Life Cycle

The 'kanga' plays an important role in each of the following aspects of a woman's life:

Birth → puberty → marriage → Death.

When a baby is born the 'kanga' acts as a receiving blanket whether the baby is a boy or a girl. The 'kanga' can be used as baby diapers, as a belt to tighten the mother's stomach in order to reduce the effects of pregnancy, and as a baby carrier. A woman becomes an experienced 'kanga' user because of the training she got when she was growing up. In Moslem communities, a young girl of five or six years of age going to Qur'an school uses the 'kanga' to cover her head. At puberty, she starts using a pair of 'kanga' to tie one at the waist and one to cover the head and shoulders when she starts praying which is obligatory when a girl reaches puberty. When a young woman becomes a bride she gets dozens of kanga. Some to use with her husband who can wear the kanga only in the privacy of the bedroom. A bride is given a special kanga called 'kisutu' – a black, red, and white. Hamid (1995) and Zawawi (2005) explain the meaning of these three colors: red signifies the blood that the bride gets the first time she has intimate relation with a man, her husband; black signifies the pain she gets, and white the pleasure which comes after the pain. Hamid (1995) provides another explanation on the significance of these colors: if there is an accidental spotting, the bride will not feel bad because the spotting will appear like the red of the 'kanga'. When it is time to pass on to the next world, a woman is washed and dried with several pairs of kanga that are later given to the washer and her assistants. The woman's casket is covered with a 'kanga' to indicate that the person who is being sent to the graveyard is a woman.

Figure 3: 'Kanga' as a baby carrier

'Kanga' and indirect communication

Indirect communication in African societies has been discussed in detail in Obeng (1994, 1997, 2003). Obeng shows that indirect communication, both verbal and written, is a communicational strategy that is used to send out messages, to obviate crises or to avoid losing face. Indirectness helps to manage conflicts and confrontations while remaining polite. In Akan discourse, people use circumlocution. innuendos, and metaphors as strategies for indirect communication. These strategies provide interlocutors with a certain degree of protection and immunity while communicating a matter of difficulty. The same strategies are used with 'kanga' writings. Yahya-Othman (1997) provides a report of her interview with women from Zanzibar on the use of 'kanga' writings as indirect communication. One of the reasons given by the women is that 'kanga' writings provide a venue to let off steam and to let their voices heard. A response to a 'kanga' name is done by another 'kanga' name. In using 'kanga' names to communicate, the women that Yahya-Othman interviewed felt that they would be able to avoid conflicts and physical contact, and at the same time they would uphold respect, or remain polite.

Types of socio-cultural messages

'Kanga' is an ideal gift to give. In buying a pair of 'kanga' as a gift particular care is taken to choose the right kind of message that is straightforward and unambiguous. 'Kanga' given as a gift may have messages of love. Traditionally, it is rare for a mother to tell her children she loves them and vice versa but this can be done through a kanga message. A kanga with the following message can be given to a mother by her daughter or by her son.

4. Penzi la mama ni tamu haliishi hamu
Mother's love is so sweet that you never have enough of it (Hassan, 1995)

And the following message from the author's collection achieves the same purpose of expressing love for one's mother:

5. Nani kama mama?
Who is like mother? (meaning: there is no one like mother)

'Kanga' can have messages of conventional wisdom providing advice and warnings. Parents can give these kinds of messages to their children, and friends can give advice to each other. One such message is that in Example 6 that encourages someone to take her time to do something well and not to rush and do it badly

6. Haraka haraka haina baraka
Haste makes waste (Hongoke, 1993)

Below are messages from the author's collection that give the receiver advice or warnings:

7. Ukitaka radhi uwaheshimu wazazi
If you want blessings you must respect your parents

8. Siri ya nyumbani usitoe nje
Secret of the home should not be taken out

9. Apendaye halipizi
S/he who loves does not revenge

10. Pombe si maji
Beer is not water

Some 'kanga' captions may convey religious messages like examples 11 to 16 below from the author's collection, and example 17 (Hantgan pc):

11. Yote yatendwayo namkabidhi mola
All that are being done I leave to God

12. Mola ndiye atakayeniongoza
God is the one who will lead me

13. Mungu ni muweza wa kila jambo
God is capable of everything

14. Ya rabi nijaaliye kila la kheri
O God grant me everything that is blessed

15. Mola ibariki ndoa hii iwe ya kheri na baraka
God bless this marriage

16. Eid Mubarak
Happy Eid (after the fasting month of Ramadan and after pilgrimage)

17. Nimenusurika
I am saved (Hantgan, pc)

Particular attention needs to be given while buying 'kanga'. The message is more important than the pattern or the color. On one of the author's visits to Zanzibar, she decided to buy 'kanga' as gifts and because she was in a hurry, she did not check the captions. It turned out that she was not able to give out some of them as gifts. Here are a few examples:

18. Vishindo vya nini na wewe si wako?
Why all the noise and he is not yours?

19. Wakerekao shauri zao watakufa siku si zao
Those who are unhappy it is their problem, they will die before their time

A 'kanga' that has a message like that of Example 18, will be worn by a woman who thinks some other woman is going out with her husband. Example 19 sends a message to people who are not happy about some thing that the woman who wears the 'kanga' has done to show that she does not care about what they think. The messages in Examples 20 and 21 could be given as a gift between two friends who are always fighting and one wants to reconcile and finish the fight.

20. Kila siku ugomvi tutapatana lini?
Daily, we are quarreling, when will we reconcile?

21. Nimesafi moyo wangu wala sioni uchungu
I have cleared my heart and I don't feel bad

Yahya-Othman (1997) provides an example of two neighbors who had quarreled and one of the neighbors decided to stop the verbal fight but to continue non-verbally using 'kanga' names. Example 22 is one of the 'kanga' names she used:

22. Maneno yako yaishe wala usiyazidishe
Not another word! (Yahya-Othman, 1997)

In her articles on the history and uses of kanga Hamid (1995) shows how a wife sends indirect messages to her husband if she thinks her husband is cheating as Example 23 shows.

23. Mke wa nyumbani ni mwangaza wa chumbani
A wife in the home is light in the (bed) room. (Hamid, 1995)

Two identical kanga of this message would be placed on the bed before bedtime. The husband may or may not comment on it. Other captions from the author's collection that convey messages connected to marital relationship are:

> 24. Sitomwacha mume wangu kwa mnongono wa mtaani (Arabic script)
> *I will not leave my husband because of the rumors in the neighborhood*

> 25. Wapendanao ni sisi hebu tupeni nafasi
> *We are the ones who love each other, give us space*

> 26. Si mizizi si hirizi kanipenda kwa mapenzi
> *It is not roots it is not amulets, he loves me for love*

Another function of the 'kanga' is to convey gratitude. Sometimes it is hard for people to show gratitude verbally and therefore the gratitude may be expressed indirectly with a 'kanga' as in Example 27 from the author's collection.

> 27. Nikulipe nini? Kwa mema ulionitendea
> *How can I pay you? For the good you have done for me*

Political symbols and messages

Women not only use 'kanga' to air issues about their lives but also to show their views of respective political parties that they belong to. They also wear kanga that have captions that promote different programs organized by government and by non-governmental organizations on health, education, economy, and culture. One prominent woman politician, the late Bibi Titi Mohammed was quoted in the Jukwaa newspaper as saying:

> "Nilijiwa na Wahindi wakanipiga picha huku nikiwa nimenyanyua mkono wangu juu, ikiwa ni ishara ya kudai uhuru. Alisema, " Bibi Titi huku akionyesha kanga iliyochapishwa mwaka 1959, yenye picha yake hiyo aliyoieleza

> *"Some Indians (kanga merchants) came to me and took a picture of me holding my hand up as a sign of demanding independence, " Bibi Titi said while showing the 'kanga' which was printed in the year 1959, which has the picture she was talking about.* (Hamid 1995)

The hand being held high referred to by Bibi Titi Mohammed was a universal symbol during the fight for independence in many countries in Africa and elsewhere.

Symbols are very important in conveying the mottos and ideologies of political parties. Obeng (2003) cites political symbols used by different parties in Ghana. These symbols include elephant, rooster, umbrella, and man and woman holding hands. Elephant signifies strength and endurance but members of the opposing party would refer to it as destructive. The rooster heralds a new day and new beginnings, but it would be referred to as soft and weak compared to the elephant. While the umbrella provides shade, it can be interpreted negatively in that it can cause accident due to having a pointed end. A man and a woman holding hands can be interpreted as gender equality and a sense of community but members of opposing parties may see the act of two people of opposite sex holding hands as promiscuous.

In Zanzibar during the fight for independence in the late 1950s and early 1960s when Zanzibar was under British rule there were two main parties: the Afro-Shirazi party (ASP) and the Zanzibar Nationalist party (ZNP). There was also a Zanzibari sultan of Omani origin. The results of the elections that were held in 1963 declared that ZNP, the party that favored the sultan, won. Independence was declared on December 9th, 1963. A month later, on January 12th, 1964, a revolution led by the ASP took place in Zanzibar and the king went into exile in Britain. During these electoral campaigns there were no women who ran for office but they played an important role in sending out messages of their respective parties through the 'kanga'. The two main parties had the following logos or symbols: the ASP had a well as its logo and the logo for the ZNP was a rooster. For the ASP, the well symbolized the struggle of the people. The majority of Zanzibaris led a hard life. The water in the well symbolized better life to come. The rooster for the ZNP signified new life and a brighter future. At dawn the cry of the rooster hailed a new beginning.

There happens to be two Kiswahili proverbs that are linked with the well and the rooster. These proverbs have been in existence long before the political parties:

28. Jogoo wa shamba hawiki mjini
A country rooster would not crow while in town (wider meaning: some things only fit in some environments) (Hassan, 1995)

29. Mchimba kisima huingia mwenyewe
He who digs a well gets himself inside (wider meaning: if you have bad intentions against others, chances are, you will be affected directly or indirectly) (Hassan, 1995)

These proverbs were used as 'kanga' names and became two important messages in the 1963 electoral campaigns. Women from the ASP used the 'rooster' proverb to send a message to ZNP leaders that they were not capable enough to govern the islands and women from the ZNP used the 'well' proverb to inform ASP leaders that they had bad intentions for the islands and they would pay dearly for this. These two messages seemed to have had a certain kind of prophecy. The ZNP leaders won the 1963 elections and formed a new government but they were in power for one month only. The revolution took them by surprise. The ASP took control of the islands but things did not go well for some ASP members. During the initial years of the revolution several ASP members holding opposing views were imprisoned and killed by the revolutionary government. In 1972, Mheshimiwa Abeid Amani Karume, the first president of Zanzibar, was assassinated. The saying '*He who digs a well gets himself inside*' seemed to have been true to some extent and so did the saying on '*The country rooster can not crow in the city*'.

Zanzibar got its independence from the British after Tanganyika. Tanganyika African National Union (TANU) was the party that led Tanganyika to Independence on December 9, 1961. Peg Snyder (pc) emailed the author the caption in Example 30 with description below it.

30. Africa si Ulaya, Tanganyika ni kwetu
Africa is not Europe. Tanganyika is our home (Snyder, pc)

'It's green and gold and black. Large map of Africa with "Africa si Ulaya" printed on it. And below: "Tanganyika ni kwetu". There are giraffes in the corners, and palm trees on the border.'

Example 30 indirectly told the British colonizers to get out of Africa in general and Tanganyika in particular. It told them that their continent was Europe and not Africa and that Tanganyika was not their home. Also the map of Africa signified the vision for Africa that Mwalimu Nyerere, the first president of Tanganyika and later Tanzania, had. This vision was that of unity among African countries. Soon after the Zanzibar revolution Tanganyika united with Zanzibar islands in April 1964 to form the United Republic of Tanzania. This vision of unity is seen in the Tanzania Coat of Arms motto shown in Example 31.

31. Uhuru na umoja
Independence and unity

When Mwalimu Nyerere died on October 14, 1999, a kanga was printed with the following caption:

32. Majonzi tunayo Tanzania (Mayrene Bentley pc)
We have sadness in Tanzania

The era of one party ended in 1995 when for the first time since independence and Zanzibar revolution there were multi party elections. The main parties that we will discuss in this section of the paper are Chama Cha Mapinduzi (CCM) that is a union between the ASP of Zanzibar and the TANU of mainland Tanzania that took place in 1977. In 1995 and in subsequent multi party elections in 2000 and in 2005, it was always the CCM presidential candidate that won the elections. So Civic United Front (CUF) came up with the caption in Example 33 that encouraged CUF members to be patient and that change would come one day.

33. Subira yavuta kheri
Patience brings blessings

The caption in Example 34 indirectly points out the alleged unequal treatment that exists in some situations. It is alleged that there is discrimination in allocation of scholarships for Zanzibari students to continue with higher education. It is students with links to government officials that get priority.

34. Haki sawa kwa wote
Equal rights for all

And the message in Example 35 encourages CUF members to hang in there and not lose hope:

36. Ari mpya nguvu mpya
New motivation new strength

During previous electoral multiparty campaigns there were tensions that sometime led to violence between CUF and CCM members and government security forces intervened and it was alleged that victims of shootings by the government security forces were CUF members. So CUF members fought back indirectly with kanga captions:

37. Hamadi kibindoni silaha mkononi
Place your reserve safely and take arms

38. Akutendaye mtende (Ummi Bawazir nad Zayna Omar, pc)
Tit for tat

39. Si mkuki si bunduki CUF siibanduki (Ummi Bawazir and Zayna Omar, pc)
Not an arrow not a rifle I won't leave CUF

In the midst of the violence CCM came up with a kanga with the following caption:

40. Amani na utulivu Zanzibar (Ammal Salim, pc)
Peace and tranquility in Zanzibar

In addition to indirectly conveying a message of peace, the message in Exaple 40 plays with words. 'Amani' is also the name of the current president of Zanzibar 'Amani Abeid Karume', the son of the first president of Zanzibar who was assassinated in 1972. And the CUF caption in Example 37 also plays with words. The word *'Hamadi'* in *'Hamadi kibindoni silaha mkononi'* is the last name of the opposing presidential candidate Seif Shariff Hamadi.

The ruling party in Zanzibar produced the following kanga captions to show that because it had been in power since the 1964 revolution it must be doing well.

41. Heko miaka 30 ya uhuru wa mapinduzi Zanzibar
Congratulations 30 years of revolutionary freedom in Zanzibar

42. Miaka 40 mapinduzi ni kielelezo cha ufanisi
Forty years of the revolutionary indicates success

And because CCM has continued to rule for a long time, it has become care provider 'mlezi' for Zanzibaris.

43. CCM mlezi wa Wazanzibari
CCM is the care provider of Zanzibaris

The caption in Example 44 also shows that CCM leaders are patting themselves on the shoulder for what they think is a job well done:

44. CCM NO 1 (Ammal Salim, pc)

On the other hand, CUF, the opposing party in Zanzibar, does not agree with CCM statements of success and they indirectly respond with the following kanga caption:

45. Alaa Kumbe
Is that so?

The following CUF captions encourage Zanzibaris to vote for a better future:

46. Nikopeshe kura yako nikulipe
Lend me your vote so that I can pay you back

47. Kwa raha zetu
For our relaxation

48. Ipigie kura CUF uishi bila ya hofu (Ammal Salim, pc)
Vote for CUF so that you live without fear

Promotion of different programs

As pointed out earlier, kanga captions are also used to promote different programs by the government as well as non-governmental organizations. The following captions promote health.

49. Mtu ni afya
A person is health

50. Ondoa kipindu pindu
Eradicate cholera

51. Jihadhari na ukimwi
Protect yourself drom HIV/AIDs

Examples 52, 53, and 54 are used to promote education, agriculture, and culture respectively:

52. Elimu ni ufunguo wa maisha
Education is the key to life

53. Kilimo ni uti wa mgongo
Farming is (our) backbone

54. Tutukuze utamaduni wetu
Let's value our culture

Another caption is that of promoting housing:

55. Afro Shirazi Imefanya Kazi Kutupatia Malazi" (William Bissel pc)
Afro Shirazi has worked to provide us with housing
(with a picture of large housing blocks in the background)

Pedagogical Application

The kanga and its many uses is an important pedagogical resource in the teaching and learning of Kiswahili. In this section, the author provides different ways that the kanga can be integrated in the language classroom to reinforce the 5 Cs of the National Foreign Language Standards. See Appendix 2 for detailed description of these Standards:

1. Communication: Communicate in languages other than English

The interpretive communicative skills of the learners will be greatly enhanced by reading captions used in different socio-cultural and socio political situations. Assignments linked to these captions can be given to enhance interactive and presentational communicative skills.

2. Cultures: Gain knowledge and understanding of other cultures

Learners will be exposed to the 'kanga' as a cultural product. They will learn different cultural practices that are linked to the 'kanga' as discussed in section 3 above.

3. Connections: Connect with other disciplines and acquire information

Learners can make connections to other disciplines like History, Politics, and Gender relations using 'kanga' captions and 'kanga' as a cultural product.

4. Comparisons: Develop insight into the nature of language and culture

Learners can compare the use of the 'kanga' in indirect communication with different ways of communication in their own cultures like writings on T-shirts, walls, and messages on cars

5. Community: Participate in multilingual communities at home and around the world

Learners can participate in community events outside the school or during campus language festivals and demonstrate multiple uses of the kanga.

Teachers can introduce the 'kanga' at different levels of language study. At the lower levels, teachers can dedicate one 'kanga' as the 'kanga of the week' with an accompanying caption possibly a proverb with its meaning. At lower levels, teachers can demonstrate different uses of the kanga and can provide pictures from 101 uses of the kanga by Hanby (2006). At higher levels, the textbook by Omar and Rushubirwa (2007) can be used. In this textbook, one chapter focuses on the kanga and provides different activities that enable learners to reinforce their communicative as well as other skills. The following activity, for example, reinforces the C of *Community* as well as those of *Communication and Cultures*.

Mchezo wa kuigiza *Role play*

> Darasa lenu la Kiswahili limekaribishwa katika maonyesho yaliyotayarishwa na chama cha walimu wa Kiswahili kusherehekea siku kuu ya utamaduni wa kimataifa chuoni kwenu. Mmeombwa mwonyeshe namna mbalimbali kina mama huko Afrika Mashariki wanavyotumia kanga. Katika matayarisho hayo, kwanza, kila mwanafunzi afanye utafiti kuhusu angalau namna moja ya utumiaji wa kanga. Pili, kila mwanafunzi aeleze utumiaji huo unaashiria nini au kwa nini watu wanatumia kanga kwa namna hiyo. Tatu, wanafunzi wazingatie matumizi ya methali zilizopo katika kanga.

> *Your Kiswahili class has been invited to participate in a festival organized by Kiswahili teachers' association to celebrate international cultures in your university. You have been asked to show different ways in which women in East Africa use the kanga. In your preparation, each student should explain at least one use of the kanga. Second, each student should explain why the kanga is used in that way. Third, students should discuss the uses of the sayings on the kanga.*

Conclusion

In this chapter, we have seen that the 'kanga' also known as 'leso' is a very important cultural product in the lives of Swahili women in all walks of life. We have seen how it evolved historically from a black piece of cloth to the multi-colored one that communicates. It is a powerful vehicle of indirect communication socially and politically affecting men, women, and children. Only women can wear the kanga in public domain, hence women are a powerful force in disseminating opposing political views as well as promotions of different social programs. Socially, women communicate with each other through kanga messages. They argue, they offer solutions to problems, they send messages of love, they warn and advice, and they show appreciation. The kanga is a light piece of cloth with heavyweight interpretations and meanings. Pedagogically, it is a crucial cultural product and a great resource to Kiswahili language teachers and learners. An array of activities can be used in and outside the classroom to reinforce all skills encompassed in the 5Cs of the National Foreign Language Standards.

Notes

[1] A version of this work was presented as part of Wednesday seminar series at Indiana University, Bloomington in Spring 2007.

Web resources

Kanga History and Writings: http://www.glcom.com/hassan/kanga.html, Page maintained by Ali Hassan

TAMWA: http://www.tamwa.org/

National Foreign Language Standards http://www.discoverlanguages.org/i4a/pages/index.cfm?pageid=3392#standards

References

Beck, Rose Marie. 2000. Aesthetics of Communication: Texts on textiles (Leso) from the East African Coast (Swahili) in Research in African Literature Volume 31, number 4.

_____2001. Ambiguous Signs: the role of the 'kanga' as a medium of communication in Afrikanistische Arbeitspapiere, 68, pp 157-169.

Cohen, Steven. 2005. Textile as commodity, dress as text: Swahili kanga and women's statements. In Ruth Barnes (Ed.). *Textiles in Indian Ocean Societies*. New York: Routledge Curzon.

Hamid, Mahfoudha. 1995. Nini historia na matumizi ya kanga, kwenye gazeti la Jukwaa, matoleo ya Julai 3-9, Julai 10-16, Julai 17-23, na Julai 24 – 30, 1995, Zanzibar. (What is the history and use of kanga, in the newspaper Jukwaa, July 3-9, July 10-16, July 17-23, and July 24-30 issues, Zanzibar).

Hanby, J. 2006. Kangas: 101 Uses. Nairobi, Kenya: Haria's Stop Shop Ltd.

Hongoke, Christine J. 1993. The Effects of Khanga Inscription as a communication vehicle in Tanzania, Research report, 19. Dar es Salaam, Tanzania: Women's Research and Documentation Project.

Linnebuhr, E. 1997. Kanga: Popular cloths with messages. In Karin Barber (Ed.). Readings in African Popular Culture. Bloomington: Indiana University Press, pp 138-141.

Ngoji, Idrisa Haji. 1995. Burudani kwa majina ya kanga, kwenye gazeti la Jukwaa toleo la Agosti 7-13, 1995, Zanzibar. (Relaxation with Kanga names, in Jukwaa newspaper, August 7-13 issue.).

Obeng, Samuel Gyas. 2003. Language in African Social interaction: Indirectness in Akan communication. New York: Nova Science Publishers, Inc.

Omar, A. S. and Rushubirwa, L. 2007. Tuwasiliane Kwa Kiswahili: Let's Commuincate in Kiswahili. A text book for Advanced Learners. Madison, Wisconsin: NALRC Press.

Yahya-Othman, Saida. 1997. If the cap fits: 'kanga' names and women's voices in Swahili society. *Afrikanistische Arbeitspapiere,* 51, pp 131-149

Zawawi, Sharifa M. 2005. *Kanga: The Cloth that Speaks.* New York: Azania Hills Press

APPENDIX 1

(UNITED STATES OF AMERICA) NATIONAL FOREIGN LANGUAGE STANDARDS

*http://www.discoverlanguages.org/i4a/pages/index.cfm?
pageid=3392#standards*

1. Communication: Communicate in languages other than English

1.1 Interpersonal: engage in conversations, express feelings, exchange opinions
1.2 Interpretive: understand and interpret written and spoken language
1.3 Presentational: present information, concepts, and ideas to listeners/readers

2. Cultures: Gain knowledge and understanding of other Cultures

2.1 Practices: understanding of relationship of practices and perspective of the target culture
2.2 Products: understanding of relationship between products and perspective of target culture

3. Connections: Connect with other disciplines and acquire information

3.1 Making connections: reinforce further their knowledge of other disciplines
3.2 Acquiring information: recognize distinctive view points that are only available through the foreign language and culture

4. Comparisons: Develop insight into the nature of language and culture

4.1 Language comparisons: demonstrate understanding through comparisons of language studied and own language
4.2 Cultural comparisons: demonstrate understanding through comparisons of culture studied and own culture

5. Communities: participate in multi lingual communities at home and around the World

5.1 School and Community: use language both within and beyond school setting
5.2 Lifelong learning: use language for personal enjoyment and enrichment

Chapter 9

LANGUAGE CONTACT AND LANGUAGE USE: A STUDY OF IGBO UNDERGRADUATES IN SELECTED NIGERIAN UNIVERSITIES

Harrison Adéníyî and Rachael Bello

Introduction

Nigeria is linguistically a complex nation and the number of languages spoken within the country cannot be given with a degree of certainty. This derives from the problems of indeterminacy between language and dialect. However, majority of the authors claimed that we have between 300 and 510 languages in Nigeria. (K. Hansford, J. Bendor-Samuel, and R. Stanford 1976; J. Bendor-Samuel 1989; D. Crozier and R. Blench 1992; R. Blench 1998 2004; Raymond Gordon, G. Jr. (ed.), 2005). However, two of these languages, i. e. English and French, function as second language without mother tongue speakers. We can broadly divide the entire languages into three viz. major, semi-major and minor. Yorubá, Hausa and Igbo are categorized as major languages because of the numbers and spread of the speakers, their development as written languages; they are used as media of instruction and are taught as subjects in the curriculum. The speakers, because of the numerical strength, exert a lot of political influence within the country. (cf: Igboanusi and Peters 2005).

Languages such as Edo, Nupe, Fulfulde, Efik, Ibibio, Idoma, Itsekiri, Izon, Kanuri, Urhobo, Idoma, Ebirra, Tiv, etc. are classified as semi-major language. They are classified as such because they are only confined to the regions that they are spoken. These languages are oftentimes used in the media and are taught at the primary and junior secondary schools within the regions where they are spoken. Some of them are even offered at Diploma and Degree levels at the University, just like the majority languages. They equally have a sizable number of speakers; some of them run into a few millions. They play the roles of 'major' languages within the regions that they operate. Igboanusi and Peter (2005) however refer to them as medium languages.

The third category is the minor languages and they are spoken by small ethnolinguistic groups that are scattered throughout the country. They constitute up to about 85% percent of the entire languages in the country. Some of these include Ogu, Emai, Ghotuo, Ahan, Iyayu, Lokoo, Ika, Ikpeshi, Horom, Margi, Sukur, Obolo, Yala, Bokyi, Ukwa, Yekhee, Waka, Zedi, Oloma, Iguta etc. As noted by Oyetáde (n. d), majority of the languages in this group have lately become prominent in their respective states because of creation of new states. In most cases, the population of speakers of languages in this category does not exceed 100, 000 speakers.

English is the official language for business and administration in the country. Official government records are written in English. Although Nigerian languages are spoken in government offices, such language use more or less indicate familiarity, for in strict transactional relations, the more official the situation, the less likely is the use of non-official language. Parliaments both state and national conduct its deliberations in English. Although the Nigerian constitution also allows the three major languages i. e. Hausa, Igbo and Yoruba to function alongside with English in the parliamentary discourse, the government is yet to implement the sections of this constitution because of an escape clause that has already been built into it thus: "the business of the National assembly shall be conducted in English and in Hausa, Igbo and Yoruba when adequate arrangements have been made thereof (underline mine) (section 55, 1999 constitution). Also in the States House of Assemblies, the constitution says that: "The business of a House of Assembly shall be conducted in English, but the House may in addition to English conduct the business of the House in one or more other languages spoken in the State as the House may by resolution approve" (section 97, 1999 constitution). Since up till now adequate arrangements have not been made for the stipulated measures, it follows that English will continue to be the sole language of legislation. (Oyetáde n. d).

The laws of the country are written in English. In this connection, the mastery of English has also played a role in the destiny of those who aspire to achieve or "make" it in the country. English is the medium of instruction at virtually all levels of education. In fact, English is the single most important subject for anyone willing to aspire in the field of education. A pass at credit level in the English language in West African School Certificate/General Certificate in Education or National Examination Council is a sine qua non for any candidate wishing to study any course (even a degree in Edo, or any indigenous language for that matter) at any of our tertiary institutions in Nigeria. Even in these tertiary institutions, English language is mounted under the General Studies Program, and for students to be awarded any certificate or degree, he or she must, apart from fulfilling other requirements in the course of study, pass English language. Since knowledge of English guarantees academic advancement in Nigeria, mastery of the language is indicative of one being educated and, therefore, knowledgeable. Further, as Myers-Scotton (1993a) points out, English has the status of being an international language; the language of science and technology and by extension, the language for expressing forms of advancement and modernity (cf: Simango 2000). For the above reasons, no single Nigerian language rivals English for prestige.

French language has recently been given a national role in the constitution. For reasons best known to our government, French is now the second official language after English. The language has already been given a vital role to play in the educational sector. Thus, according to the National Policy on Education (2004:10) which says that; "For smooth interaction with our neighbors, it is desirable for every Nigerian to speak French. Accordingly, French shall be the second official language in Nigeria and it shall be compulsory in Primary and Junior Secondary Schools but non-vocational Elective at Senior Secondary". Pidgin on the other hand, readily complements English and the local languages in urban centers where the population is not homogenous.

Universities in Nigeria, just like in other countries of the world can be broadly classified into two, publicly or privately owned. The public Universities are either owned by the federal government or state governments, while the private universities are either faith based or owned by individuals. Some of these Universities are highly specialized in science and technology while majority run courses in almost all areas of human endeavor.

Background to the study

This research was informed by the unconscious but prevalent attitudes of members of the 'minor groups' in Nigeria to the mainstream language groups in the country. They would like to function or at least insist on functioning without dictates from other groups considering the linguistic rivalry amongst them. It is obvious, however that it is difficult if not impossible for members to live outside the world in which they find themselves.

The Igbo speech community is known not only by its determination to distinguish themselves as an economically relevant group in the country but also by its linguistic 'stubbornness'. However, the linguistic fortitude shown by this group does not seem to be carried all they way. Such is the behaviour of the Igbo undergraduates in the south-western universities examined. Naturally when languages come in contact, they work on each other. In some instances, however, a group may resolve not to be influenced by other groups with which they are in contact. This attitude may be brought about by different reasons. The linguistic behaviour of our informants, in spite of their wish to distinguish themselves, precipitated us into doing the research.

Theoretical Framework

The framework on which the study is anchored is Winford's (2003) model of contact language, language come in contact physically when members of the language in question naturally interact or through book learning via literature, religious texts, dictionaries etc. To Winford, language contact situations generally are subject to two often conflicting forces, which are the need to achieve communicative efficiency adequate for the purpose of interaction, dynamic of accommodation and the need to preserve a distinct sense of group identify. In his view, contact between people speaking different languages could have varied outcomes depending on several factors which include, the length and intensity of contact between the groups, the types of social, economic and political relationship between them, the functions which communication perform between them must serve and the degree of similarity between the languages they speak. (group loyalty) To him, the former encourage convergence or compromise between language, while the latter encourage divergence or preservation of language boundaries.

In Winford's opinion, dynamics of accommodation is at work in cases of borrowing in the spread of features across language and in the willingness of bilingual to switching and mixing codes. On the other hand, group loyalty features in the efforts of language purists to proscribe foreign influences on a language, in an attempt to maximize differences between language so as to assert cultural or ethnic differences and in the refusal to accommodate through code switching.

Methodology

Four major methods were adopted in gathering data for the research. They include participants' observation, natural recordings of discourses of informants' association meetings, the interview and the questionnaire.

Four universities in south-western part of the country were the targets. These Universities are University of Lagos, University of Ibàdan, Ogùn State University and the Lagos State University. Both researchers had been lecturers in some of the universities for a number of years. Consequently, they had observed both linguistic and non-linguistic behaviours of the informants. In fact, the study is the outcome of a research that has been on for at least four years. Furthermore, the informants were recorded at their various association meetings. The essence of our recording these transactions is to know how much loyalty they demonstrate as claimed. Moreover, some of our informants were interviewed to see if they consciously try to keep their languages apart, and to find out their attitudes to language other than the Igbo language.

The questionnaire, one of the methods employed, is made up of three sections. The first section sources the biographical data of the informants. The second section comprises fourteen (14) questions to which informants may or may not agree with to varying degrees. The third part, consisting of the open end questions simply examine informants' attitude to the languages they already speak or do not speak at all, and all these were analyzed.

Data Presentation and Analysis

From the informants' responses, there seems not to be age distinction for the respondents. Our analysis of informants' ages, for instance, shows that fifty nine (59%) of the informants are 16-25, thirty-six (36%) are between the age of 26 and 35 while the remaining 5% are above 35 years. The parity between respondents whose ages are below thirty-five and those above this age may be connected with the category of members of this group who have a need of having a university education.

Similarly, our analysis shows that seventy-seven (77%) of the respondents are female while thirty three (33%) are male. The difference again may be linked to the volition and or vocation members of the group under study are titled to. It is usual, for instance, to have the male members engage themselves more in trade while they leave the business of academics to the female members.

The respondents' languages of first contact range from Igbo, English, Yorubá, Hausa to Adon (Ghanaian language). Eight-one (81%) of the respondents acquired Igbo as their first language, sixteen (16%) of them came in contact first with English, the remaining three respondents' language of first contact are Yorubá, Hausa and Adon (Ghanaian language).

Strangely enough, however, going by the respondents' first languages, eighty seven (87) of the respondents, accounting for 87% of the total population predominantly use English. Nine (9%) of them mainly make use of Igbo in discourse while only three (3%) would opt for Yoruba in a situation they have a choice. These findings show that the first language a person acquires may after some time cease to be his dominant language, By implication, the language with which a person is most comfortable in is his dominant language. For example, the Canadian census defines first language for its purposes as the first language acquired in childhood and still spoken, recognizing that for some, the earliest language may be lost as a result of a process known as language attrition. This could result from various factors such as migration, vocation, attitudes by speakers, etc.

There are fourteen (14) questions in all in the section II of the questionnaire. They are closed-end question types. The analyses are presented below. For easy referencing, we number the questions in this section starting with the Roman numeral number (i). Ninety eight (98) of the respondents hold that the English language has succeeded in performing a unifying function among the different native University undergraduates on campus. However, two of the respondents representing only 2% of the total are of a contrary view. The unifying role of English talked about here may go beyond linguistics to include both psychological and emotional bond that the various native speakers enjoy. The result of the analysis of question (ii) vividly shows the emotional tie language users have with their first languages. Ninety nine (99) of the respondents either strongly agreed or simply agreed that irrespective of the status and linguistic functions of the English language in the country they are still emotionally entwined to their indigenous language.

Every linguistic group desires to be recognized and distinguished. The question of identity is of significance to a person as the need to have a language with which to communicate his/her thoughts is also required. Following this, Eighty four (84) of the respondents hold that the Igbo speech community stands out on campus irrespective of the population of the Igbo students. The remaining sixteen (16) students are of a contrary opinion. Related to the need for identify in the formation of associations which range from religions, social, linguistic to academic.

The question whether or not the non-verbal forms much more than the verbal form as a better means of identifying a person produced varying responses. While sixty three (63) of the respondents are of a contrary view, thirty seven (37) are of a positive opinion. It is believed generally that words alone are inadequate to convey the strong feelings behind the words. In this case, language users need other tools of communication which are classified as nonverbal behavior. Simply put nonverbal language deals with those things that the speaker does not say. Thus, members of the group under study were found to communicate unsaid, sometimes unimaginable messages through their artifacts, gestures and even look. Types of clothing generally, especially on days members of the Igbo students association have to meet, were found to denote both communal as well as signs of sharing.

Section (v) of the questionnaire sought to know if one of the yardsticks an Igbo student will identify with the larger group is on the overall population of the Igbo speakers on campus, fifty-six (56) of our respondents hold that the numerical strength of the Igbo speaking community even outside their geographical location whether or not members population is reasonable or not.

Forty-six (46) of our respondents agreed that other major languages pose a threat to the Igbo language on the various campuses in the southwestern part of Nigerian. However, fifty-seven (57) are of the view that other major languages do not pose any threat to the Igbo language. The insignificant difference in the two positions simply helps to show that language users could change existing claims or happenings. Thus, a group could choose to stay alive even in the face of threats.

Our analysis of question (vii) supports our immediate position above. For instance, while forty six of the respondents assert that the Igbo-English undergraduates are a minority group on campus; fifty three (53) believe that they are a majority group on campus.

In question (viii), the respondents are to take a position on whether the Yoruba'-English bilingual undergraduates are linguistically domineering on campus. This question indirectly tests the ability of major groups to use their codes functionally. Our analysis shows that seventy-two (72) of our respondents feel that they are linguistically domineering while twenty eight (28) feel otherwise. The implication of this is that the major linguistic group uses its language indescrimately not mindful of the setting larger community.

Fifty-nine (59) of the respondents agreed that it is easy for a user to separate his code as the situation of their use demands without mixing codes. The remaining forty-one (41) are of a contrary opinion. The ability of a multilingual/bilingual to separate his codes could be considered a linguistic expertise.

Languages influence one another when they are in contact although to a varying degree. In this paper, Ninety-one (91) of the respondents believe that English has more effect on the Igbo language. On the other hand, nine (9) are of a contrary view. The result complements when they use English lexis in contexts that ordinarily demand that their Igbo equivalents be used.

Ninety-four (94) of our respondents are of the opinion that they can manage the Igbo language effectively in communication in spite of competing languages. Six (6) submit that they cannot separate the Igbo code from other codes in their repertoire. It must be said however, that the ninety-four (94) respondents may not at all times use the Igbo language at a stretch without mixing it with other codes. This attitude may not be unconnected with natural and not mechanical properties languages possess especially in rapid speech.

The analysis of item (xii) reveals that eighty one (81) of the respondents either strongly agreed or simply agreed that the various Igbo associations on campus are a veritable avenue for promoting the Igbo language. Eighteen (18) of the respondents feel otherwise.

The group language users keep could influence their attitudes to their language. It in little wonder than that fifty three (53) of the respondents are of the view that their room-mates determine how they identify with the Igbo language. However, forty-seven (47) of them have a contrary opinion.

In the third section of the questionnaire, the respondents were asked if they would opt to learn the Yoruba' language should the need arise. From our analyses, the following were arrived at.

Seventy three (73) of our respondents are of the view that they will learn the Yoruba' language. The reasons they adduced vary. Some say that they want to be bilingual', some say that 'they like the language, ' some say that 'because of effective communication because they are in Yoruba' land', some say that 'just because they want to know more about Nigerian language'.

Nineteen (19) of our respondents are of the view that they do not want to learn the Yoruba' language because there is nothing to learn in the language, others within this group say that they are proud to be associated with the Igbo language, hence they do not see anything spectacular about learning Yoruba'. Eight (8%) of our respondents don't even know whether they want to learn the Yoruba language or not.

General Findings

The following findings were discovered from the study:

- There are more Igbo females than males in the southwestern Nigeria.
- The results show that Igbo students frequently code-switch/code-mix where all members are expected to understand discourses in the English language.
- From our interviews and observations during their meetings, discussions, deliberations are initiated in Igbo, however, after a period participants are forced to mix codes not only to carry all members along, but because of their inability to make a complete sentence in the Igbo language.
- Code switching and mixing are natural phenomenon of Igbo bilingual speakers.

Implications of study

In this section, we examine the implications of our findings for various concepts ranging from linguistic, social to language planning. The act of code-mixing and code-switching as exemplified by this group of language users especially in contexts where members do not have a need to so code-mix or code switch has implication for how language users relate their choice of language to their participants and even to contact these days. not many distinguish between formal and informal contexts in their choice of code.

Furthermore, the findings reveal the possibility of the Igbo-English community, with its increasing formal education, becoming ignorant of certain Igbo lexis. This is obvious in their replacement of Igbo items with their English equivalents even when the linguistic situation does not demand this.

Moreover, our findings suggest that major language groups may become minority outside their immediate linguistic environments. Thus, a group may choose to be alive by not migrating from its original position. This, of course is highly difficult if not impossible.

Recommendations

The recommendations of this paper are useful both to speech communities as well as to the Government Speech groups may actively have to aspire to be distinct both within their immediate as well as their non-immediate geographical locations.

Similarly, multilingual societies, especially those which have English as their official language should be educated on the importance of identifying with their indigenous languages. After all, these indigenous languages are indices of identity.

Moreover, if the country, Nigeria really desires national integration, the idea of catchment areas and quota system where an outrageous number of those candidates of the State where a University is situated and only share the remaining insignificant percentage among candidates from other parts of the nation should be discouraged.

Conclusion

We have, from the foregoing, studied the verbal as well as the non-verbal behaviors of the Nigerian-Igbo undergraduate in selected Nigerian universities. We examined how members of this speech community are able to retain linguistic identity in-spite of their claim to be a unique group on campus. He observed that it is difficult it not impossible for members of this group even in their indigenous meetings to separate themselves from the English language even when their artifacts and ornaments portray how strongly they would want to be distinct.

References

Adégbìjà, E. 1994. The context of Language planning in African: An illustration with Nigeria. In Martin Putz, (Ed.). *Language Contact and language conflict*, pp. 139-163. Philadelphia: John Benjamins.

Adékúnlé, M. 2005. English in Nigeria: Attitudes, Policy and Communicative realities. In Ayo Bámgbósé et al (eds). *New Englishes: AWest-Afriacan Perspectives*. Ibadan, Nigeria: Masuro

Bendor-Samuel, J. (Ed.). 1989. *The Niger-Congo Languages*. Maryland: University Press of America.

Crozier, D. H. and Blench, R. M. (Eds.). 1992. *An Index of Nigerian Languages*. 2nd Edition. Texas: Summer Institute of Linguistics.

Federal Government of Nigeria. 2004. *National Policy on Education*. Lagos, Nigeria: National Educational Research Development Council.

Gordon, G., Jr. (Ed.). 2005. *Ethnologue: Languages of the World*. 15th Edition. Texas: SIL International.

Hansford, K., Bendor-Samuel J, and R. Stanford. 1976. An index of Nigerian Languages. *Studies in Nigerian Languages*, No. 5. Accra, Ghana: Summer Institute of Linguistics

Igboanusi, Herbert & Lothar Peter. 2005. Languages in Competition: The Struggle for Supremacy among Nigeria's Major Languages, English and Pidgin. New York: Peter Lang.

Myers-Scotton. 1993. The Social motivations for code-switching: Evidence form Africa. Oxford, England: Oxford University Press.

Oyetáde, S. O. n. d. The linguistic situation in Nigeria. Mimeograph.

Simango, R. S 2000. 'My Madam is fine': The adaptation of English loans in Chichewa. *Journal of multilingual and multicultural development*. Vol. 21. No. 6.

Winford, D. 2003. *An introduction to Contact Linguistics*. Malden, M. A: Blackwell Publishers.

Chapter 10

LANGUAGE RESTRICTION IN RADIO PROGRAMMING AS A SOURCE OF INDIGENOUS LANGUAGE PROMOTION: THE ORISUN FM AS A CASE STUDY

Adeola Adijat Faleye

Introduction

As one of the agencies of education, radio plays important roles in promoting the use of languages amongst people living in a society. Programmers and presenters on radio stations can therefore be regarded as informants and educators as well as entertainers. For the purpose of reaching larger audiences, specific dialects and major languages can be used as vehicles through which messages are conveyed to listeners. The radio station *Orísun* FM operates from the ancient city of Ilé-Ifè, with the intent of reaching different ethnic groups in Òsun state and across Nigeria. This paper investigates the extent of the role played by *Orísun* FM radio station in promoting and preserving Yoruba language use amongst its listeners.

Data Collection Procedure and Methodology

This study set out to analyze the extent to which "language restrictions" have promoted the use and revival of Yorùbá language as one of the three main languages used for official communication in Nigeria. The data used for this study were collected from interviews conducted with three levels of stakeholders in the *Orísun* FM radio station: presenters, participants and audience members. A key fact revealed by the data was that no language other than Yorùbá is used in *Orísun* FM's programmes. Evidence provided by the interviewees demonstrates the positive influence of this radio station in championing the revitalization of Yorùbá language throughout the country. The analysis of the data collected made use of the existing literatures on endangered languages to investigate the status of dialects and languages involved in the study. Data was also collected through a one-on-one interview process with key employees of the radio station. This was an important technique because it was most effective in gathering information from the people directly involved with a long list of programmes on *Orísun* FM radio station. Ten of such presenters, both men and women, were purposely selected. In addition to the interviews, more than ten different main programme segments were analyzed and listened to in full, this provided the necessary information for a determination of the level of adherence to the guiding principle of the station. Most of the programmes reviewed fall into the category of phone-in programmes. That is, the programmes tagged "Live" programmes/presentations.

For us to make for proper comparative study on the intent of the Orísun FM station among its pairs, other four radio stations within Òsun, Òyó, and Lagos state regions were also visited. This is conduct similar processes so that a proper placement of the *Orísun* FM station can be made. Finally, we employed the psycho-sociolinguistic theory for our analysis.

Figure 1: Nigerian map showing the 36 states, the Federal Capital Territory and the Yorùbá Speaking States /Locations

Source: http://www.motherlandnigeria.com/geography.html#Map

Literature Review

Yorùbá is the general name given to the language spoken in the Osun, Lagos, Oyo, Ogun, Ekiti, Ondo, and Edo states of in Southwestern Nigeria (see figure 1). Though a common language is recognized, Yorùbá exists in many different dialects, for example: Ìgbómìnà, Òyó, Ifè, Ìjèsà,

Èkìtì, Ègbá, Ìjèbú, and Òwò among others. The names of dialects are directly associated with the towns in which they are spoken and are used as ethnic designations for their speakers. However, because of shared language, a widely accepted common mythological origin and historical developments during the Atlantic Slave Trade, colonization, and Independence, the Yorùbá people now identify as one group: "Yorùbá people. " The illustration as found in figure 2 below indicates the size of the ethnic groups that can be found in Nigeria and the people who speak or use the various languages/dialects found in the country. The chart clearly shows the three main ethnic groups recognized in Nigeria: Yorùbá, Hausa-Fulani and the Ibo/Igbo.

Figure 2: Ethnicity in Nigeria

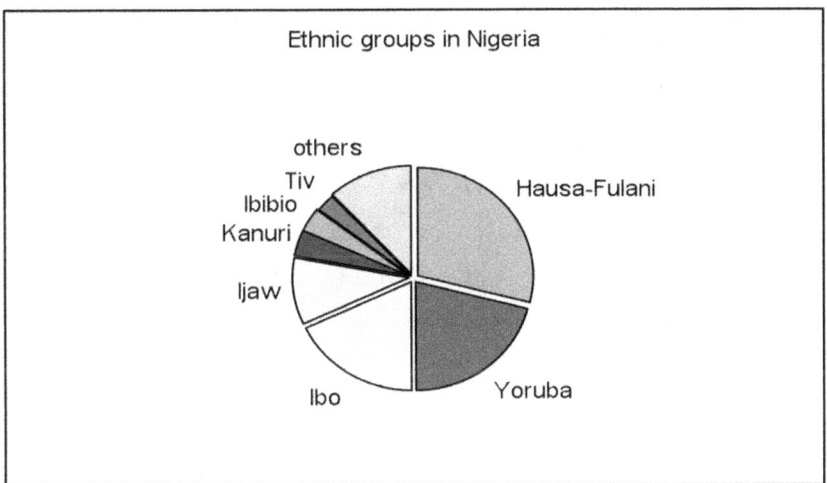

Significant works of scholars like Bamgbose (2003 & 2006), Jubril (2007), Adegbite (2007 and 2008) show that both academia and non-academia hold the view that Yorùbá language is nearing extinction. Many reasons are accountable for this. For instance, Bamgbose (1993 and 2003) reflects on the status of the role played by each major language identifiable within the Nigerian context thus:

(1) The Official language: English language

Inter ethnic and intra-ethnic languages:

- Pidgin, (which is restricted as a Lingua Franca)
- Edo, Igala, Nupe (these are languages found usable on network news).
- Arabic, Latin, German and French (religious and personal, official and transnational)

(2) Regional lingua franca: Hausa, Igbo and Yorùbá.

The indication from the data above is that English language, which is supposedly second language (L2) in the Nigerian context, has overtaken the originally recognized first languages (L1) of the environment. In another assessment made by Bamgbose (1993), the roles of the main languages of Nigeria are classified in four categories:

(a) the dominant: English language

(b) the deprived: Hausa, Igbo and Yorùbá (the major languages)

(c) the endangered: Edo, Efik/Ibiobio, Itsekiri, Tiv and

(d) the dying: Bassa, Emai etc.

This classification further supports the conclusion that despite its classification as an (L2) language in an African (Nigerian) environment, English has continually gained more recognition and broad usage above and beyond that of indigenous languages of Nigerians (L1). Alarmingly, this is the case amongst all levels of society, and is no longer restricted to the highly educated or elite.

Babalola (2005: 20) also reiterates this view in his analysis of the place of English language, in contemporary Nigeria:

> English is generally regarded as the world's most important language. The pre-eminent status of English is not in doubt given the varied roles it is performing in the world. Whenever it is being spoken alone (as in most monolingual nations like England and America) or used together with another language (as is the case in bilingual nations like Canada and Swaziland), or used in a multilingual setting (as in Nigeria and Ghana), its supremacy is well established. (Babalola, 2005: 20).

What concerns Yoruba speakers here is the increasing use of English at the expense of the indigenous language. The efficacy of English proficiency has threatened the very survival of indigenous language. When the two languages are forced to complete with one another, the dominance of English is essentially unquestioned. In the interest of developing a local and national language to compete with English, extraordinary actions are required.

When a language is said to be deprived, it is following a path of declining utilization. In some cases, a "deprived" language is actively discouraged from attaining its communicative prowess by the very people who speak the language. An important example of this is the designation of Yorùbá as 'vernacular' and therefore inferior by some Yoruba speaking elites Adegbite (2008). The same elites often impart English as a first language to their children, and discourage or even forbid the use of Yoruba in the home, the workplace, or the classroom.

By the time a language is identified as "dying" as classified by Bamgbose above, that language's survival is threatened in the immediate future. A lesson that must be taken from this classification is the urgent need to take necessary steps to reverse the abstinence of speakers from that language. Simply stated, action should be taken before a language ever reached this classification. All necessary steps must be taken to prevent Yoruba from falling into the "endangered" or "dying" categories, because once the language reaches the state of "dying, " the urgency is inestimable. The results of inaction are the rapid death of languages and increased difficulty in rescuing them from extinction. Recent examples of rapidly dying languages are: Edo, Efik/Ibiobio, Itsekiri and Tiv.

Evidence abounds that speaking the Yorùbá language is fast becoming a challenge amongst under-graduates, graduates and the artisans. My own observation shows that English is fast becoming the mother tongue and Yorùbá is treated as an L2 spoken with strange accents! One consequence of this is that even students studying the Yoruba language at home or school do not demonstrate proficiency with the language. The majority of students shy away from associating with a Yoruba course of study, as they hardly introduce themselves as students of Yorùbá/-Hausa/Igbo in the tertiary institutions, except when they hide under the glorious name of "Linguistics" or "communication arts. " This desperate situation calls for a pragmatic approach towards the restoration of indigenous language(s). This is why *Orísun* FM's decision to provide exclusively Yorùbá-oriented radio programming and their innovation in doing so becomes a source of pride to all language preservationists.

Introduction to the *Orísun* FM Study

This study is inspired by scholarly and anecdotal evidence that despite its status as one of the most widely researched African/Nigerian languages Yoruba is too quickly becoming a deprived language. For proper justification, the analysis is primarily based on Bamgbose (1993) and (2003), Arohunmolase (1998), Jubril (2003), Adegbite (2003 and (2008) and Adegbija (2004). The study posits that the *Orísun* FM radio station can function as a powerful force in correcting the ways in which individuals and collective efforts have assisted in demeaning Yorùbá language and its use, effectively resuscitating the power enwrapped in spoken and other forms of Yorùbá.

This study recognizes the exceptional functions of the media to the public. Because the electronic media, and the radio in particular, serves in different capacities, (informant, educator, and entertainer) it reaches an extensive audience across varied types of relationships. For this reason, the role played by the *Orísun* FM radio station in articulating the culture and literature of the Yorùbá through exclusively Yorùbá language use can not be underestimated. This study therefore emphasizes the importance of radio stations in communicating and encouraging communication to the general populace on different topical issues.

More importantly, the study also pays particular attention to the reasons behind the choice of language of communication on the radio programmes of *Orísun* FM radio station in Ilé-Ifè. One key question that is addressed by the study is the effect of conducting various programmes in Yorùbá language as well as other local dialects. Since the culture and literature of any race is best identified through spoken language, which serves as an icon for superb-element of identification to individual and the collective race, the results of the study commend the role played by the radio station for its effectiveness, both in methods of promoting Yorùbá language from the local to international levels, and for curbing all factors that may lead the language to a level of total extinction.

In the final analysis, we are suggesting that there is the need to employ an aggressive method of total abstinence from foreign tongue in programme presentation campaign to enliven the use of Yorùbá language locally and at a global level. It makes further suggestions of ways to promote the local dialects for the purpose of building a national and international identity for the users of the language. A call for emulation of *Orísun* FM radio station by other local and international radio stations in Nigeria and in the Diaspora is recommended to assist the evolution.

Historical Background of *Orísun* FM Radio Station in Ilé-Ifè on Yorùbá Language

The radio station called *Orísun* FM that now operates on 89. 5frequency modulation KHz is located in the center of Ilé-Ifè, the mythological source of the Yoruba people, at Òkè-Ìtasè, a walkable distance from the traditional royal palace of the incumbent Oòni of Ifè: Oba Síjúwadé Olúbùse II. Following the creation of Òsun from the old Òyó state between 1991/92, the station sprang up as a radio station under the supervision of Òsun state government with ten media, cultural officers and experienced members as the Governing Board of its operation. The parent radio and television stations were then located in Òsogbo, the capital of the Osun State, having about four outlets of operations: Òsun Broadcasting station, operating on *104. 5 KHz*: Ilé-Àwíyé, *32UHF: Òkè-baálè, 22UHF: Ìbòkun* and the last is the one under study.

The radio station originally transmitted from *Ilé-Àwíyé* in Òsogbo as one of the main radio stations in Òsun State. However, in the quest of the station's Board members to meet the demands of the community and as a way of meeting their goals as educators, informants and entertainers to the public; *Orísun* FM station was relocated to Ilé-Ifè in 2005. This enabled the achievement of its objective of promoting indigenous African values and languages. At the time of its inauguration, the Ilé-Ifè station made use of virtually all the local dialects of the Yorùbá speaking states, including the English language. This was purposefully done, with the intentions of reaching a wider audience residing in the suburbs and the main cities around the location of the radio station: Òyó, Òsun, Ògùn, Èkìtì, Ondo, among others. The main staff consisted of fifteen classified permanent officers, and almost twenty personnel as other assisting hands. The radio station from our findings, aired numerous programmes daily between 6am till 12midnight, and these could be categorized into three main areas as illustrated below in Figure 3. A sampling of the programs aired on the station and some of the renowned presenters are given in Figure 4.

Figure 3: Categories of Daily Programming on Orisun FM

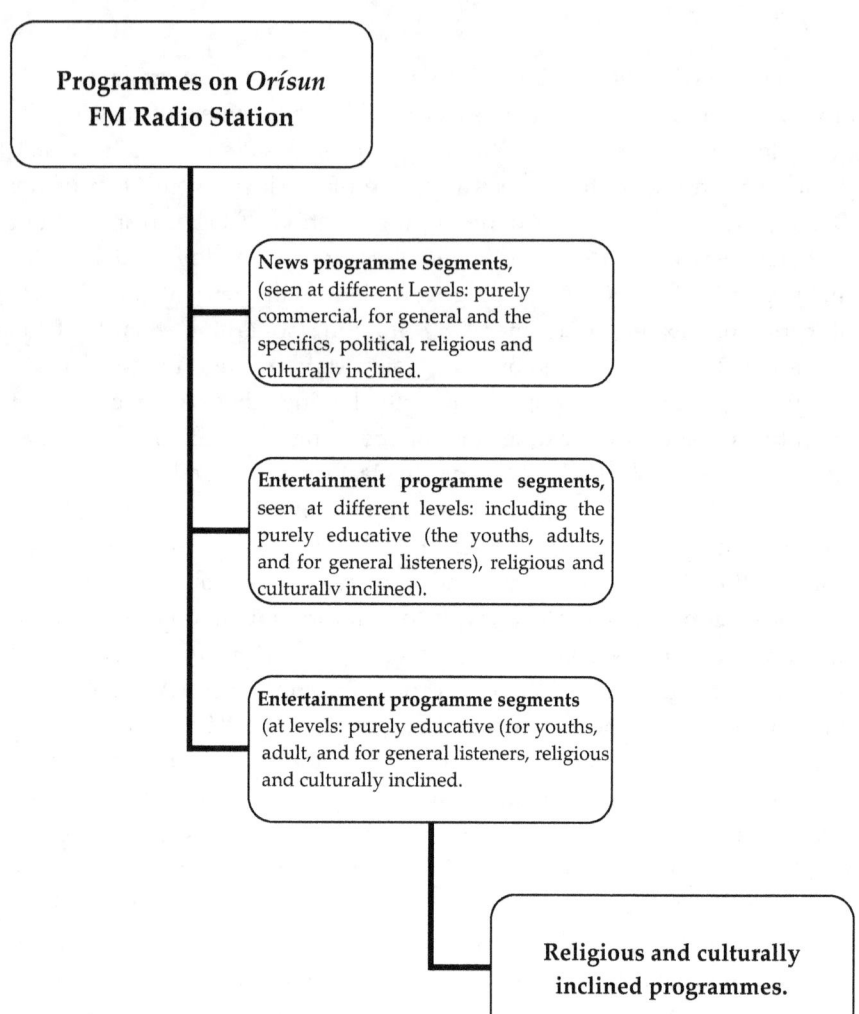

Figure 4: Sample Programmes and the Presenters on *Orísun* FM Ilé-Ifè

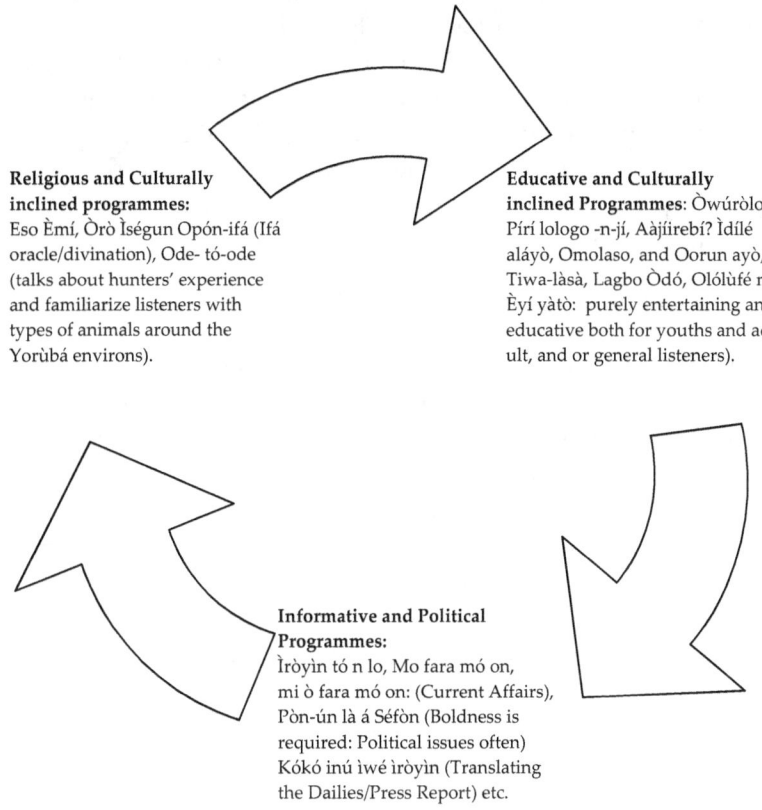

Religious and Culturally inclined programmes: Eso Èmí, Òrò Ìségun Opón-ifá (Ifá oracle/divination), Ode- tó-ode (talks about hunters' experience and familiarize listeners with types of animals around the Yorùbá environs).

Educative and Culturally inclined Programmes: Òwúròlojó, Pírí lologo -n-jí, Aàjíirebí? Ìdílé aláyò, Omolaso, and Oorun ayò, Tiwa-làsà, Lagbo Òdó, Olólùfé mi, Èyí yàtò: purely entertaining and educative both for youths and adult, and or general listeners).

Informative and Political Programmes: Ìròyìn tó n lo, Mo fara mó on, mi ò fara mó on: (Current Affairs), Pòn-ún là á Séfòn (Boldness is required: Political issues often) Kókó inú ìwé ìròyìn (Translating the Dailies/Press Report) etc.

Presenters: Most of these programmes mentioned in the three divisions are anchored by our informants: Bósè Bamgbóyè, Adéoyè Bákàrè, Aráfémi Àlàbí, Délé Amúsàn-án, Délé Jímoh, Tájùdeen Àkànmú, Olákúnbi Ìdòwú, Fúnmi Kalèjayé, Bùkólá Owólabí, Abimbola Babátúndé and others.

Steps towards Reviving the Endangered or Deprived African (Yorùbá) Language

From the evalation of the data, this study determined that the intensive broadcasting of language restricted programmes on radio air through seems to have more impact than other approached suggested and implemented in Nigeria and Africa generally. Some concerned scholars such as Kola Owolabi, (1999 and 2007) and other stakeholders in Yorùbá studies have begun to evolve ways of fighting the factors that could lead or have led to language deprivation. One such method is the running of workshops on the use and advantages of speaking indigenous languages. Another is advocating for translation of the Nigerian constitution into Yorùbá and other major indigenous Nigerian languages. A partner to the translation would be the utilization of indigenous languages at important legislative and other political settings. *Orísun* FM in Ilé-Ifè has become a special and symbolic icon in the promotion of Yorùbá language because it appears that it has had more impact on preservation than all of the above techniques.

Principles and Effects of Choice of Yorùbá Language for Broadcast

The positive effects of the *Orísun* FM station are difficult to measure, but easily recognizable. In assessing all the pros and cons of the effects of the choice of medium of broadcast language of the station, one can point to several positive outcomes. From a close monitoring of and, in some cases, direct involvement in different programmes on the station, such as "*Tiwa Làsà*" (We own the culture or the culture is ours), one can say that the caliber of speakers that the presenters bring to the radio station is high. *Orísun* FM today in Ilé-Ifè, can boast of wining many hearts to the station. Additionally, apart from the recognized Yorùbá speaking states, the station has developed a wide listening audience. People are tuning in and listening to *Orísun* FM from as far as Aba (Imo State), Kaduna, Maiduguri and other parts of the Northern states in Nigeria and outside the nation.

The success of the station in promoting, preserving, and improving Yoruba language skills is evident in the quality of speakers who phone-in during air time at different hours of the day. The recognition given to the station during the celebration of its 2nd anniversary of existence in February 2008 also helped to promote the station and recognize its important role in language preservation. This event highlighted the station's emphasis on Yorùbá language and culture through language restrictions and innovative programming. One of the special approaches highlighted was the use of language instruction on the station. Private, public, secondary and tertiary intuitions have participated in quiz competitions through the use of Yorùbá language in all subjects. This has distinguished the station from others as a thorough and true promoter of indigenous culture and language.

At another level, the approach employed by the *Orísun* FM radio station which can be classified as a bottom-top and top-bottom approach has also shown some levels of achievements in making sure that the

Yorùbá language use is seriously revived. The high level of public recognition of people such as top officials in government, and economic representatives, whom the presenters invite to participate in the phone-in programmes such as *"Pòn-ún làá-séfòn", Òrò tó n lo"* among others (all are centered towards current issues politically and economically) has affected the respect and influence of the station's language restriction policies. The high level of language competence has increased the ability of most of the stations' presenters to strictly enforce participants to speak the native language, and this has in many ways added value to the development and sustenance of the language and social interaction required in this democratic era. More importantly, through the varied programming, the "commoners" and under-privileged citizens in the society also have gained access to information that could have been shared solely among elites if "foreign tongues/languages" were encouraged on the radio station as in other avenues of media broadcast. In essence, the non-elite have also been given access to a wide range of space to participate in the country's development. They can air their views through phone-in programmes on all levels of issues: including politics, business, religion and entertainment because of the choice of language use on this radio station. The programmes such as *Lábé Òrun (Under the world), Ojú-àwo-làwo fi-n gbobè (Eye for an eye), and lágbo òsèlú (At Political Setting)*, and the popular *Kókó inú ìwé ìròyìn (Press Review/reports)* are typical examples of the programmes which allow the less privileged the opportunity to communicate with important personalities on crucial and general issues in the society, as well as having access to current information in the daily news.

In spite of *Orísun* FM's success in promoting Yoruba language, the less positive effects of the language restriction policy can also be analyzed by this study. One of the more obvious negative effects encountered was the station's limited audience. It is a natural consequence of the language restriction policy that the audience will be limited by the exclusive use of Yoruba. This decision has of course limited the station's ability to reach out to all shades of audience(s), around the location of operation. *Orísun* FM is certainly not 100 percent in reaching all the populations living in Ilé-Ifè and its suburbs. As a major city, Ilé-Ifè boasts a diverse ethnic, religious, and linguistic population. The other side of this is that heritage and non-heritage citizens who might have lived in a Yorùbá language speaking environment but could not speak the language very well and have little understanding, are able to turn to the station as a linguistic and cultural authority.

In very pragmatic terms, I can say that the commercial value of the station is also limited by the language restriction policy. From the information gathered from the Head of the station (Mrs. Bósèdé Bámgbóyè) and the view as shared by majority of our informants, I determined that at the initial stage of operation in 2005, it was very difficult for the station to make tangible financial gains. The reason for this is that the choice of language limits the type of advertisements received from people, and patronage was very low. This resulted in repeating some already aired programmes, which affected the audience enthusiasm and participation by making the station's presentation very monotonous. Yet the commitment to the language restriction policy remains strong. In fact, close friends to the workers of the station and of the Board members were reportedly turned down for their promotion requests in the English language or other foreign languages as a matter of principle to make sure that no language interference pollutes the identity that the station has carved for itself as a pioneer in the use of African indigenous language on air.

The station also faced the challenges of coping with participant guests or callers-in for live programmes at the initial stage of operation because they were censured whenever any languages apart from Yorùbá or other variants of the dialects were spoken. The censoring was done through the presenter by asking the guest or the home participants to say whatever he/she has in mind in English language in Yorùbá if he/she wished continue to participate on the programme.

Inferences

In the course of the analysis of data produced in this study, the various roles of the *Orísun* FM Ilé-Ifè as a strong and aggressive promoter of language and culture through language restriction has been demonstrated. One of the important results inferred from the study is that the radio station has promoted the democratic process by including a previously marginalized segment of society by communicating in the language of that group, and creating a space for that group to interact with powerful people in the society. This seems to the researcher an appropriate and laudable result, and one that should be expected from Ilé-Ifè- the Cradle of the Yorùbá civilization.

Despite the negligible minuses of the choice of broadcasting exclusively in local languages, it has also been demonstrated that language is a significant source of identification for the individual and collective linguistic and cultural group, with language as the key preserver of literature and culture. The need to encourage sponsorship has also been identified, especially for students who chose to study any African indigenous language. This is also to ensure the training of man-power who will eventually staff these stations to ensure that the achievements of the language restriction policies can be sustained. Finally, this study intends to honestly communicate to government, individual radio, and media broadcasting stations, that too much premium should not be placed on the monetary values at the inauguration of their stations. Simply stated, English should not be chosen over (L1) languages for simple monetary gain. The study suggests that improved usage of indigenous languages will yield advertising revenue in time. The initial development of radio stations should primarily be concerned with the legacies of developing and protecting the language and culture of the environment. Programmers/presenters on radio stations across the African continent and in the Diaspora are advised strongly to emulate the *Orísun* FM station, as it is evident by at least three stations in Lagos, (T*iwa-n-tiwa FM* radio station), Ìbàdàn and at Ìwó in Òsun state now.

Internet and Newspaper Sources:

http://www.motherlandnigeria.com/geography.html#Map

http://nigeriaworld.com/focus/documents/vision2010.html

Daily Sun, June 10, 2008: Coverage by Sola Balogun.

References

Adegbija, Efurosibina. 1989. Lexico-semantic Variation in English. *World's Englishes*, Vol 8, No. 2, pp 165-177.

_____1994. Language Attitudes in Sub-saharan Africa: A Sociolonguistic Overview. Clevedon: Multilingual Matter Ltd.

_____2004. *Multilingualism: A Nigerian Case Study*. Trenton, NJ: Africa World Press.

Adegbite, Wale and Akindele, Femi. 2005. *The Sociology and Politics of English in Nigeria*. Ile-Ife: OAU Press.

Awoniyi, Adedeji. 1995. Determining Language in Education Policy: The Dilemma in Africa. In Owolabi, Kola (Ed.). Language in Nigeria: Essays in honour of Ayo Bamgbose. Ibadan, Nigeria: Group Publishers. pp. 441- 454.

Bamgbose, Ayo. 1971. The English Language in Nigeria. In J. Spencer (Ed.). *The English Language in West Africa*. London: Longman.

____1993. Deprived, Endangered and Dying languages. *Diogenes* 161: 19 – 26.

____1996. Speaking in Tongue: Implications of Multilingualism for Language Policy in Nigeria. Nigerian National Merit Award Winner Lecture.

____2006. *Linguistics and Social Responsibility: The Challenge for the Nigerian Linguist*. Port Harcourt, Nigeria: M & J Ground Orbit Communications Ltd. & Emhai Press.

Babalola E. T. 2006. The Place of English in the Contemporary History of Nigeria. In Akin Alao (Ed.). *The Nigerian State: Language of its Politics*. p. 20-28.

Dada, S. A. 2005. Anomie: Another view of Language endangerment in Nigeria. *Journal of Language, Culture and Communication* Vol 1. No 3. pp. 33- 41.

Dell Hymes. 1972. *Models of the Interaction of Language and Social Life*. In *Directions in Sociolinguistics: the Ethnography of* Communication. John Gumperz and Dell Hymes (Eds.). New York: Holt, Rinehant and Winston, Inc. pp. 35 -71.

Egbokhare, Francis. 2004. Language and Politics in Nigeria. In Owolabi, Kola and Ademola Dasylva (Eds.). *Forms and Functions of English and Indigenous Language in Nigeria*.

Federal Republic of Nigeria Press. 2004. National Policy on Education

Gordon, Avery F., and Christopher Newfield. (Eds.). 1996. *Mapping Multiculturalism*. Minneapolis: University of Minnesota Press.

Jubril, M. 1995. The Elaboration of the Functions of Nigerian Pidgin. In Bamgbose A. et. al. (Eds.). *New Englishes: A West African Perspective*. Ibadan, Mosuro Publishers, pp. 232-247.

Oyetade, S. Oluwole. 2002. Language Policies and Planning in Nigeria. *Research in African Languages and Linguistics*, Vol 18 pp. 581 – 610.

Owolabi, Kola (Ed.). 1995. *Language in Nigeria: Essays in honour of Ayo Bamgbose*. Ibadan, Nigeria: Group Publishers.

Ruiz, Richard. 1995. Language Planning Considerations in Indigenous Communities. *The Bilingual Research Journal*, Vol 19, No. 1, pp. 71-81.

Chapter 11

THE ORIKI (PANEGYRIC) PHENOMENON AS ARCHIVAL MATERIAL FOR YORUBA HISTORY

Oladayo Akanmu

Introduction

Oriki is unarguably the most popular of Yoruba oral poetic genres. It remains the only genre that features in the performance of all Yoruba chanters as they address members of their audience. However, our concern in this paper is to show how this phenomenon preserves records of the past as well as giving detailed explanations on some of its hidden meanings. This is necessary because in oriki, references are often made to historical or mythological events and they usually require an explanation before their full significance can be grasped (Adeboyeje et al 1987). Unfortunately, this phenomenon is gradually losing popularity among the Yoruba due to the effect of our so-called 'civilization' and wholesale acceptance of anything and everything western. Today, when a Yoruba man is traced to his great grandfather as *'Omo Ekun'* meaning, the offspring of leopard, the response is always that Jesus or Mohammed has erased such a name from his life. This is sheer ignorance and a great mistake that is tantamount to a loss of identity. Oriki provides information about a person's origin, how powerful his ancestors were, how wealthy they were, and all the noble things that they have done and therefore, should not be seen either as a curse or spell. It is something one should be proud of. It is evident that many of our people do not appreciate the importance of oriki because of their lack of knowledge of the events and meanings embedded in it. Several types of oriki are recognized on the basis of the subject matter. They are oriki of lineages, towns, places, chiefs, kings, divinities, individuals, plants and animals. It is possible to begin someone's oriki with her oriki soki (a brief panegyric) and still trace her to her place, town and lineage:

1. Abeni
   Abeni

   Omo Atenigboye
   Offspring of Atenigboye

   Omo Aborogboye
   Offspring of Aborogboye

   Omo Adeyeye
   Offspring of Adeyeye

   Omo Adeyemi
   Offspring of Adeyemi

   Omo Adeyemo
   Offspring of Adeyemo

   Omo Adegoroye
   Offspring of Adegoroye

   Omo Adegoriite
   Offspring of Adegoriite

   Omo Ejigbara Ileke
   Offspring of the double string of Ejigba beads

   Omo Arowomeweewa-gboye-l'owu.
   Offspring of He who is entitled to receive the title with both hands (ten fingers) in Owu

Looking at the excerpt above, one discovers that 'Abeni' is the short oriki (one-word oriki) of the person being praised. The numerous references to the title and the crown, in the names of the subject's ancestors, and the *Ejigba* beads which royalty dons all attest to the royal blood of the Olowu lineage and its offsprings. Such is the explanation of event and meaning embedded in oriki.

Perspectives on Oriki (Panegyric)

Oriki as a literary genre is comparable to the Greek's 'panegyric'. According to the New Encyclopedia Britannica (2003), 'panegyric' is a eulogistic oration or laudatory discourse, which originally was a speech, delivered at an ancient Greek general assembly such as the Olympic and panathenaic festivals. Speakers frequently took advantage of these occasions, whenever Greeks from the various city-states gathered together to advocate Hellenic unity. With this end in view and also in order to gratify their audience, they tended to expatiate on the former glories of Greek cities, hence came the encomiastic association that eventually clung to the term panegyric.

Oriki is not a virgin ground for scholarship as several scholars have worked extensively and tenaciously on it. Babalola (1966) and Olatunji (1979) assert that oriki, especially oriki orile (lineage oriki), is the most decisive factor in assessing the competence of an artists, and that, this account for why every Yoruba oral poet strives to know the oriki of important people in his locality. Awe (1974) sees oriki as a feeling of solidarity with one's blood relation and of pride in one's ancestors as well as confidence for the present and courage for the future. Awe's position is corroborated by Babalola (1966) when he says:

> It is traditionally believed that the correct performance of oriki in honour of a progenitor gladdens the progenitor in the world of spirits and induces him to show blessings on his offspring on earth. The reciting or chanting of the appropriate oriki in honour of the ancestors of a particular family causes members of that family who hear the performance to feel very proud of their pedigree, and if they are then away from home, they also feel exceedingly homesick.

Olatunji (1984) gives several examples of oriki as oriki soki (Akanmu, Akande, Abeni, Aduke), the amutorunwa (name brought from heaven/name which the child said to be born with Ogidi Olu for Ajayi, Olukuloye for Ojo, Adubi for Ige, Orosun for Aina), oriki inagije or alaje, igbo-fi-dudu-sola (the forest is resplendently dark), Adumaadan (He whose skin is dark and smooth). He stresses further that oriki can also be played on the drum as the speech tones are reproduced with the drum in a kind of surrogate language. Ayanlowo (1978) opines that it is possible to beat oriki on the drum as we can see in Odubitan (1964) which contains the oriki of all the Timi of Ede up to the late Oba Adetoyese Laoye I. Citing research works on oriki is incomplete without noting the efforts of Babalola (1967) and (1975), Lasebikan (1958), Odubitan (1964), Atilade (1963), Aremu (1979) and Adeoye (1973) on oriki and Alaje. It can be deduced that scholars' views about oriki are all-encompassing, however, in the context of this work, oriki is perceived as an item of oral tradition used to define its subject (human and non-human) by extolling good qualities and playing down, as much as possible, the unflattering ones.

Oriki (Panegyric) as Archive

Though oriki is not a physical structure or a concrete building that one can see with the eyes. It is "concretized" here as an archive because of its lofty role in the life of the Yorubas. An archive, as we all know is a place where a large number of historical records are stores. Going by this definition, it is not out of place to say that oriki (panegyric) can be equated with an archive in that, it serves as a reservoir of knowledge of the Yoruba worldview. In short, oriki is comparable to a store of knowledge about happenings in the Yoruba past that cannot be easily recollected except through it. The moment an oriki is chanted in the direction of some events, those who are knowledgeable and versed in oriki would remember not only the happening but also the place, time and the year. Consider this example:

2. Omo Apaja funwonrawo
   Offspring of the one who killed the dog so that people might have its skin

   Ela omo oko n ko gbodo jeran ega
   Ela, offspring of the triplet, I must not eat weaver birds' meat

   Omo Layimese apejaye
   Offspring of Layimese who was begged to reign.
   (Babalola, 1967: 30).

It takes only those who are deeply rooted in Yoruba culture to comprehend the meaning of the above excerpt and also, what led to the incident. The excerpt above is the oriki of the Oluoje lineage. 'Apajafunwonrawo' refers to the legend about the death of the Oluoje while on a hunting expedition. His corpse was found some days after his death, and his faithful dog, which was keeping watch over his corpse, had to be killed and skinned to provide a wrapper for its owner's corpse. Oluoje offsprings abstain from eating weaver birds' meat because Oje town was saved from a night attack by weaver birds which alerted Oluoje's guards by flying at night when their nests were disturbed by invading Fulani. This abstinence is also due to the legend that weaverbirds were chattering on the locust-bean tree under which the Oluoje's corpse was found. Layimese Apejoye refers to the legend about the third son of the Oluoje whose aim was bad during a duiker-shooting contest. He was later asked to reign after his two brothers had become the Onpetu and Awoyira respectively. 'Oko' alludes to the legend, which states that Oluoje, Onpetu and Awoyira were triplets.

Also, it is not news that the Yoruba people have at varied intervals punctuated the peaceful flow of their history by resorting to arms. Indeed, the nineteenth century was particularly notorious for warfare in Yoruba land. Therefore, in oriki it is possible to get records of some activities and many innovations that took place during the war. For instance, in the lifetime of Akeredolu, the son of Baale Oroowusi, who died in 1871, many innovations took place:

3. A bi o were la ri ota
   Soon after you were born bullets came on the scene

   A n we o lowo la retu
   As you were being washed soon after birth, we became familiar with the gunpowder

   Ojo ta a ko o jade la ri Felegun
   At your naming ceremony, we saw Felegun.
   (Akinyele, 1950).

The excerpts above gives insight into the types of weapons used in Yoruba land prior to the birth of Akeredolu. Locally made weapons were used before his birth. Although, the exact year of the innovation is not mentioned, those who are knowledgeable about oriki will comprehend easily and eventually fix the date. This is because the innovation is symbolic. By the time Ajayi Osungbekun came on the scene at the tail end of the century 1893-5, many new weapons had been introduced and had gained general acceptance:

4. Bankole yita metu
   Bankole, the innovator, who mixed gunpowder with bullets at one go

   Oke ko le duro, igbo ko le duro
   The hills retreat before you, the forest also cannot stand.

   Afi kara omo aluganmbi
   Only Kara, son of Alugambi

   To duro de poopoo ni popo
   Who waited for your poopoo on the highway...

O fogolo bemo lese kan alonge
He cuts a man's foot with the ogolo sword.
(Akinyele, 1950).

The locally made weapons were also in use prior to the time this oriki was chanted. In personal oriki of Laoye Ogunwemide of Ogbomoso we see the description of his weapon and techniques of killing enemies at war front:

5. Onikumo afofun oko Aawa
    The white-washed club, husband of Aawa,

    Abosan-gbomo-ni-warapa baba Akinkunmi
    He that has a cudgel that makes a child epileptic, The father of Akinkunmi

    Ojikutu-pa-meji loke Onpetu
    He who wakes early in the morning to kill two people in upper Onpetu

    O fi t'Areeago se'bose re
    He used those from Areago as his stockings

    O pa Tela nipa esin
    He killed Tela in a disgraceful manner

    O pa Abidogun kankan biku ogun
    He killed Abiodun immediately as war kills a man

    O p'Arepoponda omo Sango
    He killed Arepoponda; offspring of Sango

    O p'Olopade o fowo re wole geere
    He killed Olopade and dragged his hand about

    O kanri ole, kanri a kunle
    He nailed the head of the robber, nailed the head of the arsonist
    (Oyerinde, 1934: 129).

The excerpt above extolled the military might and prowess of Laoye Ogunweminde of Ogbomoso. He is described as a mass killer of men in battle and an instant judge of social deviants. The validity of this oriki can be seen in the names of some of the areas mentioned in the excepts. For instance, Areago and Onpetu and the names of some areas in Ogbomoso till today. Apart from this, the name 'Laoye' is from one of the five royal families in Ogbomoso. It should be stressed here that the incidents in most of the excerpts discussed earlier happened in the 19th Century, the period when oriki gained immense popularity (Biobaku, S. O. (ed), 1973). However, the explanation of happenings in oriki which is quite different from those discussed earlier is embedded in the personal oriki of Anikura:

6. Ogboju ole ti n daboro
   The great robber that wears fez

   Agba ole abasunwon gbooro
   The renowned robber that has a long purse

   Jaguda kekeke lolopa Eko n mu
   It is petty thieves that the Lagos police can arrest

   Anikura mbe nibe won o le mu u
   Anikura is there, they dare not arrest him

   Bi won ba m'Anikura,
   If they arrest Anikura

   Owo nla
   Big sums of money

   Aso nla
   Big garments

   Nii fi di baba won lenu
   Are what he uses to block their fathers' mouth

   Ayinla bale wayo
   Ayinla, master fraudster

   O gbowo Ijebu
   He stole an Ijebu's money

   O fi dewu etu sile
   And spent it to make an expensive etu woven garment for himself.
   (Olajubu, 1977: 10).

It should be affirmed here that the world of oriki is amoral and that the literary imagination that gave birth to the oriki readily accepts the extolling of human bravery and courage at the expense of everyday or commonplace morality. This is exactly the picture painted by the personal oriki of Anikura, a notorious robber in Lagos in the 1940s. Those who witnessed Anikura's nefarious activities must have forgotten by now, but at the chant of his personal oriki it becomes fresh again in their memory. Also, this oriki reflects the act of bribe-taking on the part of the Nigerian police as an age long issue. The police could not arrest Anikura because they had collected bribe from him (as reflected in the lines:

b. Bi won ba m'Anikura,
    If they arrest Anikura

    Owo nla
    Big sums of money

    Aso nla
    Big garments

    Nii fi di baba won lenu
    Are what he uses to block their fathers' mouth - that is bribe them all.

Apart from bringing the foregoing issues to the fore, oriki can also refresh our memories even with relatively recent issues. In contemporary times oriki is used to capture the ugly incidents of September 11, 2007 in America:

7. ...Amerika
    ...America

    Loogunlekoo
    The War lord

    Okunrin ogun
    The man of war

    Eni a a le mu
    The indomitable (defies all weapons and enchantments)

    Ta a ran Alajangbila si
    Hence, Alajangbila (an aimless fighter) was petitioned to deal with him

    Oju t'eni ti won ran
    The one petitioned to deal with him experienced the fear and defeat of his life

Oju t'eni to ran won
The petitioner as well surrendered in shame.
(Akanmu, 2002:7-8).

The excerpt above is a reminiscence of the personal oriki in Yoruba. It is taken from a poem entitled 'O-gbebo-bebo-rin' (suicide bomber) in *Jongbo Oro* (Akanmu, 2002). In the poem, a pictorial view of the ugly incidents as well as a deeper understanding of the activities of the suicide bombers who the Americans alleged were sent by Osama bin Ladin[2] is given. The poetic composition of this oriki extols America's unrivalled bravery, unique martial spirit and excellence in warfare. Although, this poetic depiction is designed to sympathize with the American government, it is not an exaggeration. This is because immediately after the incidents, the American government declared war on Osama bin-Ladin and his Al-Queda group as well as their supporters. This must have been one of the reasons for the death of Saddam Hussein, former Iraq president who was also believed to be the number one supporter of the Al-Queda group. Indeed, 'the petitioner as well surrendered in shame'. This is because up till now Bin Laden the leader of the Al-Queda and other members of the group are still in their various hide-outs.

Looking at the oriki of some towns in Yoruba land, most especially Ibadan, meanings are hidden. It takes those who are very perceptive and fully conversant with Ibadan people to understand their oriki.

For instance:

8. Ibadan maja, maja koo kara iwaju leru
   Ibadan need not fight to enslave his victims.

   Eyi too ja nijosi nko?
   What about your previous battles?

   Gbogbo aladuugbo lo hun
   The entire neighbourhood was affected
   (Olajubu, 1971:12).

Issues of fighting in the above oriki may not be clear to someone who does not have deep knowledge of Ibadan people. Research shows that incessant battles gave birth to Ibadan. Ibadan people never seem tired of fighting. History had it that a Baale, and not a crowned Oba[2] was the head of the land and that, most of the people that lived there were immigrants. Perhaps, this is the reason for the incessant crisis among them (Agbaje, 2001). Also, right from the then Western Regional government when Ibadan was the seat of government to this moment, the issue of fighting among Ibadan people is on-going, political matters are always serious issue in Ibadan especially during the lifetime of Chief Adelabu (a. k. a. peculiar mess) and Chief Adelakun (a. k. a. eru o bodo) even up to the time of Chief Lamidi Adedibu, a P. D. P. (the ruling political party in Nigeria) chieftain.

The Proliferation of local government may also be one of the reasons for the spread of crisis in Ibadan. History also had it that Ibadan people waged war against the Ijebus, Egbas and Ekiti people. Even, of recent, there was a serious feud between Adedibu and the former Governor of Oyo State Alhaji Rashidi Ladoja, which spread to neighbouring towns. The fight eventually took Ladoja out of power. Presently, it is difficult to say that the incessant crisis, which Ibadan is known for has become a thing of the past because the workers in Ibadan have just suspended an industrial strike embarked upon over the non-increment of their salary.

Conclusion

It is hoped that this work has broadened our knowledge of the personal, town and lineage oriki in Yoruba land. It shows also that the oriki is comparable to an archive where culture related matters are kept, and that whenever we need information about age long or forgotten issues, oriki brings them to our memories.

As viable as oriki is, it has limitations. Oriki cannot answer all questions on the Yoruba worldview. It is at best only another contributory source for building up the panorama of Yoruba history and it can only serve to shed light on those aspects of events, which have been highlighted here. Therefore, this paper suggests a return to the basics by the Yoruba people. They should be proud of their cultural heritage, embrace what belongs to them and strive to improve upon them. Also, African friends from the other part of the world should know that the entire world relies on culture and that the entire world needs to look at all world cultures with respect to appreciate the totality of human knowledge and wisdom.

References

Adeboyeje Et al. 1978. *Eko Ede Yoruba Ode Oni (3)*. Lagos, Nigeria: Macmillan Nigeria Ltd.

Adeoye, C. L. 1972. *Oruko Yoruba*. Ibadan, Nigeria: Oxford University Press.

Agbaje, Bode. 2001. Ifiwadi Sotumo Iyanrofeere Ayolo Lati Inu Esa Egungun. *A Journal of Yoruba Studies Association of Nigeria*. Vol. 2, No. 1.

Akanmu, D. 2002. *Jongbo Oro*. Lagos, Nigeria: Olomun Printing Press.

Akinyele, J. B. 1950. Iwe Itan Ibadan ati die Ninu Awon Ilu Agbegbe re bi Iwo, Osogbo ati Ikirun. Exeter: James Townsend.

Aremu, A. 1979. *Asayan Oriki*. Ibadan, University Press Limited.

Atilade, E. A. 1963. *Iwe Oriki Awon Orile Yoruba*. Lagos, Nigeria.

Awe, Bolanle. 1974. Praise Poems and Historical Data: The Example of the Yoruba Oriki. *Africa* XLIV, No. 4, pp. 331-349.

Ayanlowo, P. B. 1978. Language of the Drum among the Yoruba People. Unpublished B. A. Thesis. Department of Linguistics and Nigerian Languages, University of Ibadan.

Babalola, A. 1966. *The Content and Form of Yoruba Ijala*. Oxford, London: Clarendon Press.

____1967. *Awon Oriki Orile*. Glasgow: Collins.

____1975. *Awon Oriki Borokinni*. Ibadan, Nigeria: Hodder and Stoughton Educational.

Biobaku, S. O. (Ed.). 1973. *Sources of Yoruba History*. Oxford, London: Clarendon Press.

Lasebikan, E. L. 1958. *Ijinle Ohun Enu Yoruba*. Ibadan: Government Printers.

Longman Dictionary of Contemporary English. 2005. England: Pearson Educational Limited.

Odubitan, S. 1964. *Oriki Awon Timi Ede*. Osogbo, Nigeria: MBARI MBAYO Publications.

Olajubu, O. 1972. References to Sex in Yoruba Oral Literature. *Journal of American Folklore*, Vol. 85, No. 336.

____1974. Iwi Egungun Chants: An Introduction. *Research in African Literature*, Vol. 5, No. 1, pp. 31 – 51.

Olatunji, O. 1979. Issues in the Study of Oral Poetry in Africa. *Journal of African Studies*, UCLA, Los Angeles, Vol. 6, No. 2, pp. 112-119.

Olatunji, O. 1984. *Features of Yoruba Oral Poetry*. Ibadan, Nigeria: University Press Limited.

Oyerinde, N. D. 1934. *Iwe Itan Ogbomoso Nipa N. D. Oyerinde*. Jos, Nigeria: Niger Press.

Chapter 12

PHONOLOGICAL DEVIATION IN SPOKEN ENGLISH AMONG STUDENTS IN NIGERIAN TERTIARY INSTITUTIONS: DRAMA AND THEATRE TO THE RESCUE

Ezekiel Tunde Bolaji and Kehinde Abimbola Adeniyi

Introduction

Kachru (1985) has conveniently categorized the users of English around, the word into three concentric circles: the "norm-producing" inner circle comprising the native speakers who use English as their first language (L1); the "norm-developing" outer circle, comprising second language (L2) users of English who use it for official purposes; and the "norm-dependent" expanding circle, made up of foreign language (FL) users of English, who use it for commercial purposes. Nigeria falls eminently in the second category of users of English. its arrival in Nigeria has made English inter mingled with Nigerian indigenous languages and this in turn has precipitated lexico-semantic, grammatical and phonological variation and changes in the norms and forms of English spoken within the country when compared with its native variety. This chapter investigates phonological deviation or variation- a critical important dimension of how the English language in Nigeria, especially among Nigerian higher institution students in Nigeria English when compared with other native and non-native varieties.

The chapter aims primarily at achieving four main goals: first, to examine the causes and types of phonological deviation in the use of English among Nigerian tertiary institution students; second, to exemplify such variation; third, to offer theatre and drama as a remedy to the identified deviation; four, to highlight some of implications. Several kinds of studies have been carried out on the English language in Nigeria (Bamgbose 1995, 2003; adegbija1989, Adegbija 2004, Afolayan, 1995, Adekunle 1995). However very few of these have attempted a consistent systematic focus on phonological deviation in Nigerian English per se, though, earlier studies (e. g. Bobda, 1995, Essien, 1995, Williams, 1995, Adetugbo, 1987 Awonusi 1987) have acknowledged it to be important in characterizing the uniqueness of the variety of English spoken in Nigeria.

It is important for such deviation to be thoroughly documented in order to pinpoint exactly what we mean.

Causes and Types of Phonological Deviation

In the outer circle countries, implantation of English was a consequence of colonial rule. As a result of its former mode of introduction and because it is an imposed L2, only a minority of the population may be said to be proficient in English. Whatever statistics of speaker provided will at best be "guesstimates" (Bamgbose 2003). For example, Crystal (1997: 59) credited Nigeria with 43,000,000 speakers of English out of a population of 95,000,000. About this figure, Bamgbose (2003: 420) observes:

> As someone who is professionallyInvolved in language studies, I do not know where these millions of speakers are to be found! It is truer to say that in Nigeria, as in all other former British colonies, English remains a minority, but powerful language used by an elite.

Hence, this is one of the reasons for deviation from the (standard) norm; literacy in English or competence in it is acquired through formal education and use. Unfortunately in Nigeria not all schools are conducive for learning the language to the point of becoming competent as it for most students. Most public schools in Lagos are over populated making it impossible for the English teacher to teach meaning fully. Besides, they lack enough benches, chairs and desks for students to sit on and learn. Adejare (1995:168) identify other reasons responsible for incompetence in English among Nigerian students:

- The ESL user has another language with different systems resulting in interference.
- There is a serious time constraint for the ESL user in the acquisition of L2
- While EMT (English as Mother Tongue) is a biological or sociological 'mother' tongue, ESL is, properly speaking, English as teacher tongue or ETT; it emphasizes the centrality of the teacher in the acquisition of ESL; and
- The ESL user is essentially bicultural and there are two bicultural variables: ESL in EMT cultures and ESL in an indigenous language culture.

Bolaji (2007:4) observes that the structures of the English language say the syllable structure, are different. In addition to this is the problem of teachers who are poor modes of English language teaching because they too are often incompetent. Also included are lack of readiness for English language tasks expected at the beginning of secondary education and teachers who reinforce the learning errors of their students by their own poor pronunciation (Bamgbose 2003; Akere 1995). It is clear from the above that the reasons responsible for phonological deviation in Nigerian English are a legion.

The rest of this section will consider the types of phonological deviation in Nigerian English. But before then, we would like to explain what we mean by deviation. The words deviance and deviation are terms used in linguistics analysis. Deviance is a term usually used in linguistic analysis to refer a usage that does not conform to the rules of grammar or phonology. Ebeogu (1998:139) simply calls it "a total departure from the norms. " Hence it is the case that deviance is regarded as the form of usage which "reflects the users" ignorance or failures in the application of the rules which dictate correct usage in a language (Ikonta & Maduekwe 2006:3). Deviation on the other hand is adjudged a positive and acceptable departure from the norm. It is viewed as an institutionalized expression that is not in conformity with the norms of a language (Adeniran 1987).

In this chapter we are in good company with Bada & Yaounde (1995:255) who talks of "deviant stress" or "stress deviations" in Nigerian English using both terms synonymously and Jowitt (2000: 45-47) who considers both terms as departure "from SE" by using the terms interchangeably. To us, both deviance and deviation "indicate a shift from standard English" (Ikonta &Madueke, 2006: 3), accordingly, the two terms are synonymous and are used interchangeably. Below are the groupings and examples of deviation noticeable in the English of students of Nigerian Universities.

Deletion

This is a situation in which L2 users of English in Nigeria remove a phoneme from a word thus changing the form and meaning of the word. Deletion Nigerian English (NE) is observable in the following:

1. Initial Consonant Deletion

This relates especially to the glottal fricative /h/. Awonusi (2004: 214) calls this 'Categorical H-Dropping. ' "It is the non-articulation of /h/ in h-full words".

Examples of such words include:

hat	is pronounced as at
hear	is pronounced as ear
heard	is pronounced as eard
hello	is pronounced as ello
home	is pronounced as ome
help	is pronounced as elp
heave	is pronounced as eave

One can observe that while the deletion results in different words at times, in some cases, it results in meaningless words (in writing) e. g. ome, ello, elp etc.

2. H – Insertion

This is usually occurs when the language user inserts or adds on in words without the orthographic "h".

Examples of such words include:

egg	is pronounced as hegg
at	is pronounced as hat
every	is pronounced as hevery
accuse	is pronounced as haccuse

3. Final Consonant Deletion

Here, the language user drops off the final sounds in a word, usually a suffix.

Examples of such words include:

speaks	is pronounced as speak
passed	is pronounced as pass

worked	is pronounced as work
asks	is pronounced as ask
slapped	is pronounced as slap

Simplification

This is done by the L2 user in order to make complex sounds easy to pronounce.

1. Cluster Reduction

Here, the language user reduces English language clusters by inserting vowels to ensure that the word(s) conform to the Yoruba language syllabic structure.

Examples of such words include:

dignity	is pronounced as diginity
school	is pronounced as sukul
enmity	is pronounced as enimity

2. U – Insertion:

Another inserted vowel in the simplification of English language clusters is the vowel [u]:

Examples of such words include:

article	is pronounced as artikul
table	is pronounced as tabul
angle	is pronounced as angul
people	is pronounced as peopul
title	is pronounced as titul
entitled	is pronounced as entituld
hospital	is pronounced as hospital

3. Final Consonant Simplification

An L2 user of English does this by deleting the final consonant forming the cluster.

Examples of such words include:

post   is pronounced as pos
cold   is pronounced as col / cool
hands   is pronounced as hans

Devoicing

Voiced sounds, especially consonants are devoiced whenever an L2 user comes across them, making them sound voiceless.

Examples of such words include:

	Zoo	sue	
[bægz]	bag[z]	[bags]	
	Robe	rope	
	Leave	leaf	
boy[z]	bɔIz	bɔIs	boy[s]
	Exam	eksam	
	Leg[z]	leg[s]	

Voicing

In Standard British English, for example, the "x" in the following words is realized as /ks/ or /kʃ/ whereas in Nigerian English, it is realized as [gz], voiced consonants usually before vowels.

Examples of such words include:

Flexible   is pronounced as [flegzible]
Maximum   is pronounced as [magzimum]
Laxity   is pronounced as [lagzity]
Luxury   is pronounced as [luzuri]

Substitution

The speaker who substitutes, replaces an item which is absent in the phonology of his first language with a closer one in is native tongue. This is done in various ways:

1. Affrication / De – affrication

This is the substitution of a fricative or the yord at times for an affricative. In Nigeria English, it takes place because the sound substituted for does not exist in the language user's native language.

Examples of such words include:

Pleʒə	plʃə	or	plejə
Meʒə	meʃə	or	meʃə
Chip	ship		
Matches	mashes		
Chalk	shock		

2. Gliding

This occurs when a language user substitutes or replaces the consonants /w/ or /j/. Our observation shows that this seems to be more of a habit that may be overcome with much effort. Surprisingly, more students in Nigerian tertiary institutions now suffer from this problem.

Examples of such words include:

Road	woad
Right	wight
Rotting	wotting
Rabbit	wabbit

Our examples do not include lateral /l/. This is deliberate since we do not find any instance of such with adults, except children.

3. Transposition (Metathesis or Intervention)

This is the process in which two sounds coming immediately after each other swap places. Although called an aspect of child Phonology, Transposition was found in the adult speech of some students in Nigerian higher institution, among these were graduates.

Examples of such words include:

detestable	destetable
ask	aks

4. Spelling Pronunciations

This occurs when the language user pronounces words as spelt irrespective of whether all the letters making up the words are actually pronounced by the native speaker / included in the dictionary transcription of the word or not. This especially so where there are combinations as "mb', "dt", "nd", "st", / "stl", "wh"/"sw".

Examples of such words include:

(i) "mb" spelling pronunciation. The silent letters are bracketed.

clim(b)	climb
bom(b)	bomb
plum(b)	plumb
thum(b)	thumb
lam(b)	lamb

(ii) "bt" spelling pronunciation. The silent letters are bracketed.

De(b)t	debt

(iii) "h" spelling pronunciation. The silent letters are bracketed.

anni(h)ilate	annihilate
(h)our	hour
Ve(h)ement	vehement
(h)eir	heir
ve(h)icle	vehicle
(h)onour	honour

(iv) "st" spelling pronunciation. The silent letters are bracketed.

apos(t)le	apostle
nes(t)le	nestle
epis(t)le	epistle
lis(t)en	listen
whistle	whistle
waist coat	waist coat

(v) Wh/sw spelling pronunciation. The silent letters are bracketed.

ans(w)er	answer
(w)hole	whole
s(w)ord	sword
(w)hoop	whoop

5. Merger

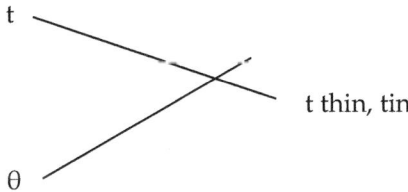

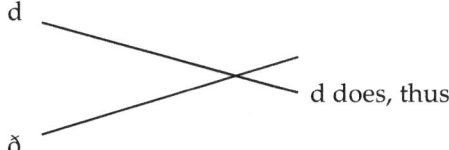

We now want to take a look at phonological deviation in the vocalic aspect of phonology.

1. Merger & Neutralization

In Nigerian English some vowels are merged or neutralized. The result of this, according to Adejare (1995:175) is that "a large number f English words become hard to distinguish as pairs in the language".

Examples of such words include:

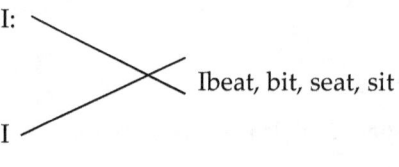
I: beat, bit, seat, sit

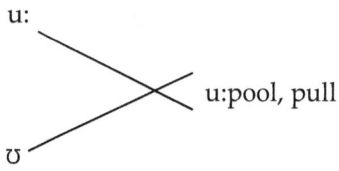
u: pool, pull

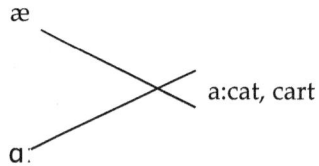
a: cat, cart

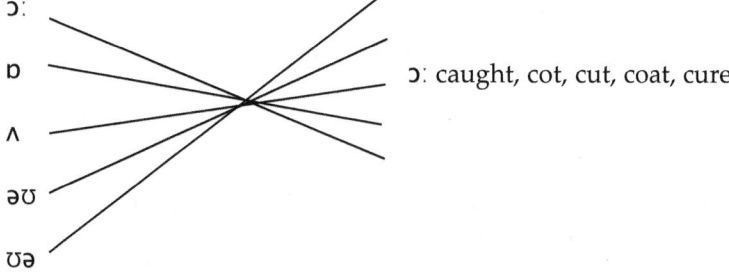
ɔ: caught, cot, cut, coat, cure

2. Spelling induced split

This occurs when the schwa /ə/ is realized as any of the sounds below. In other words, the schwa splits into different segments which are often suggested by the spelling.

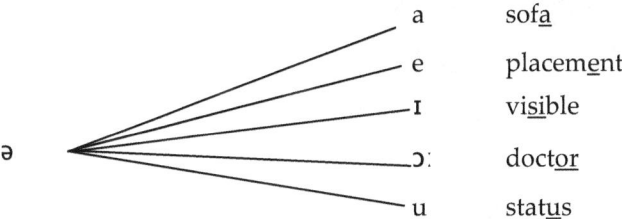

3. /ɜː/ split

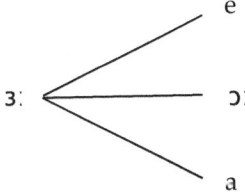

E. g. first, shirt, girl, curl, stern. The spellings are "ir", "ur", "er" and perhaps others.

4. Gliding vowels

fire	faya
lion	layon
power	pawa
higher	haya
liar	laya
lower	lowa

Lastly, we move on to suprasegmentals:

Stress Placement

1. Word initial stress assignment

In Nigerian English, words that normally receive stress on the first syllable take the stress on the final syllable.
Examples of such words include:

'Colleague	Col'league
'Petrol	Pe,troll
,madam	ma'dam
'Bedroom	Bed'room
'Background	Back'ground

2. Word with stress on final syllable.

These words in Nigerian English receive their stress word initially
Examples of such words include:

Plan'tain	'plantain
Hy'giene	'hygiene
Suc'cess	'success

These are just some samples of the many instances of phonological deviation or deviance in the speech of educated Nigerians. It is our belief that the field of drama and theatre, because of its focus on performance and its enhancement, can provide the needed mechanisms to address some of these deviation or deviance in speech of educated Nigerians. Drama and theatre techniques are thus discussed in the rest of the chapter as the remedy to the problems highlighted.

Advantages of the Techniques

Drama and Theatre techniques in language teaching have a number of advantages. First, they emphasize action or doing. The learner is able to hear, see and be emotionally involved in what is going on as he sees this demonstrated; he in turn may demonstrate this for others to imitate. Second, drama and theatre techniques emphasize vision or seeing. The learner does not only hear but he also sees the action being demonstrated. Third, he is allowed to imitate or 'replay' what he sees. This is represented by the triangle below. Fourth, Drama is fun. It enriches purposeful experience lightens the academic mood and enlightens the learner. Fifth, relaxes the nerves. Heldenbrand (2003:29) is of the view that with drama "the learner can remain enjoyable relaxed" and "step out of the box" as the right answer /wrong answer concept is removed and communication becomes more informed". And finally, Drama helps the learner to pronounce properly and intonation correctly. Godwin (2001:126) says that "Drama is a particularly effective tool for pronunciation teaching".

Figure 1: Triadic Representation of Features of Theatre /Drama Techniques

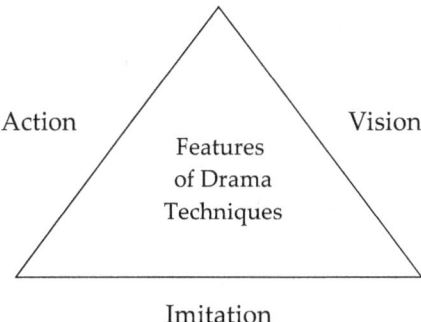

Let us now consider three of the techniques below:

Breathing

Bolaji (2007: 6) have identified four components are necessary in order to articulate sounds as expected; breathing and other three components – vocal folds, resonators and oral cavity. **Breath** functions as a force of power for the sound about to be produced or speech about to be made. Efficient breathing supplies the needed air for sustenance of the voice and it aids good projection. The **vocal folds** are the main sound producers; hence hey need to be properly used. There is no need to tense them unnecessarily as this affects speech quality. The language users need to relax the **resonators**- the neck cavity, the head cavity, the throat, shoulder and the entire body-which amplify the resulting sound. The **oral cavity** moulds the sounds which combine to form words. The language user may need to draw these consonants.

To succeed using this technique, hold your head up, and open your mouth sufficiently when you speak. Practice relaxing your neck, jaw, lips, facial muscles, and throat muscles.

Tongue –Twister

The teacher can also help his pupil to master the skill of good communication by asking them to say some tongue twisters. Tongue-twisters are difficult to say phrases or sentences with many similar sounds. The sounds difficult for the learners to pronounce may be concern of the teacher.

Example: She sells sea-shells on the sea shore [ʃ, s]

Throwing a poem around the class

According to Bolaji (2007: 10) this exercise demands that the teacher gets a poem or a text from a well written play and numbers the lines to indicate each line's place in the sequence. This may help him to achieve two things:

(i) Stress placement

(ii) Sound contrast or minimal pairs

He will look for words that rhyme. Any of the above may be acted or performed. The teacher may also get or prepare short scenes from a drama text for this purpose.

Implications

One obvious implication of phonological deviation is that it fails the test of intelligibility since it can generate **Semantic Confusion** like examples shown above. Closely related to this is that it fails the test of international acceptability in as much as to what is acceptable as educated usage in Nigeria what is not always acceptable by other users of English around the world. Next, is that it can make the listener feel irritated, spark up amusement, prevent good communication and embarrassed the speaker even if he can be understood. In conclusion, as educated Nigerians use English, they should not forget to always let their usage be measured against the three criteria of grammaticality, intelligibility and acceptability, and for this to be achieved we have proposed the integration of drama and theatre into ESL classroom.

References

Adejare, O. 1985. Communicative competence in English as a second language. In Bamgbose A, Banjo, A. & Thomas. A. (Eds.). *New Englishes: A West African perspective*. Ibadan: Mosuro

Adekunle, M. 1995. English in Nigeria: Attitudes, Policy and Communicative realities. In Bamgbose A, Banjo, A. & Thomas. A. (Eds.). *New Englishes: A West African perspective*. Ibadan: Mosuro

Adetugbo, A. 1987. Nigerian English Phonology: is there any Standard? *Lagos Review of English Studies*. Vol. ix pp. 64-84

Afolayan, A. 1995. Ineffectiveness in the Presentation of English in Nigeria: Sources and Remedies. In Bamgbose A, Banjo, A. & Thomas. A. (Eds.). *New Englishes: A West African perspective*. Ibadan: Mosuro

Akere, F. 1995. Languages in the curriculum: an Assesement of the Role of English and other languages in the Education Delivery process in Nigeria. In Bamgbose A, Banjo, A. & Thomas. A. (Eds.). *New Englishes: A West African perspective*. Ibadan: Mosuro

Awonusi, V. O. 2004. Some characterisitics of Nigerian English phonology. In Dadzie, A. B. K & Awonusi, S. (Eds.). *Nigerian English: Influences & Characteristics*. Lagos, Nigeria: Concept Publications.

Awonusi, V. O. 1987. The Identification of Standard within institutionalised Non-Native Englises: the Nigerian Experience. *Lagos Review of English Studies* vol. ix pp47-63

Bobda, A. S. 1995. The phonologies of Nigerian English and Cameroom English. In Bamgbose A, Banjo, A. & Thomas. A. (Eds.). *New Englishes: A West African perspective*. Ibadan: Mosuro

Bamgbose, A. 2003. A Recurring Decimal: English in language policy and planning. In *World Englishes* Vol. 22, No4 pp419-431. UK: Blackwell

Bolaji, E. T. 2007. Drama and the teaching of Pronounciation: A bottom-up Approach. A paper presented at the monthly Seminar organized by the school of Arts and Social Sciences, Adeniran Ogunsanya College of Education Oto/Ijanikin, Lagos on August 29

Crystal, D. 1997. English as a Global language. Cambridge: Cambridge University Press

Essien, O. 1995. The English language and code-mixing: A case study of the phenomenon in Ibibio. In Bamgbose A, Banjo, A. & Thomas. A. (Eds.). *New Englishes: A West African perspective*. Ibadan: Mosuro

Godwin, J. 2001. Teaching Pronunciation. In Ceke-Murcia, M (Ed.) *Teaching English as a Second or Foreign language* (3rd ed.). Boston: Heinle & Henle.

Heldenbrand, B. 2003. Drama Techniques in English Language Learning. Retrieved February 14, 2007, from http://www.kotesol.org/publications/journal/2003/kj6_027-38.pdf

Ikonta, N. R & Madueke, A. N. 2006. Lexical Deviations in written English among Nigerian High School Students: Impact and Implications for Language Instruction. A paper presented at the International Conference on "Preparing Teachers for a changing context: at the institute of Education, University of London on May, 3-6

Jowitt, D. 2000. *Nigerian English Usage. An Introduction.* Lagos, Nigeria: Longman

Kachru, B. B. 1985. Standards, codification, and socio-linguistic realism: the English language in the outer circle. In Quirk, R & Widdowson, H. G. (Eds.) *English in the World: teaching and learning the language and literatures.* Cambridge: Cambridge University Press.

Chapter 13

INTERPRETING THE LANGUAGE OF THE DRUMS: A CASE STUDY OF YORUBA TRADITIONAL BATA AND DUNDUN

Jeleel Olasunkanmi Ojuade

Introduction

The art of dance is said to be "as old as man and his desire to express himself, to communicate his joys and sorrows, to celebrate and to mourn with the most immediate instrument: his body" (Sorell, 1967:9). It is a universal phenomenon that serves a vital function in human society in an effort to achieve social cohesion or togetherness, causing them to feel a deep sense of communion with one another. Based on the aforementioned premise, people are liberated from the bonds of individuality (Lange, 1975:92). However, dance creates such platform for people of diverse origin or background to exercise their rights of appearance in the dance arena. It is our observation therefore that 'drums' play significant roles in such exercise. Thus, this paper is confronted with the interpretation of the language of the drums by the dancers. Here, the focus is on the two important traditional music idioms of the Yoruba of the Southwestern people in Nigeria (Bata and Dundun). It raises questions about the dancer's ability to decode easily the assumed knotty, difficult and complex language of such drums with accurate movement of their bodies. Equally, it examines the interplay of the super-rich communication and variations that come into play between the drummers and dancers in performance(s). The study in its conclusion recommends further inclusion of the drums in our daily activities.

Dance Performance in Africa Vis a Vis Nigeria

Historically, dance is believed to be one of the first human activities which did not directly serve the mere survival. Starting with instinctive movements, as a reaction to physical or psychic situations, via the first shaped and repeated rhythmic movements, men started to experience dance as a possibility of expression of individual and collective feelings and an instrument which could influence the natural forces. The existence of dance in the early periods of human history may be witnessed only by pictorial representations, carved by the hands of primitive people on the walls of the caves, the only dwellings of men at that time. The impressions which the pictures form show that they were created in a phase of human development.

In Africa, dance is believed to have originated from two human activities namely the religious/ritual worship or recreation/social activities. This is generally believed to be true of most areas of the performing arts in many African societies. Dance is regarded as a major art and an essential element in the celebration of events connected with every aspect of human life. These events range from birth of a new baby, the transformation of youths into adulthood and farewell or display of last respects for the dead. It thus symbolizes the profound truths about the complex human existence and gives meaning of life. The dance therefore in application in Nigeria is inborn, communal-oriented, participatory by all and natural. In Nigeria therefore, dance is popular, widespread and may be practiced by all, regardless of age, sex and social status. The social and cultural occasions at which these dances are performed have to do with individual or group celebrations. For example, most rite of passage dances deal with individuals who move from one status of life to another. It may be accompanied by friends and relations. Also, at naming ceremonies, coronation, festivals, feasts, communal purification and cleansing, title takings etc. It suffices then to say that the nature of dance in Nigeria, considering the ethnic configuration belongs largely to the category of ethnic dance, which is popularly known as traditional dance (where Bata and Dundun- the focus in this work- belong). Dance forms could also be classified and analyzed in varying categories-those that survived and thrived within the communities (traditional) that are raw, those making waves in the academic environment (modern oriented) and the prototype of the western world that is in vogue now. Considering these, dance performance may be regarded as an artistic expression predicated on movement; it has also been aptly described as a dramatic phenomenon induced by a psychological state (Layiwola, 1991:19-27). However, it has been observed that the Nigerian people and indeed other peoples of Africa had hitherto been subjected to slavery and colonialism by the so called superpowers of the Northern hemisphere before the new dawn of independence. Thus, our general psychological state, especially as it relates to aspects of our culture has been distorted.

However, religious or ritual which is one of the major sources of dance in Nigeria as mentioned earlier, regulates the relationship between the members of the society and the supernatural powers which there is strong believe that they are in control of human activities. Such examples are in the famous Osun Osogbo festival dance, Olojo festival dance in Ile-Ife, Sango (god of thunder and lightning) worship, Obatala worship, Egungun (masquerade) festival dance etc. It is a central element in a ceremony or festival which is an act of worship for the members of a particular religious cult. The dance is usually performed by the initiates and may include the leading members of the cult.

Social dances on the other hand change with time, based on the creative ability of the various dance artists. In its function as an expression of social organization, dance safeguards the traditionally established social and political hierarchy and equally emphasises the standard of behaviour and instructs on orals within the society. Such examples are the dances that are purely restricted to the royal personalities, elder dances and age grade dances. It is often performed by groups or teams of dancers, which clearly states their status in the enabling society. It may be a part of a festival performance or simply for entertainment. Moreover, re-creative process dance are informally a free for all affair to the members of a particular community. It could be an expression of talent or display of expertise. The dance gives room for improvisation, while such dancers are usually found at various relaxation centers and social functions, or in their private homes and at times on disco floors of hotels in the urban centers.

The Bata and Dundun Examples from Nigeria

Bata and Dundun are music cultures that are not confined to the phenomenon of dance. Historical documentation relating to the origin of Bata and Dundun are very remote and are of various forms. However, this study is particular about their interpretations by dancers. In African societies, music making ranks as one of the major events. The participation in such event may be a voluntary activity or an obligation imposed by one's membership in a social group. The social group may be a descent group (that is a group of people who trace their ancestry back to the same person), or it may be any group based on the broader societal classifications of age, sex, interest, or occupation (Nketia, 1974:35). However, Bata and Dundun music culture are one of the popular music/dance in Yoruba land in Nigeria and most of West Africa that may be performed on any occasion, feasts, festivals, social, religious, political, ceremonies and rites. In their various applications, the actual music that may be performed in Bata or Dundun ensemble depends on the social event and those involved in it. Thus, it is appropriate to organize the music/dance in relation to the different phases of community life or in terms of the needs of special situations.

Bata and Dundun drums, which the Yorubas call Ilu Bata or Ilu Dundun, belong to the membranophone group- it comprises of the musical instruments that produces sound through the vibration of a stretched animal skin. On the other hand, Bata belongs to the class of drums that assembles people together. In fact, placing Bata side-by-side with other drums like Dundun in performance, it is Bata that will attract or pull the larger number of crowd together. This is simply because of its sound (shrill and sometimes harsh). Dundun drums were originally employed for entertainments but Bata drums were exclusively in the worship of Sango. However, owing to its secularization and patronage by the people, Bata drums now features in other contexts such as political campaigns and rallies, house warming, birth and naming ceremonies, installations, coronations, death, funeral and burial of kings, chiefs or any other person of rank. Bata and Dundun are equally applicable in the worship of other Yoruba deities such as Oya, Ogun, Osun and so on.

The Bata drum ensemble consists of four or sometimes five drums, which are;

- Iya Ilu – The lead drum (wittingly, the term means mother drum)
- Omele Abo – Female drum
- Omele Meji – Twin drums, which are again sub-divided into two namely:
    - Omele Ako - male twin drum
    - Kudi – female twin drum
- Ijin – An accompaniment to the lead drum (Iya Ilu).

The Dundun drum ensemble consists of three or sometimes four drums, which are:

- Iya Ilu – The lead drum
- Kanango or Gangan – A smaller version and main support to the lead drum
- Isaju – the lead accompaniment to the lead drum
- Gudugudu or Kerikeri – Other accompaniments to the lead drum

Significantly, all the drums in both ensembles are directed by the Iya Ilu which is the lead drum, in performance. This is because the drums in Africa speak and they have languages of their own. However, the drums cannot talk on their own except through the dictate or the instructions of the drummer. There is usually a message that the drummer is passing through fabrications or instructions. It is the message that is received and interpreted in the movement of the dancer(s). In many African societies, dance serves as a major aspect of their modes of expression. Dance was used to highlight the kinetic logic, as well as to portray the cultural interpretations of the history and reality of the people from which it came. Dance therefore achieved the above through a functional language medium. In order to have an adequate exposition of the dancers, it would be necessary to consider the mode of interpretation of the language of the drums by the dancers.

The Language of the Drums

The word language has been described by several scholars in different ways. For instance Adedimeji (2002:2) defined language as "a system of signs, verbal or non-verbal, through which human beings in their varying cultures and contexts exchange ideas and communicate feelings". Equally, Leonard Bloomfield, a linguist, simply defined it as the "totality of utterances that can be made in a speech community (cited in Chomsky, 1986:16). While Edward Sapir, a language scholar of repute defined language as " a purely human, non-instinctive method of communicating ideas, emotions and desires by means of voluntarily produced symbols" (Crystal, 1997:400).

The definitions above indicates that language is an asset to man, and is by far one of the greatest, most complex and most enigmatic possessions, the quintessence of his humanity, without which individuals and nations lose their mental and cultural heritage (Essien, 1990:168). The transferred effect of the complexities of language as it relates to drums is the focus of this paper. What then is the language of the drums?

In application, the language of the drums can take different forms, which are:

The Direct Language of the drum – This is a situation whereby the drums are modulated into speaking/making a particular speech or words.

The Drum Language that comes as a Metaphor – This is the metaphoric use of drum linguistically to make speech. For instance, the drums could be used pre-meditatively to motivate the people and subsequently spur them into dancing actions.

The Indirect Language of the drum – On the other hand, Indirect Language could be employed which easily elicits intended interactive mode between Drummers, Dancers or the audience at times. Though the audience may not understand the indirect language except those that are familiar with the language medium or that are natives of such environment. The example is the occasional situation in some Yoruba palaces in Nigeria, where the drummers use their drums to herald the arrival of visitors in and out of the palaces. Such drumming activity usually informs the King of the arrival and the exact departure of his guest/visitors.

In Africa, language creates a typical identity, which is a source of distinction. It has been observed especially in Nigeria that the difference in language from one ethic configuration to another is very imminent. Such is a reflection of their culture and ways of life. Interestingly, the differences as observed reflect in their drumming patterns and the subsequent interpretation of the drums by their dancers. In an interview after a performance, Lateef Adedapo, who is an expert Dundun drummer, explained that the sounds of drum are transformed into speeches or languages based on the lead drummer's experience and ability to construct sentences. He stated that:

> The drummer's mother tongue assists him to ably play around with words, sentences etc. While his knowledge of relevant 'adage' is an added advantage.

It is amusing to note that language affects drummers as he works or practically demonstrates his skills on the instruments. For instance, a lead Bata drummer on the Iya-Ilu, darts around the arena in order to support, instruct/command, make statements or express his feelings through the medium of his drum.

However, the activities as it unfolds can only be meaningful to the audience member who is verse in the knowledge of the ensuing language and can decode the drummer's own drums language. The above example is equally applicable to a Dundun drummer in the performance arena, who uses his technique on the drum to interact with the dancer without making audible statements except via the drums. For example in a performance, the lead drummer on Iya Ilu instructs as follows:

1. "...ma se b'o ti to, b'o ba se b'o ti to ija ni o da, ma se b'o tito"

Meaning:

"...please don't reveal your personality now, if you do so, it will cause trouble"

2. "B'oba se p'emi ni iwo ni, n'iwo ni, mo ba fi apa jo, f'apa jo, f'apa jo.
B'oba se p'emi ni iwo ni, n'iwo ni, mo ba f'ese jo, f'ese jo, f'ese jo.
B'oba se p'emi ni iwo ni, n'iwo ni, mo ba fi gbogbo ara gbon on ri ri ri ri ri..."

Meaning:

"If I were to be you in the dancing arena, I would have danced with my hands.
If I were to be you in the dancing arena, I would have danced with my legs.
If I were to be you in the dancing arena, I would have danced with the whole of my body shaking, shaking, shaking..."

In other words, the methodologies involved in the trade, which leads to linguistical meanings in communication, are essential to language formations. This aspect can be compared with a learner of a new language or a baby who is in the stage of making/forming statements. There are basic steps to follow in such situations, which includes identification of alphabets, syllables, words and sentences. The step here as mentioned, if well followed, assists the drummer in his direction and to approximately take charge of the performance(s).

The dancer in his interpretation/efforts to decode the language of the drum makes use of his expertise. Here, the experience comes into play; his competence in the native language becomes an asset, his kinesthetic sense (it is that which makes it possible for emotions, thoughts or views as conceived by the dancer to be expressed accurately through dance movements. Hence, it can be called 'movement sense') and the consideration of the knowledge of his body. Depending on the form of language, whether Bata drum language or Dundun drum language, the interactive experience between the drummer and the dancer is a scene to behold. It is a place where both try to outplay one another. It serves as an avenue to display one's talent or gift as a drummer or dancer. The dancer on the other hand employs the use of various body parts to adequately interpret the language of the drums as dictated by the drummer.

Meanwhile, the language communication through drumming in performance can equally extend to or lead to interactive experience between the drummer and chorus or chanters. It is a typical example of the situation in Nigeria, where the chorus joins in the experience, contributing positively to the success of such performance. At times, the chanter leads or dictates to the lead drummer in performance. He (the chanter) uses his linguistic prowess aesthetically and brings in the drummer to complement such in action. For instance, Alabi Ogundepo (a famous Ewi poet and director of a dance group based in Osogbo, Osun State in Nigeria) is known for this type of strategy in language communication, where his dancers interpretes the drum language. Occasionally, the experience takes the toll of language communication between the drummer and the audience. Here, the drummer in performance invites, through his drumming, the audience to be a part of the ensuing experience. This unique experience takes the form of improvisation, where the dance is usually a free for all.

Conclusion

The above discussion emphasizes that the language factor is a human factor. It therefore suffices to say that in the application of drums in performance in Nigeria, there are certain communications or terminologies/messages that are passed across by the drummer to the dancer or by the drummer to the audience. Importantly, there is need for adequate response (in movement) that is logical, meaningful and appropriate. It is not just aesthetic application alone, but well interpreted dance movements. The response may convey positive recognition of the message or it may be a repugnant response to the message by the drummer. Such response makes adequate application of kinesthetic sense, which is meant to relate exactly what is happening in any part of the body being used in a particular movement. It equally alerts the dancer on which parts of the body are not functioning properly and the manner at which they are functioning. Therefore, practitioners, individuals, dancers, would-be dancers and all need further inclusion of the drums (Bata and Dundun) in our day-to-day activities as explained in this study for clearer interpretations of the drums in dance.

References

Adedimeji, M. 2002. Language as Missiles: A Pragma-Semiotic Study of the Fireworks against Military Rule in Nigeria (1989-1999). Unpublished M. A. Thesis. University of Ilorin, Ilorin.

African Notes. Journal of the Institute of African Studies, University of Ibadan, Ibadan, Nigeria, Vol. xv Nos. 1&2, 1991, 19-27. (Referenced: Article by Layiwola D.)

Chomsky, Noam. 1986. *Knowledge of Language.* New York: Paeger Publishers.

Crystal, David. 1997. *The Cambridge Encyclopedia of Language.* 2nd Ed. Cambridge: Cambridge University Press.

Essien, O. E. 1990. The Future of Minority Languages. In Emenanjo, N. E. (Ed.). *Multilingualism, Minority languages and Language policy in Nigeria.* Agbor, Nigeria: Central Books Ltd. pp. 155-168.

Idowu, Bolaji. 1962. *Olodumare: God in Yoruba Belief.* London: Longmans

Johnson, S. 1921. *The History of the Yorubas.* Lagos, Nigeria: C. S. S. Bookshop (reprinted in 1956).

Nketia, K. 1974. *The Music of Africa.* New York: W. W. Norton & Co., Inc. (Reprinted in 1982 by Victor Gollancz Ltd, London).

Roderyk, L. 1975. The Nature of Dance: An Anthropological Perspective. London: Macdonald &Evans.

Sorell, W. 1967. *Dance through the Ages.* New York: Grosse

Chapter 14

AFRICAN LANGUAGES USE AND PEDAGOGY: THE ROAD AHEAD

Lioba Moshi and Akinloyè Òjó

Introduction

There is no doubt that indigenous languages play a critical role in language pedagogy and linguistic research. Their visibility and viability lies in the hands of scholars of African languages and linguistics, many of them Africans. The African experience has continually affirmed the belief that the level of linguistic loyalty toward a specific language comes from within the society and its attitude will significantly affect the extent to which the language is revered and respected by outsiders. Thus, "the less nationalistic" a society is about its indigenous language the more vulnerable the society and its languages would be (Mazrui and Mazrui, 1998). Examples come from registered success of nations that respect their indigenous languages with a designated national language that unites its people under one cultural, political, social, and economic umbrella. Not many nations in Africa can boast to be such a nation and this can be explained by the fact that many African countries have two or more dominant languages and a multiple number of other languages that represent the numerous ethnic compositions of the populace. The multilingual situation in most countries is, unfortunately, often exploited solely for political gains by the ruling class. Consequently, linguistic nationalism, which is mainly about having pride in the value of one's language, its use and enrichment, is wrongly characterized in most African countries. Language is continually dismissed as not being core to the issue that are of great interest to its speakers as long as the ruling class is satisfied that their needs are met. They, the ruling class, are often more interested in developing a unity of effort in economic reconstruction but not necessarily in forms of total national unification.

It is therefore important for pedagogists and linguistic researchers to help the world understand that 'World democracy' is unattainable when the role of language and culture is not factored into the configuration of what it is that a people cherishes and assumes to be the fabric that unites them all. This task must unavoidably begin within the different countries such as those in Africa in which the interwoven relationship between language and culture is regularly celebrated but hardly ever considered crucial to national socio-economic development. This role of compelling the nation and the World to appreciate the centrality of language and culture to the social wellbeing and progress of the country is not an optional task for those involved in the teaching, researching and promotion of the various African languages on the African continent and in the Diaspora. It is part of what Ayo Bamgbose identified in 2002 (and further expanded upon in 2006) as the social responsibility of the (African) linguist. As he noted, linguists and other language scholars in developing countries (especially in Africa) must strive to be more than theoreticians but must be fully invested and involved in applied research and activities such as addressing problems of language teaching, devising of orthographies, producing language teaching materials, contributing to the nation's language policy and generally contributing to the 'linguistic welfare' of the communities among whom they work. The central message being that every language researcher in Africa must strive to be 'a sociolinguist at heart. ' Bamgbose (2006) further highlights the dimensions of social responsibility for (African) linguists along eight specific domains of language corpus, language policy, education, justice, health, rural development, politics, and information.

Fundamental to the dimensions of social responsibility of (African) linguists in the first four domains identified by Bamgbose (2006) is the critical issue of English as the medium of instruction in the language policy in most Africa countries. The issues of national language policies as well as the language in Education policies across the African continent has been seriously and variously examined in this book by Elugbe, Dzahene-Quarshie, Arasanyin, Ojo and Amoloye (see Chapters 3 through 7 respectively). These examinations have variously highlighted the unjustifiable elevated status of English (and other colonial languages) in the language policies of most African countries to the detriment of indigenous languages as well as the harmful impact, in many cases, of the use of English as a medium of instruction. Increasingly from these discussions, it also appears that even the status of English in these language policies are not well thought out in some cases and not best implemented in others. All these findings appear to echo parts of Bamgbose's call to action regarding "the educational failure engendered by inappropriate language policy, particularly in relation to English as a medium of instruction. " (Bamgbose, 2006: 9).

The marketing of English in Africa seems to get its support from the rise of globalization. However, there is a dark side of globalization in Africa which is the erosion of linguistic national pride. Nkrumah (1st President of Ghana) and Nyerere (1st President of Tanzania), realized this dark side before the term globalization became a popular lexical item in the politics of the World. Nyerere worked very hard to impress on his people on the need to develop a national language without infringing on the rights of other indigenous languages. He demonstrated the potential power of Kiswahili by authoring several books in Kiswahili (an English translation was, also made available) which include: *Ujamaa* 'Familyhood/Socialism', *Uhuru na Umoja* 'Freedom and Unity', and *Uhuru na Maendeleo* 'Freedom and Development'. In addition, he translated two Shakespeare plays that he considered influential in the way he articulated his policies to a young nation emerging from colonialism: The Merchants of Venice '*Mabepari wa Venice*' and Julius Caesar '*Julius Kaisari*'. Nyerere challenged other scholars to do likewise. Many scholars in Tanzania and Kenya have done so, enhancing literary publications in Kiswahili and other languages like Kikuyu (by Ngugi wa Thiongo). Language textbooks as well as textbooks for other disciplines are in abundance in Kenya and Tanzania to be used by elementary and secondary schools. A few books can be found in the areas of linguistics and literature at the college level: Moshi (1988, 1996, 1998), Moshi and Omar (2003), Mwita and Mwasoko (1998), and Ohly (1987) among others.

In the case of the Yoruba language in Nigeria, it has had a significantly extended literary tradition compared to other languages in the country and the region. It has also enjoyed the status of being a national language in the multi-lingual and multi-ethnic nation and the development and use of the language was one of the bedrock of the liberation and post independence politics of many politicians in the old Western region of Nigeria such as Obafemi Awolowo, S. L. Akintola and Adegoke Adelabu. The surge of nationalistic (Nigerian) patriotism and the political chaos of the late 1960s in Nigeria would temporarily arrest the momentum of the development of the Yoruba language in the country. There was however a remarkable re-emergence of interest in the development and use of the Yoruba language in the 1970s as speakers and scholars began to change their attitudes towards the language. This change led to the increased adoption of the language in formal domains such as education, government and mass media. It also brought about the clamor for the adoption of the language (and the other national languages: Igbo and Hausa) as the medium of instruction under a mother-tongue education policy. Subsequently, the development of educational materials increased and the study of the language became a momentous enterprise at all levels of education. With the development of the Yoruba metalanguage in the 1980s, technical publications increased in the language including dissertations and academic research findings in linguistics and literature such as Olabimtan (1969), Isola (1970, 1974), Faleti (1972), Arohunmolase (1986), Owolabi (1989), Bamgbose (1990), Ojo (2004) and Adeniyi and Ojo (2005) among others.

What was noteworthy was that all these were against the backdrop of increased focus on the global languages such English and French. Africa, like the rest of the developing World was in the uncertain era of 'transferred' economic development policies. The economic development packages being delivered to Africa were prepared with non-indigenous economic models that were exclusively supported by the languages such as English. In essence, these policies provided the opportunity for the development and increased usage of English in these countries. The notion of globalization would not take hold until decades later but the seeds in the globalization of languages such as English (and its economic advantages) were already germinating in Africa. Notwithstanding, a significant number of African languages were getting renewed attention, increased development and increased usage at home and abroad towards the end of the twentieth century. Some notable African languages such as Hausa, Swahili, Yoruba, Lingala, and Zulu became the focus of academic studies as well as second language courses in places like North America, South America, and as far as various parts of Asia. The efforts of the civil rights movement in North America and members of the African Diaspora who 'resettled' back in Africa must be recognized in this enterprise. The fervent interest in the rest of the World, particularly the African Diaspora appeared to have further galvanized interest in the indigenous languages on the African continent. It would appear, late into the last century that indigenous African languages were gaining ground and that ethnic language empowerment was on the rise. It is, therefore, disconcerting to see that wheel of ethnic language empowerment reversed as more and more middle class families resort to English medium schools for their sons and daughters.

As we consider the globalization of World languages such as English, one would expect Africans to find the national will to invest in their indigenous languages. Though on a small scale, there is movement to incorporate some indigenous languages in technological advancement, but this is coming from outside of the continent. For example, the investment made by Microsoft millionaire Bill Gates in African languages for the development of a version of the Microsoft (July 2004) and the utilization of new technologies like the cell-phones are encouraging aspects that create opportunities for indigenous languages as well as establishing an important role for African languages in the 21st Century. It is also a testimony to the current and future power of African languages, dispelling the myth that technology and modern science can only be achieved through colonial or European languages, something that is a concern to many as the winds of globalization surge on. All these developments give a glimmer of hope that would perhaps encourage African leaders and their citizens to resist the temptation to continue to succumb to the pressure to de-emphasize African languages by promoting European languages such as English, French, and Portuguese as national or official languages. This can be achieved with the help of scholars in the Diaspora whose power of advocacy for the inclusion of African languages in the company of designated global languages.

These scholars and other members of the African Diaspora can also enhance the visibility of African languages by refraining from being contented with the minimal utilization of African languages as is often demonstrated in the US in the adoption of African names, words, and phrases in naming practices, the scattered use of words from African languages such as KiSwahili in children's books, children's theatre and films, and product labels (especially beauty products). While the use of African languages such as Yoruba as part of the liturgy of New World religion is encouraging, practitioners should do more to provide practical World advocacy for these languages. As scholars we need to encourage serious research, usage, and learning of African languages. Serious learners would also produce life-long learners, those who are willing to go beyond the object naming exercise. Accuracy in usage and the need to be functional in the language should be the key objectives both for the teacher and the learner of African languages. The continent and the Diaspora have reached a point where the blame game no longer produces world sympathy. It is the point in time where Africans on the continent and in the Diaspora must make a language attitude change in order to eradicate the harmful impacts of colonialism and European economic expansion on the languages and cultures of Africa. In this era of globalization, the survival and increased use of African languages will depend on two key factors. First is the collaborative work done (between Africa, its Diaspora and other supporters of African languages) to ensure that African languages are able to meet the increasing and changing needs of their users in a networked (global) World. The second factor will be the positive adjustment of attitudes of speakers (especially policy makers) towards indigenous African languages. Lightheartedly, there must be work done and a positive twist of ethno linguistic sentiments in Africa.

The present competition in Tanzania and other parts of East Africa between English and Kiswahili, for instance as noted by Dzahene-Quarshie (Chapter 4) in this book, is heightened by language attitudes, national consciousness, and the preference accorded to English by established elites. As she noted, speakers' sentimental value of Kiswahili in East Africa did not translate an advantage over English. Nyerere (1st President of Tanzania) marketed Kiswahili before and after independence as the only trans-ethnic link. It became an instrumental link in the urbanization process. During his administration, Kiswahili was embraced more than English in both the urban and rural areas. However, the rural people considered Kiswahili the language of urbanites and therefore its ability to erode ethnic customs and rituals, was limited. This is true of many other parts of Africa especially where there is an absence of a strong generalized opposition to imperial languages which in turn allows for a lack of a strong commitment to local languages. Unfortunately, a weak linguistic nationalism breeds a higher demand for imperial languages and less demand for indigenous languages. The positive attitude towards the demand/use of imperial languages is by and large 'instrumentally' motivated while that of indigenous languages is integratively motivated. Speakers associate advantages and disadvantages of a particular language with educational opportunities and the market. Local conditions determine the language that would be considered an advantage. For example in Tanzania, Kiswahili may hold a higher advantage in the local job markets while in Kenya or Uganda English holds an advantage over Kiswahili. In Kenya for instance, English proficiency is taken as a marker of good education and modernity (Abdul Aziz, 1989: 32 – 49).

It appears that all things considered, the proficiency in English in many African countries continues to be advantageous to the average individual (Ngugi wa Tiongo (1986), Banjo (1995), Ojo (1997), Mazrui and Mazrui (1998), and Igboanusi and Peter (2005). Describing the dominance of English in Nigeria, Igboanusi and Peter (2005) noted that the 'dominance of English has been institutionalized from the days of the colonial administration on' (pg. 9). In discussing the role of English in most of the developing World, Phillipson (1992) elaborated on the 'exploitation theory' which makes the point that the use of English in developing countries causes more harm than good. This is because the spreading English language contributes to the downgrading of local languages, the limitation of popular participation in public affairs, and the transmission of foreign worldviews to the other societies and cultures. A study on the choice of lingua franca in Kampala (Scotton 1974) showed that English in Uganda is considered a language of socio-economic ascent and is valued as useful because proficiency in English translates to a high economic status. Interestingly, Luganda, an indigenous language in Uganda, is revered and is considered to have generated more ethno-linguistic nationalism among its speakers than Gikuyu, for the Kikuyu people of Kenya, an equally powerful ethnic group. This can be explained by the fact that Luganda is to the Baganda people what Kiswahili is to the people of the coastal states of Kenya and Tanzania. Luganda speakers have always opposed the Kiswahili language and consider it a foreign language associated with the Ugandan military power.

As noted previously, the inter-territorial role of Kiswahili has served the neighboring countries in East Africa well. Africa as a continent does not have an inter-territorial language, an explanation for the popularity of English, even though the continent is divided into Anglophone, Francophone, and Lusophone due to the different colonial legacies. This condition has allowed English to expand beyond its instrumental role into the arena of now playing the integrative role of meeting the linguistic needs of migrant labor communities in sub-Saharan Africa, displaced populations in refugee communities in Africa and beyond, including Britain and the United States. Needless to say, the role expansion serves as an encouragement to African leaders to further their attitude towards English, a language of 'documented' civilization, the literate, and the 'educated elites.' Such attributes create political capital to leaders seeking political positions in most African countries. In Kenya, for example, the highest government post in the country (the Presidency) has to be occupied by someone who is trilingual: competent in English, Kiswahili and any one of the major ethnic languages. This is encouraged by the fact that the Kenyan constitution is written in English although it can be deliberated in Kiswahili. Tanzania does require its president to be proficient in Kiswahili but proficiency in English is encouraged to allow ease of communication with world leaders. In Uganda, like in Ghana, and Nigeria, English has remained the undisputed qualification for the highest office on the land. Preference on ethnic languages has always been avoided since such a suggestion would be a political risk in these deeply divided societies. Uganda exhibits an interesting case. It encourages the development and use of all languages. Thus, its linguistic advantage has been enhanced by the people's readiness to be linguistically be united, not through a single lingua franca like the case of Tanzania, but rather through a concerted efforts by the citizens to learn each other's Afro-ethnic language. The rich diversity of languages has created an opportunity to develop a more polyglottal national culture.

The dilemma of African nations with respect to imperial languages is their instrumental role and the more recent acquired integrative role across borders. In the case of English, its power is unmatched around the World. Thus its instrumental role is very high across the globe. However, unlike French and Portuguese, not many speakers can exploit this instrumental role. Cristal (2005) notes that although English is the language of the elite those who speak it do not always achieve communication because there is no clear common ground for all speakers whether native or non-native. Despite its dominance in Nigeria for instance, it is only spoken proficiently by only about 20% of the population. It has however attained economic, military, and communication power on the continent of Africa compared to French or Portuguese, both imperial languages whose powers were developed on the continent in the 19th Century. Currently, the most challenging dilemma in many Anglophone African countries is the continuation of English in the legal system. This has been the slowest to change from an imperial setting to one that embraces earlier indigenous judicial traditions (See Arasanyin in this book, Chapter 5: for the case of Nigeria). In East Africa, English has continued to be the primary language of legal discourse. Because the legal culture is itself derived from the British legal system, the English language finds itself in the legal system in Africa and the relationship between the English language and the law almost throughout Anglophone Africa is one of maximum *convergence* (Mazrui and Mazrui 1998).

It is disconcerting that the constitution is interpreted through colonial languages: every right, every civil liberty, and every law in terms of its meaning. The constitutional law is linguistically Eurocentric. The area of civil rights has been the area that is often used to justify the sustainability of the use of English in the legal system. The argument is that using English enables the legal system to draw lawyers from different parts of Anglophone Africa and the African Diaspora to serve in the judicial system. For example, Tanzania had a judge from West Indies, Uganda had a judge from Nigeria, Kenya had several Chief Justices from Guyana and Ghana. In addition, Nigerian and Kenyan, lawyers have been able to pursue justice across Anglophone Africa due to their status as vanguards of defending human rights and democratic processes. They have used this opportunity to execute the law without fear of the affected government having the power to victimize them since they are protected by the international networking of jurists and constitutionalists from other Anglophone nations. However, the negative effect of this system of justice has been the promotion of a dependence syndrome. Kenya, for example, has been very slow in relinquishing the dependence on judges from outside of Kenya. This has created an image in the minds of the citizens that shows this lingo-legal convergence as the true justice, causing the people to believe that an effective system is the one that is imported from outside their society. It is acts such as these that undermine the confidence of the African people in using their languages for African business. The loss of confidence has also contributed to the negative attitude from the outside World towards African leaders and scholars.

Schmied (1991) observes that the inability of African scholars to write in their own languages is downplayed by the outside world. He notes that African scholars face sociolinguistic and grammatical problems as they try to express their ideas in Imperial languages, particularly English. A substantial number of works by Africans across the continents written in English remain unpublished due to sociolinguistic stereo-typing of both the authors and the texts. Those written in indigenous languages cannot find audience outside their local jurisdictions. Unfortunately, as long as native English-speaking countries have the power to sustain and further influence the domination of English, the dominance of English in Africa might continue through the 21st century (Igboanusi and Peter, 2005). It is therefore apparent from these discussions and the expressed opinions in the chapters in this book that there is the need to reconfigure the role of African languages in a global society. African scholars (and others) must strive to re-direct the African consciousness to the problem of shielding cultural insecurity and timidity in scholarship. Interestingly, much of this timidity can be explained by Henri Tajfel's (1974, 1978, 1981) theory of social grouping.

Within the preview of the theory of inter-group relations and social change, Tajfel shows how perceived inferior/minority groups operate in comparison to a superior/majority group. He notes that, a minority/inferior group is often viewed in negative terms when comparing them with other groups. Because they are aware of this negative perception, members within the inferior group always look for ways to stay visible and to coexist within the social structure. Tajfel suggests two strategies available to the inferior group: (1) to accept the minority/inferior status or (2) to reject the minority/inferior status. Each strategy yield different outcomes. When a group or an individual accepts the perceived inferior status they attempt to assume an individualistic stance. This means that they get out of their group circle in order to achieve a personal positive image. They also attempt to measure themselves against members of their own group to create a superior status of their own in relation to the group they wish to isolate themselves. In the case of the second strategy, namely rejecting the inferior/minority status, the group attempts to change the status quo by seeking equality with the superior (majority) group, This can be done adopting the values of the superior group, a process known as assimilation. An individual or group that adopts the rejection strategy would try to redefine the negative characteristics that identify them as a group by creating positive characteristics for their group. They can attempt to create new dimensions for comparison with the superior group as a way to create an identity for themselves.

How does this apply to the African consciousness? Based on the prevailing status quo among African scholars and leaders, it is not unreasonable to assume that for the most part, the first strategy is often selected when confronted with an identity choice. Both Ali Mazrui (1986) and Henry Louis Gates (1999) in their documentaries about Africa (*The Africans* and *Wonders of the African World* respectively) have alluded to this tendency. It is not uncommon to hear someone say that the Ivorians, Congolese, and Algerians are more French than the French. Also, in the 70s, one Kenyan politician refused to fly in an aircraft whose pilot was not an Englishman meaning that an African from Kenya was incapable of taking command of the aircraft with him on board. In his documentary, Henry Louis Gates was shocked when he found out that in Lamu and Zanzibar, a good percentage of the people did not consider themselves Waswahili but rather Persians or Shiraz. Cognizant of the "consciousness" factor, Gates, laughingly, commented in the documentary that African Americans in America have issues with identity too, and that some claim ancestry from many places except Africa and presumably for the same reasons, their need not to be associated with slavery. Like some of their brothers and sisters in Lamu and Zanzibar, some African Americans do not want to be considered descendants of slaves.

These illustrations offer us a window through which we can view the African society as a social group. If the Swahili people were the indigenous people of the coastal states of East Africa, they cannot escape affinity with the slavery experiences of different ruling eras on the east coast of Africa. Henry Louis Gates' interlocutors in Lamu and Zanzibar could not denounced their prestigious status as *waugwana* (member of the 'elite' group) because y doing so they would be accepting membership in the class of the inferiors, *watumwa* 'slaves'. By isolating themselves from the perceived inferior group they are able to create a superior social group of their own in the eyes of other superior group that they have interestingly considered Henry Loius Gates to be a member. As *waungwana* they could compare themselves with the *watumwa* 'slaves' or the *wazaliwa* 'free born/offspring of the slaves'. As Persians and Shirazi descendants, Gates' interlocutors also denounce Kiswahili as their indigenous language and adopt Arabic which is considered the language of the 'Islamic scholarship'. Because the Swahili people are not considered elites, Kiswahili identifies them as inferior making it necessary to learn Arabic in order to be elevated to the *waungwana* status. The Lamu and Zanzibar people who shocked Gates by identifying with the Persians/ Shiraz and the Arabic language wanted to dissociate themselves from the *watumwa*, the indigenous Swahili people by emphasizing their affiliations with the scholarship of the Arabic languages needed by scholars of Islam and interpreting the Koran. Thus, a claim to Islam requires that one shows proof of their proficiency in the Arabic language. It is important to note that this tendency is not unique to Islam. Catholicism was closely associated with Latin until 1965 when the Council of Catholic Bishops resolved that churches around the world could use their local languages for religious services. Until then, knowledge of Latin was used to claim a superior status in the church as well as a requirement for all clergy who were entrusted with the power to interpret the Bible 'Word of God' to the heathen.

How does this relate to the marginalization of African languages? Africans have been conditioned to believe that their indigenous languages are inferior to other foreign languages. As such, some Africans try to adopt Tajfel's strategies as described above. During the colonial period, the education system emphasized the use of colonial languages such as English, French, or Portuguese, at the expense of the local languages. Consequently, an attitude was developed in the minds of the people that their local languages were inferior to the European languages. This attitude has not changed and has been perpetuated by the affluent, even in a country like Tanzania where its first leader, President Julius Nyerere worked hard to change that attitude. The affluent and elite have adopted the 'group acceptance' (accepting the inferior status) strategy by identifying with the system that downplays the importance of their indigenous languages and cultures. This is demonstrated in the discussions by Moshi (Chapter 1) and Dzahene-Quarshie (Chapter 4) on the mushrooming of English medium schools in Kenya and Tanzania for the children of the affluent and elite. This development sends a negative message about Kiswahili to the larger majority of the citizenry. The elites and the affluent confirm the superior status of English and signal that proficiency in Kiswahili is not as important. Scholars and other elites who have achieved membership in the superior group need to evaluate their African consciousness with respect to the development of African languages and cultures.

Conclusion

Language reflects its power in the way it is exploited by its speakers. Accepting the role of a non-powerful participant, through constraining contents of usage, relations entered into, and subject position occupied will remain the major impediment to the efforts of establishing and maintaining a visible status of African languages. Crystal (2005) points out the dangers of accepting one language and consciously or subconsciously rejecting others. Downplaying the power of a language contributes to the limitations imposed on other sources of knowledge from and about the target nations. The blame and burden to advocate for African languages resides with the African leaders. The only leaders, who give their speeches abroad in languages other than their own, even where they run a risk of embarrassing themselves because of limited fluency, come from Africa. Other leaders take pride in their language and culture and are provided with translators when they need them, not because they are not fluent in the language but because they choose to take pride in their indigenous languages and cultures.

To enhance the needed transformation, the African languages and cultural studies as well as African languages and cultural understanding must receive a fair representation in the popular media and the academy. Patriotic and nationalistic efforts in Africa must also be constructively channeled towards linguistic and cultural development. If Africans do not speak or promote their own languages; if they seek to educate their children only in foreign languages while they ignore and belittle the importance of their indigenous languages as the avenue for cultural understanding and assimilation; if Africans continue with the attitude that African languages have nothing to offer to other world languages and that all that can be learnt has to be learned in foreign language, then Africans cannot continue to blame colonialism as the sole source for under developing Africa. African attitudes about the continent and its potentials contribute to the exploitation that the continent suffers. It is also the underlying reason for the outside World's resolve to continue ignoring the accomplishments made by the African people. The erosion of Africa's cultural and linguistic pride is a reality in the 21st Century due to globalization and therefore requires major steps to prevent it from escalating.

Langer (1953, 1979) notes that language transforms speakers from biological creatures, who respond to the concrete world as it exists, into thinking beings that interpret, interact with, and remake the world through symbols. The symbols used shape our understanding of the world and our own places within it. The power of symbols lies in the kind of thought and action they enable. Symbols allow us to define, organize, and evaluate experiences and people. At the same time, they enable us to think hypothetically and to reflect on ourselves. Thus, the language that we use, selectively, shapes our perceptions and the names we apply emphasize particular aspects of reality and neglect others. Language names what exists and those with power name and define the world in their own terms. Furthermore, those with power to name the world use names and words rooted in their language to acknowledge what affects them. Therefore, when we talk about "the power of a language" we are talking about how it reflects its speakers and how the speakers exploit that power. It is also important to note that language conventions and acceptance replicate and validate the existing power structures. Powerful participants (attempt to) control and constrain the distribution of non-powerful participants, through constraining contents of usage as well as relations entered into and the subject positions occupied. What becomes of a language depends on its users and advocates. It is, therefore, incumbent upon speakers and scholars to look for ways to grow the languages that are the root of the African symbolic place in the world. Part of the goal of making a language visible should be to expose its existing and powerful achievements in the global society.

References

Abdul Aziz, Mohamed H. (1989). Development of Scientific and technical Terminology with Special reference to African Languages. In *Kiswahili 56*, 32-49.

Adeniyi, Harrison and Akinloye Ojo. (Eds.). *Ìlò-Èdè àti Èdá Èdè Yorùbá* (Yoruba Linguistics and Language Use). Trenton, New Jersey: Africa World Press

Aróhunmólàse, O. (1986). *Àgbéyèwò Àwon Àkotó Yorùbá láti odún 1875 sí 1974.* (mimeo)

Bamgbose, Ayo. (1990). *Fonólójì àti Gírámà Yorùbá.* Ìbàdàn, Nigeria: University Press Ltd.

_____(2006). Linguistics and Social Responsibility: The Challenge for the Nigerian Linguist. Port Harcourt, Nigeria: Linguistics Association of Nigeria (LAN).

Banjo, Ayo. (1995). On Language Use and Modernity in Nigeria. In Kola Owolabi (ed.). *Language in Nigeria: Essays in Honour of Ayo Bamgbose.* Ibadan, Nigeria: Group Publishers.

Crystal, David (2005). Globalizing English. In Keith Walters and Michael Brody (eds.). *What's Language Got to Do With It?* (pp. 504-514). New York, NY: W. W. Norton and Co.

Fairclaugh, Norman (1989). *Language and Power.* New York, NY: Longman.

Fálétí, A. (1972) *Basòrun Gáà.* Ìbàdàn, Nigeria: Oníbonòjé Press Ltd.

Henry Louis Gates (1999). *Wonders of the African World* (A made for TV documentary about Africa).

Igboanusi, Herbert and Lothar Peter. (2005). Languages in Competition: The Struggle for Supremacy among Nigeria's Major Languages, English and Pidgin. Frankfurt: Peter Lang GmBH

Ìsòlá, Akínwùmí. (1970). *Ẹfúnsetán Aníwúrà.* Ìbàdàn, Nigeria: Oxford University Press.

_____(1974). *Ó Le Kú.* Ìbàdàn, Nigeria: Oxford University Press Ltd.

Langer, S. K. (1953). *Feeling and Form, a theory of Art.* New York: Scriber's.

_____(1979). Philosophy in a New Key: A Study in the Symbolism of Reason, Rite and Art. Cambridge, MA: Harvard University.

Mazrui, Ali A. (1986). *The Africans.* A BBC and PBS TV Documentary.

Mazrui, Ali A. and Alamin M. Mazrui. (1998). *The Power of Babel: Language & Governance in the African Experience.* Binghamton University, Binghamton, NY: IGCS Publications.

_____(1999). *Political Culture of Language. Swahili, Society, and State.* Binghamton University, Binghamton, NY: IGCS Publications.

Moshi, Lioba (1988). Tuimarishe Kiswahili Chetu (Building Proficiency in Kiswahili) A textbook for Second and Third Year Students. Lanham, MD: University press of America.

_____(1996) *KiSwahili Lugha na Utamaduni*: A 23 Lesson Video Series for the Teaching KiSwahili Language and Culture. Athens, Georgia: University of Georgia, OISD.

_____(1998). *KiSwahili, Lugha na Utamaduni (Swahili, Language and Culture).* Hyattsville, MD: Dunwoody Press.

Moshi, Lioba, and Alwiya Omar (2003). Kiswahili kwa Kompyuta (KIKO): a series of computer assisted lessons for Kiswahili learners at the elementary, intermediate, and advanced levels. http://www.africa.uga.edu/Kiswahili/doe/.

Mwita, A. M. A and D. N. Mwansoko (1998). *Kamusi ya Tiba.* Dar Es Salaam, Tanzania: GTZ.

Ngugi wa Tiongo (1986). Decolonizing the Mind: the Politics of Language in African Literature. London: James Currey.

Ohly, Rajmund (1987). *A Primary Technical Dictionary English-Swahili.* Dar Es Salaam, Tanzania.

Òjó, Akinloyè. (1997). *Incorporation of English Words in Yoruba: A Sociolinguistic and Phonological Analysis.* Unpublished M. A. Thesis, Department of Modern Languages and Linguistics (DMLL), Cornell University, Ithaca, NY

_____(2004). Akoyege Yoruba Lori Ero (AKOYE): a series of computer assisted lessons for Yoruba learners at the elementary, intermediate, and advanced levels. http://www.africa.uga.edu/Yoruba

Olábímtán, A. (1969). *Àádóta Àròfò.* Lagos, Nigeria: Macmillan Nigeria, Ltd.

Owólabí, K. (1989). Ìjìnlè Ìtúpalè Èdè Yorùbá I: Fònétíìkì àti Fonólójì. Ìbàdàn, Nigeria: Oníbonòjé Press.

Phillipson, Robert (1992). *Linguistic Imperialism.* Oxford: Oxford University Press.

Schleicher, Antonia and Lioba Moshi (2000). *The pedagogy of African languages: An Emerging Field.* Pathways Series. Ohio State University.

Schmied, Josef (1991). *English in Africa: An Introduction*. New York, NY: Longman.

Scotton, M. Carol (1974). Choosing a Lingua Franca in an African capital. *In Language in Society,* 3: 147-154. Cambridge: Cambridge University Press.

Tajfel, Henri (1974). Social Identity and Inter-group Behavior, In *Social science Information 13 (2): 65-93*.

____(1978). Differentiation between Social Groups: Studies in the Social Psychology of inter-group Relations. London: Academic Press.

____(1981). *Human Groups and Social Categories*. Cambridge: Cambridge University Press.

ABOUT THE CONTRIBUTORS

ADENIYI, Harrison is a senior lecturer in the Department of African Languages, Literatures and Communication Arts at the Lagos State University, Lagos, Nigeria.

ADENIYI, Kehinde Abimbola is an academic staff in the Department of Theatre Arts at Adeniran Ogunsanya College of Education (AOCOED), Ojo/Ijanikin, Lagos, Nigeria.

AKANMU, Samuel Oladayo is an academic staff in the Department of Yoruba at Adeniran Ogunsanya College of Education (AOCOED), Ojo/Ijanikin, Lagos, Nigeria.

AMOLOYE, Bilqis Ajoke is a faculty member in the Department of Nigerian Languages, School of Languages, Kwara State College of Education, Ilorin, Nigeria.

ARASANYIN, Olaoba F. is an associate professor of Linguistics in the Department of Writing and Linguistics at the Georgia Southern University, Statesboro, Georgia.

BELLO, Rachael O. is lecturer in the Department of English at Lagos State University, Lagos, Nigeria.

BOLAJI, Ezekiel Tunde is an academic staff in the Department of Theatre Arts at Adeniran Ogunsanya College of Education (AOCOED), Ojo/Ijanikin, Lagos, Nigeria.

DZAHENE-QUARSHIE, Josephine is a Lecturer and Coordinator of the Swahili Program in the Department of Modern Languages, Faculty of Arts at the University of Ghana.

ELUGBE, Ben Ohi is a professor of Linguistics in the Department of Linguistics and African Languages, Faculty of Arts at the University of Ibadan, Ibadan, Nigeria.

FALEYE, Adeola Adijat is a lecturer in the Department of Linguistics and African Languages, Faculty of Arts at the Obafemi Awolowo University, Ile-Ife, Nigeria.

MOSHI, Lioba is a professor of Comparative Literature in the Department of Comparative Literature at the University of Georgia, Athens, Georgia

ÒJÓ, Akinloyè is an assistant professor of Comparative Literature and African Studies in the Department of Comparative Literature at the University of Georgia, Athens, Georgia.

OJUADE, Jeleel Olasunkanmi is a lecturer in the Performing Arts Department, Faculty of Arts at the University of Ilorin, Ilorin, Nigeria.

OMAR, Alwiya S. is a clinical associate professor and the African Language Coordinator in the department of Linguistics and the African Studies Program at Indiana University, Bloomington, Indiana.

INDEX

A

Abacha, Sani, 117
Achebe, Chinua, 117
Acholi, 20
Adeniyi, Kehinde Abimbola, 6, 8, 9, 219, 248, 258
African Union, 30
Akanmu, Oladayo, 7, 9, 207, 209, 215, 217
Akinnaso, Niyi, 98, 99
Amharic, 28, 71
Amin, Idi, 20, 21
Amoloye, B.A., 5, 8, 147, 158, 159, 246
Arabic, 2, 12, 14, 17, 34, 123, 130, 131, 162, 163, 169, 196, 255
Arasanyin, Olaoba F, 4, 5, 8, 71, 75, 89, 91, 92, 100, 117, 143, 146, 246, 252
Ayo, Bamgbose, 118, 143

B

Baganda, 20, 23, 251
Bantu languages, 1, 25
Bata, 8, 235, 236, 237, 238, 240, 241, 242
Battuta, Ibn, 15
Belgian Congo, 22
Bolaji, Ezekiel Tunde, 8, 219, 221, 231, 232, 233, 243
Britain, 57, 59, 123, 170, 251
British Colonial Rule, 62

C

Cambodia, 16
Canada, 47, 196

Catholics, 13
China, 3, 11, 16, 33, 34, 35, 63
Chomsky, Noam, 243
Christianity, 12, 13, 14, 56, 163

D

Dar Es Salaam, 37, 161, 259
Democratic Republic of the Congo, 22, 34
Dundun, 8, 235, 236, 237, 238, 240, 241, 242

E

Early Exit-TBE, 66
Eastern Africa, 12, 14
Edo, 40, 42, 100, 105, 181, 182, 194, 196, 197
Ekiti, 5, 147, 194, 216
Enahoro, Anthony, 99, 118
European Economic market, 28

F

Federal Character Policy, 75, 78
Fulani, 42, 94, 195, 210

G

German East Africa Protectorate, 55
Ghana, 24, 53, 66, 68, 72, 170, 191, 196, 247, 251, 252, 261
Guosa, 40
Gupta, Das, 43, 51

H

Hausa, 3, 28, 36, 39, 40, 42, 47, 50, 85, 87, 88, 90, 93, 94, 95, 98, 100, 105, 108, 109, 111, 116, 122, 123, 124, 127, 130, 134, 147, 149, 181, 182, 185, 195, 196, 197, 247, 248

I

Igbo, 1, 3, 6, 39, 40, 42, 50, 85, 87, 88, 90, 94, 99, 100, 105, 109, 111, 116, 122, 123, 124, 127, 130, 134, 147, 149, 181, 182, 183, 185, 186, 187, 188, 189, 190, 195, 196, 197, 247
IMF, 60, 61, 64
India, 3, 11, 16, 33, 34, 35, 117
Indo-European languages, 1
Islam, 12, 14, 16, 17, 22, 255

J

Japan, 3, 11, 33, 34, 117, 146

K

Kalenjin, 21
Kambari, 42
Kanga, 6, 161, 163, 164, 165, 166, 177, 178
Kenya, 15, 19, 21, 23, 27, 28, 29, 33, 35, 36, 62, 71, 162, 178, 247, 250, 251, 252, 254, 256
Khanga, 6, 178
Kikuyu, 21, 247, 251
Kiswahili, 11, 13, 14, 15, 16, 17, 19, 20, 21, 22, 23, 24, 25, 26, 27, 28, 29, 32, 33, 34, 36, 37, 53, 54, 55, 58, 61, 71, 72, 161, 162, 164, 170, 175, 176, 177, 178, 247, 250, 251, 255, 256, 257, 259

Kogi, 6, 147
Kwara, 6, 147, 261

L

Lagos, 5, 40, 46, 50, 51, 52, 118, 119, 120, 143, 144, 145, 146, 147, 159, 160, 185, 191, 194, 205, 213, 214, 216, 217, 220, 233, 234, 243, 259, 261
Langi, 20
Language of Wider Communication, 91, 108
Language of Wider Political Access, 91
Late Exit-TBE, 66
Linguistic Association of Nigeria, 42, 48
Louis Gates, Henry, 254, 255, 258
Luo, 21

M

Malaysia, 16
Mazrui, Ali, 12, 20, 22, 23, 26, 29, 30, 32, 33, 36, 71, 117, 245, 250, 252, 254, 258
Middle East, 35, 123
Moshi, Lioba, 1, 2, 3, 8, 11, 37, 245, 247, 256, 259

N

National Foreign Language Standards, 6, 161, 175, 177, 179
National Institute for Nigerian Languages, 135, 136

National Policy on Education, 44, 51, 87, 99, 118, 119, 122, 125, 141, 143, 144, 145, 147, 148, 159, 160, 183, 191, 206
News Agency of Nigeria, 102
Niger Delta, 121, 124
Nigerian National Policy on Education, 5, 109, 122
Nigerian pidgin, 3, 39
Nigerian Television Authority, 40, 105
Nkrumah, Kwameh, 24, 247
Northern Nigeria, 78
Nyerere, Julius, 24, 25, 26, 28, 53, 54, 55, 56, 58, 59, 60, 61, 63, 64, 66, 171, 172, 247, 250, 255

O

Obote, Milton, 20
Ojo, Akinloye, 1, 5, 8, 121, 123, 130, 209, 211, 245, 246, 248, 250, 258, 261
Ojuade, Jeleel Olasunkanmi, 8, 9, 235
Ondo, 5, 147, 194, 199
Oriki, 7, 207, 208, 209, 210, 216, 217
Overseas Development Agency, 60

P

Prah, K.K., 139, 140, 146

S

Sango, 212, 237, 238
Sofala, 15
Somali, 28, 36

Swahili, 3, 4, 6, 12, 13, 15, 16, 21, 24, 36, 37, 53, 54, 55, 56, 57, 58, 59, 60, 61, 62, 63, 64, 65, 66, 67, 68, 69, 70, 71, 72, 73, 176, 177, 178, 248, 254, 259, 261

T

Tanzania, 3, 4, 6, 11, 14, 18, 20, 21, 22, 23, 24, 25, 26, 27, 28, 29, 30, 34, 37, 43, 47, 53, 54, 55, 56, 57, 58, 59, 60, 61, 62, 63, 64, 65, 66, 67, 68, 70, 71, 72, 73, 161, 162, 171, 172, 178, 247, 250, 251, 252, 255, 259
Tanzania Media Women's Association, 161
Tiv, 42, 100, 105, 181, 196, 197
Transition Bilingual Education, 66

U

Uganda, 20, 21, 23, 62, 72, 250, 251, 252
Ujamaa, 4, 53, 55, 58, 59, 60, 61, 64, 70, 247

V

Vietnam, 16

W

wa Thiongo, Ngugi, 29, 30, 31, 247
Wazobia, 40, 88, 90, 105, 112
Wolof, 42
World Bank, 28, 60, 61, 64, 95, 120

Y

Yoruba, 1, 3, 5, 7, 8, 9, 28, 39, 40, 42, 43, 47, 50, 85, 87, 88, 90, 94, 99, 100, 104, 105, 108, 109, 111, 116, 123, 124, 127, 130, 134, 135, 139, 143, 145, 146, 147, 148, 149, 150, 151, 152, 153, 155, 156, 157, 158, 159, 188, 193, 197, 198, 199, 202, 203, 207, 209, 210, 211, 215, 216, 217, 223, 235, 237, 238, 240, 243, 247, 248, 249, 258, 259, 261

Z

Zanzibar, 15, 30, 161, 162, 163, 166, 168, 170, 171, 172, 173, 174, 177, 178, 254, 255

Zimbabwe, 15

www.ingramcontent.com/pod-product-compliance
Lightning Source LLC
Chambersburg PA
CBHW070243230426
43664CB00014B/2398